The
Magic
of
a
Mighty
Memory

THE MAGIC

OF A MIGHTY MEMORY

CHESLEY V.
YOUNG

Parker Publishing Co., Inc.
West Nyack, New York

The Magic of a Mighty
Memory

by

Chesley V. Young

© 1971, BY

PARKER PUBLISHING COMPANY, INC.
WEST NYACK, NEW YORK

LIBRARY OF CONGRESS
CATALOG CARD NUMBER: 70–147171

PRINTED IN THE UNITED STATES OF AMERICA
ISBN 0–13–545053–5
B & P

How This Book Will Benefit You

Give yourself a mighty memory! With an ordinary memory, good enough for ordinary people, you can get by. But when your memory really goes to work for you, it lifts you far above average levels of life-performance.

Your mighty new memory gives you instant access to your great brain-bank of experience—always your best teacher—so you stop making many mistakes and keep moving *forward*. You can see great opportunities that other people miss. You have instant access to important knowledge; YOU are the one who knows the answers.

Also, because you remember names and faces and valuable items of personal affairs, you gain a priceless power to make others like you and want to associate themselves with you. You can influence others in many ways that bring business power and social strength.

You will find, too, that when your memory is wide awake, you awaken every other part of your mind. You increase your ability to use what you know, to get rid of much trial-and-error and proceed with boundless self-confidence. Even if your present memory is mostly a "forgettery," you can change it into a mighty tool of life-success—beginning right now.

What Is the Main Principle That Backs Up a Mighty Memory?

It is a principle you have used all your life—the *reminder* principle. One thing simply reminds you of another.

For example: In a psychological test, a random group of people were given a long list of words to memorize. Another group was given the same list to memorize in the same time; but, with this second group, one key syllable of each word was set in capitals —like this: CAPital.

Did it help? The second group averaged a much higher score in remembering words than did the first, unaided group. The second group simply had been provided a *reminder* of what they had to remember.

As you build your own mighty memory, you will use far more positive and powerful *mental* reminders. Nevertheless, these reminders will be built upon such simple, well-known bits of knowledge as the alphabet from A to Z and numbers from 1 to 100. These reminders will appear in your mind instantly, in orderly, unmistakable fashion, like signals set up in a filing cabinet.

Are you in business? You can remember every useful price, every useful specification, every important business detail. You can dominate a meeting—without notes—because you instantly recall every needed fact, name, figure, place, date, trade trend.

Are you making a speech or a sales presentation? You'll never forget a point you want to make, never fumble a story, never confuse what you have to say on a certain occasion with what you said last time—and also have in your mind a vast armamentarium of facts with which to answer questions.

Techniques just as simple can help you follow the lead of one young man who applied his new memory-might to the stock market. Merely by sitting and watching the ticker tape and calling instructions to his broker—he made more money in a few days— than he had made at his regular job during the entire previous year.

Your new mighty memory is going to give you great new reading power; the power to read two or three times as quickly as you do now, and with far better comprehension. And you'll also find plenty of fun in possessing a terrific memory. Read the chapter on memory demonstrations—after you master the simple methods— and you can make your friends whistle in amazement when they see what a *real* memory can do.

You Have the Power—Now Find It and Use It for Building a Better Life

Strictly speaking, this book does not give you a better memory. Rather, it shows you how to find and use the immense memory power that simply is *waiting* to help you. As Ralph Waldo Emerson said, we seldom use more than one-tenth of our minds. You'll be amazed to see how much you know and how much you can accomplish when that submerged nine-tenths comes to the surface.

In writing this book, I have taken pains to test every point and every method with my students and with a great many other people. Also I have used what is probably the world's largest collection of books on memory and mnemonics (memory aids). This collection is my own, and has been some decades in the making.

I have found good memory systems that are as old as Egypt! My task has been to sift every method, and to keep only those which I have been able to simplify, make easy to learn, and key to modern living.

Start reading! In a week or less you should see great results. And within a few weeks, I hope, you will see glorious proof that your mighty new memory is making your life the kind of life you want it to be.

Chesley V. Young

By the Same Author:

How to Read Faster and Remember More,
Parker Publishing Company, Inc.
1965

Contents

How This Book Will Benefit You 5

CHAPTER 1 Your Natural Memory File of Life Experience: Make It Work! . . . 19

* Importance of Memory to Success—20
* The Value of Such Memory Tabs—20
* Forming Your Own Memory File and Using It to Advantage—22
* Recognizing the Potential of a Well-Kept Memory File—22
* How to File the Right Way: The A I R Formula—24
* Historic Cases of Amazing Memory: Lightning Calculators—25
* Diversified Instances of Remarkable Memories—26
* How Such Remarkable Cases Link with You and Your Memory—28
* Using Tested Tabs as Patterns Toward Forming Your Own—30

CHAPTER 2 Ordinary Senses and Ordinary Knowledge Build a Mighty Memory . . . 33

* An Instant Aid to Memory That You Can Use Right Now—34
* Using Your Imagination and Ingenuity in the Memory Pairing Process—38
* Using a Visualization Process to Extend Your Memory Span—40
* Getting Acquainted with Your Ordi-

nary Senses for Memorization—43
* Applying the Sense of Sight Toward
  Better Memory—44
* Checking Your "Everyday" Use of
  Sight as Applied to Memory—47
* Pictorial Test for Application of Sight
  to Memory—47
* Applying the Sense of Hearing To-
  ward Better Memory—48
* Using Hearing as a Supplement to
  Sight in Building a Better Memory—
  49
* Applying the Sense of Touch Toward
  Better Memory—51
* Applying the Sense of Smell Toward
  Better Memory—52
* Applying the Sense of Taste Toward
  Better Memory—53

CHAPTER 3   **Exercise Your Imagination: The Sim-
              ple Link Method of Memory** .   .   .   **55**

* Using Your Imagination to Extend
  Memory Links to Everyday Life—56
* Putting Action and Practicality into
  the Simple Link System—58
* Applying the Simple Link Method
  Toward Remembering Essential Facts
  —60
* Injecting Humor into Memory Chains
  —63
* You Can Literally Link the Simple
  "Link" Method to Your Personal
  Needs—64
* Utilizing the A I R Formula to Sup-
  ply Key-Links in Memory Chains—
  66

CHAPTER 4   **Memory Aids in Your Own Home or
              Office: The Topical Method** .   .   .   **69**

* Applying Cicero's System to Your
  Own Daily Affairs—73

* Strengthening Your Memory Links Through Supplementary Associations —74
* Extending Your Range of Remembered Items—76
* Extending the Topical Method to Broader Scenes—77
* The Neighborhood System and Its Elaborations—79
* Steps Toward Simplification of Topical Memory Methods—80
* The Link-Place System of Remembering up to 50 Items—83

CHAPTER 5 **Get Rid of Absent-Mindedness—And Everybody Will Trust You!**   87

* Using Memory Jogs as an Impromptu Topical System—88
* Turning the Primitive Form of Count to Good Account—90
* The Calendar Count—A Perfect Type of Memory Jog—91
* Pocketing Things to Remember by the Pocket Topical Method—93
* Applying the Feminine Touch to the Pocket Topical Method—95
* Putting Yourself in the Driver's Seat Where Memory Is Concerned—96
* Extending the Topical System by Aiming for Memory Targets—98

CHAPTER 6 **Alphabet Action Makes Memory Might!**   101

* Tabbing Telephone Numbers and Addresses for Ready Reference—103
* Extending A-B-C to A-B-Z Through the Use of a Pictorial Alphabet—105
* Expanding the Alphabetical-Pictorial

Chain into a Numerical Memory Sys-
tem—107
* Figure-by-Figure Visualization Pro-
duces Alphabetical Results—108
* Interlocking Alphabet Action with
Simple Linkage to Recall a Group of
Objects—109

CHAPTER 7 **Pictures, Letters and Numbers Together Bring Amazing Memory Re-
sults!**   113

* Extending Memory Power by Expand-
ing the A I R Formula—115
* The Ten Picture Method: Retaining
Figures Visually—116
* Applying the Ten Picture Method
Toward Remembering Ten Articles—
and More—118
* Applying Catch Phrases Toward Re-
membering Historical Dates and Other
Data—119
* Develop an Actual Audio-Visual
Memory Through the Homophonic
Method—121

CHAPTER 8 **Using a Ten-Letter Figure Code to
Build Profit and Power with the 100-
Word Super-System**   125

* Forming a Ten-Word Key List from
the Figure Alphabet—130
* Extending Numerical Memory into
the Millions by Using Paired Lists—
135
* Reverting to the Original List to Add
Another Pair of Figures—138
* Using the Amplified List to Remem-
ber Population Figures—139
* Memorizing Important Business Data
Through the Figure Alphabet—139

CHAPTER 9 **How to Remember Names: First Step in Better Personal Relations** . . . **143**

* Utilizing Names as a Primary Factor in Remembering People—145
* Broadening Your Own Personal Interests Through Memory Power—146
* How Your Mental Filing System Can Deliver Personal Information—147
* Suggested Classifications for Your Cross-Reference Name File—148
  1. Occupational Names—the original memory tabs • 148
  2. Descriptive Names—a further step in simple memory tabs • 149
  3. Names of Things—a wide range of advanced memory adjuncts • 150
  4. Names of Places—a proven method of remembering personal names • 151
  5. Famous Names—a truly "jump-to-mind" classification • 151
  6. Names of Products—opening new vistas in memory expansion • 152
  7. Nicknames—a compact mental index file in themselves • 153
  8. First Names—how to turn them into memory tabs • 154
  9. Personal Linkage—teaming the new with the old • 155
  10. Actual Connections—letting names express themselves • 156
  11. Imaginary Connections—forging your own links • 157
  12. Pictorial Sequence—the rebus method, a veritable memory game • 157

CHAPTER 10 **Let's Face It: Memory Development at Its Peak—Remembering Faces and Linking Them with Names** . . 159

* *Setting Your Pace for the Future by a Selective Process of Facial Memory —161*
* *Typing Faces as an Adjunct to Your Personal Memory File—162*
* *Expanding the "Double" System into a Specialized File—163*
* *Remembering Faces by the Celebrity Linkage Method—164*
* *Advantage of Using Famous or Familiar Faces as Memory Models—166*
* *Applying the Rules of Physiognomy to Facial Memorization—166*
* *Frontal Face Formations and Their Memorization: Square, Triangular, Oval—167*
* *Three Types of Profiles That Can Be Automatically Remembered: Convex, Straight, Concave—168*
* *Additional Features Helpful to Memorizing Faces—169*
* *Linking Names with Faces: The Art of Letting a Face Announce Its Owner —170*
* *Linking Names and Faces by Step-by-Step Application of the A I R Formula —171*
* *Following Up the First Step of Attention with the Next Step: Interest— 172*
* *Repetition as a Final or Independent Step in Linking Names and Faces— 173*

CHAPTER 11 **Letting Memory Help You Build and Spell Your Word Power** . . . 177

* *Distinguishing Between Vocabulary*

Types as Preliminary to Memory Expansion—178

* Synchronizing the Vocal and Reading Vocabularies Through A I R—179
* How Word Recognition Builds Word Power Through Word Use—180
* Putting the Vocal Vocabulary to Special Use with the Reading Vocabulary —181
* The Endless Chain of Memory Links and How You Can Apply It—182
* Using Memory Keys to Increase Your Word-Span Ten to One Hundred Times—184
* Further Exploration in the Twin Realms of Prefixes and Suffixes—185
* Building These Adjuncts (Prefixes and Suffixes) into Easily Remembered Words—188
* Using Spelling as an Adjunct to Word Structure in Vocabulary Building— 189
* Ways of Applying Memory Methods to Synonyms, Antonyms and Homonyms—190
* Teaming Accepted Rules for Spelling with Simple Memory Devices—192

CHAPTER 12 **How to Read Faster and Remember Every Key Fact** **193**

* Using Pictures to Express Ideas: The Early Step Toward Reading—194
* Supplanting the Hindering Habit of Vocalization with the Helpful Practice of Visualization—196
* Mapping Your Excursions in Reading as You Would a Trip Over Modern Highways—197
* Four Speed Zones of Modern Reading with Memory Serving as Their Ultimate Aim—198

* Reading for Self-Improvement • 198
* Reading for Information • 198
* Reading for Cultural Development • 198
* Reading for Pleasure • 199

* Turning the "One-Two-Three Word" Reading Processes into Multiplex Speed—199

* Letting "Key-Words" Serve as "Eye-Signals" for Still More Rapid Reading and Use as Memory Tabs—200

* Specially Designed Techniques for Reading Faster and Remembering More—201

* The Five S System • 201
* The R T P System • 202
* The P E R U System • 202
* The P Q R S T System • 202
* The S Q 3 R System • 202

* Adapting Reading Systems to Memorization of Poetry: How to Combine Theme with Rhyme—203

* Pleasure Reading as a Step to Prestige: How to Read a Novel in a Few Hours —204

CHAPTER 13   **Now Use Your Expert Memory in High-Speed Mathematics!** . . . **207**

* Applying the Memory Factor Toward Mathematical Efficiency—209

* Doubling Your Speed in Simple Addition Through Acquired Memory—209

* From Double to Triple Speed Through Math Memory Methods—210

* Testing Your Numerical Span in Terms of Instant Memory—210

* Using "Catch Figures" as a Device in Paper-and-Pencil Addition—211

* Carrying "Catch Figure Addition" to the Tens Column and Beyond—212
* Speeding and Assuring Additions by Working from Left to Right—213
* Utilizing Memory Methods to Speed Up the Process of Subtraction—214
* Subtracting Two-Figure Numbers from Left to Right by Instant Sight—215
* Using Your Memory for Addition as an Adjunct to Quick Subtraction—216
* You Can Multiply Your Memory Power Through Multiple Memory Methods—217
* Expanding the Multiplication Table to Speed Specialized Calculations—218
* How a New Look at Number Groups Enables the Rapid Calculator to Shine in Business—218
* Putting Multiplication Methods in Reverse to Speed the Division Process—220

CHAPTER 14 **Amaze Your Friends with Memory Stunts and Games** **223**

* Calling Off Figures—224
* I've Got Your Number—225
* Master Memory—226
* Finding Concealed Names—227
* I Doubt It—228
* Concentration—231
* Authors—233

CHAPTER 1

Your Natural Memory File
of Life Experience:
Make it Work!

Importance of Memory to Success

In today's complex world of finance and progress, nearly everyone will agree with the statement: "Success is spelled with dollars and cents." Even if you don't agree, you will recognize it as the all-pervading formula and therefore something to be noted and remembered. So visualize the word like this:

$$\$ \ U \ \cent \ \cent \ E \ \$ \ \$$$

There it is, "Success spelled with dollars and cents." Will you ever forget it? You won't, because you can't. You will never again think of success, without including dollars and cents. Try and forget it; you just can't. The more that you try to dismiss that notion from your mind, the more strongly it will crop up.

This, of course, is a very exaggerated example, but it has been selected for that very reason; namely, to show how far some oddity in word formation can be carried. By backtracking to the simplest of such mental tabs, you will find that you have a whole multitude already at your disposal and that more will crop up, the more you look for them. As you proceed, you will be able to form your own tabs, sometimes automatically, which is all the better.

This is not confined to word formation. Whole systems of philosophy have been founded on aphorisms, where a truth is conveyed in a word or sentence for the mind to retain it. Empires have grown from the general acceptance of such phrases as "Go West, young man." Big businesses have won public confidence through the slogan, "The customer is always right," which is something that every customer likes to remember.

The Value of Such Memory Tabs

A well-tabbed memory file can deliver whatever information you want, instantly. Once an idea is so firmly fixed that it can spring to mind on call, it can also rouse a whole chain of recollections, thereby increasing its value as a memory tab. The same rules that applied in the past are just as important at present and will be still more valuable in the future, which is why they should be put to use by everyone.

Back in 400 B. C., Hippocrates, the "father of medicine" used aphorisms to express his findings, so that the summaries of his observations and deductions would be available to his followers in terse, pointed, easily remembered form. The so-called "Hippocratic Oath" to which modern medical students subscribe, forms a logical sequence of ideas which may be classed as memory links in themselves.

Among modern sages, Benjamin Franklin used dozens of proverbs to drive home rules and precepts. Many of these are still quoted in their capsule form and are as all-inclusive now as they were back then. But Franklin did not stop with that. He raised the value of memory tabs to a far greater degree.

In his *Autobiography*, Franklin tells how he read an article from a volume of the *Spectator*, then laid the book aside, made some notes on the subject and a few days later, tried to reconstruct the original article in his own words. That done, he compared his copy with the original and corrected any faults. Franklin did this with article after article and as he became more proficient, he scrambled his notes and tried to allocate them later.

Not only did Franklin's tabs prove their worth, but he discovered that his own vocabulary was quite limited. To expand it, he adopted the ingenious procedure of putting some of the articles into verse, because that forced him to find or think of words that would fit the meter and the rhyme. Such words in their turn became memory tabs, improving his literary ability all the more.

Among simple, direct memory tabs are quotations from the Bible, in which a person cites "book, chapter, and verse," along with the actual wording of the passage. This not only allows anyone hearing the quotation to look it up and verify it, but also the person reciting the verses can check back at intervals and refresh his memory of those passages. This accounts for the remarkable range that some gospel students have acquired.

Historians use dates as memory tabs in much the same way. So do biographical writers, who can outline the entire careers of famous men and women by simply linking the dates of their birth and death with other events of the same period. These adjuncts aid lawyers, bankers, brokers, and persons in many other walks of life. Once they recognize the rules of their profession or trade, they remember them and thereby follow them, with cumulative results.

Forming Your Own Memory File and Using It to Advantage

Analyze the average person's memory file and you will find that it is mostly hit or miss. If it falls into some special category, like those already listed, it is good, so far as it goes, yet you may find such people woefully lacking in their recollection of things outside their own range or immediate needs.

As a prime example, consider a storekeeper who has a string of steady customers and is anxious to gain new ones. He is apt to know all the regulars by name, as well as knowing what they want, the moment they come into the store. Often, he may lay aside some new item, thinking it will please Mr. So and So, and usually, it does. He may add newcomers to his mental list after their first few visits, with very much the same result.

Restaurant owners, bank tellers, and many others who have continued contact with a great many people frequently display a seemingly remarkable ability at remembering names and faces. Yet they are apt to be just as forgetful as anybody else where other matters are concerned. If you tell these persons that they are using a memory system, they generally won't believe it. They may even take the attitude that it's their business to remember such things, otherwise they wouldn't be in that business.

Also, they are apt to ask: If a system is involved, why shouldn't it work with other things as well?

The answer is, it will, if you start with whatever you can remember easily or naturally, then look for helpful tabs. From those, you can form your own memory file, adding new tabs as you proceed, giving them various "colors," so to speak, to distinguish them from one another. As with any standard filing system, there should be heads and subheads, with cross-indexing as needed. These are the "keys" which you remember to unlock a whole treasure chest of facts with which they are associated.

Recognizing the Potential of a Well-Kept Memory File

To develop any mental faculty, a positive approach is essential. As with the business slogan, "We didn't get big by thinking small," you can't build a mighty memory by insisting that you have no memory whatever. When people say, "I forget everything," try quizzing them on odd subjects with which they should be familiar, and they themselves may be utterly amazed by how much they do remember. It just happens that their files are cluttered with useless data, waiting for someone like you to provide the tabs that they should have supplied for themselves.

Here is an example of such inadequate tabbing:

Marcia Wilet regarded herself as the most forgetful of all persons, so her life was filled with apologies on that score. One night she went to a party and the next day, she called up several of her friends and asked these questions:

(1) "Tell me, Julia, who was that young man you introduced to me last night? The one you met in Miami?"

(2) "Please, Peggy, what was the name of that shop where you bought the charm bracelet for your niece, Louise?"

(3) "Give me your new address again, Helen. I was sure I'd remember it, but I forget everything—"

(4) "Jane, did you say Anne's baby was a boy or a girl?"

(5) "You said four ounces of chocolate, two cups of sugar, three-quarters of a cup of milk, but really, Grace, I can't remember when you said to add the two tablespoons of butter!"

All of Marcia's friends agreed that she was the most forgetful person they had ever met. Yet far from being a "horrible example," she really deserved a high rating. She remembered five different subjects that she had discussed with each friend, along with other persons and places involved, including a recipe for fudge; but she nullified all those recollections by missing out on the very points she wanted to remember.

Her problem: No tabs. Or if she did have any, they were all one color. If she had concentrated on the answers and found some way to peg them, she would not have had to revert to the very same questions when she called up her friends the next day. What was worse, after Marcia heard the answers for the second time, she again forgot them, because she once more failed to tab them.

If she had tabbed them at the start, concentrating upon her objective and ignoring lesser small talk, she would have had the answers the night before. Instead of calling her friends and asking them to tell her what she should have remembered, she might have met them afterward and thanked them for the information they had given her, much to their surprise, because by then, they would have forgotten all about it.

How to File the Right Way: The A I R Formula

All this resolves itself into one simple answer where natural memory is concerned. It must be related to its component elements, just as H_2O is the chemical term for water. But memory, being more variable and more volatile, is more akin to the atmosphere, which consists mostly of nitrogen, oxygen and other gases that are not combined chemically but retain their own characteristic properties.

This analogy is especially appropriate because the word A I R is the key to the elements affecting memory itself, namely:

A represents the element of Attention

I represents the element of Interest

R represents the element of Repetition

With any occupation, profession, enterprise, or even a hobby or a social gathering, a person remembers essential facts as naturally as breathing the surrounding air. He must give Attention to the subject, which is natural enough, because it is important to him. He must show Interest in it, or it would be discarded as something too trivial to be remembered. Finally, by weighing the facts thus accepted, Repetition fixes them firmly in mind.

How far can this formula be carried?

Very far.

There is an old story of a strong man who was able to lift a baby elephant. So he practiced the stunt regularly every day and, finding no appreciable difference, he decided quite logically that if he kept on, he would eventually be able to perform the unheard-of feat of lifting a full-grown elephant!

A ridiculous notion, considered within physical limitations, but in the mental realm, particularly with memory, the situation changes. Your immediate memory depends upon how much attention you give a subject, how much interest it generates in your mind and how much repetition you require to retain it. Properly tabbed, it will stay. Other facts may then be memorized by the same process without interfering with those that were acquired earlier.

Historic Cases of Amazing Memory:
Lightning Calculators

The formula A I R, as given, applies not only to normal memory, but to cases where memory may be regarded as a special faculty in itself. History is replete with instances of persons whose memories were amazing on two counts: First, the early age at which they were developed; second, the fantastic degree that they attained.

Of primary interest are the "calculating boys," whose exploits have been recorded over a period of some three centuries, though isolated instances were noted long before. Heading the modern list is Jedediah Buxton, who was born at Elmton in Derbyshire, England about the year 1707. He came from an intelligent and well-educated family, but Jedediah himself never learned to read or write and was a decidedly backward child at the age of twelve, when he began astonishing the villagers by his uncanny ability with figures.

Having no formal training in mathematics, Buxton evolved his own peculiar system which always came out right. He could walk over a field and calculate its area not only in acres, but in square inches; and he was hired to survey the entire township in that manner. In answering complicated problems by sheer mental calculation, Buxton's usual reward was free beer at the local tavern and shortly before his death in 1772, he calculated the exact number of glasses that he had earned in his lifetime.

The career of Zerah Colburn, of Cabot, Vermont, was shorter but more spectacular. At the age of six, he could recite the multiplication table so far beyond normal schoolboy limits, that his father, a local carpenter, took him on tour through the Eastern states and later abroad. One of his advertised feats was to take a number of six or seven figures and mentally determine all the factors of which it was composed.

In England in 1818, Zerah was matched against a Devonshire lad of his own age, George Parker Bidder, who could mentally divide a number like 468,592,413,563 by 9076, coming up with the answer, 51,629,838 +, in less than a minute. Honors were equally divided; but oddly, Colburn's ability faded in his early twenties and he became a teacher of languages at Norwich University in Vermont, where he died when he was only thirty-five. Bidder, however, remained a lightning calculator until his death at the age of seventy-two, and his son inherited his ability, being known as the Younger Bidder.

Diversified Instances of Remarkable Memories

In contrast to lightning calculators, there are many cases where intellectual achievements have been furthered by prodigious memories at an early age. Most remarkable was Christian Friedrich Heinecken, born in Lubeck, Germany in 1721. He could recite from the Bible at the age of one; was familiar with all of it at two; and at three could speak both Latin and French. At four, he became ill and predicted his own death which occurred in 1725. During his brief lifetime, the famous "Infant of Lubeck" faced competition from a French "wonder child," Jean Louis Cardiac, who was born in 1719 and died in 1726, outlasting the Lubeck prodigy by only one year. Jean Louis could repeat the alphabet when three months old. At three years, he could read Latin and at four could translate it into both French and English. He learned to read Greek and Hebrew at the age of six; and at seven, he was delving into arithmetic, history and geography when he died in Paris.

Obviously, fantastic memories were needed to retain all facts that these two children acquired in such little time. This led to the supposition that such infant prodigies actually matured and reached the equivalent of old age during their highly compressed lifetime. But that was refuted in the case of Jeremy Bentham, who was born in London in 1848. At the age of three, Jeremy had read many volumes of history and was learning Latin. At four, he took up French and began playing the violin. At school, he moved several classes ahead, added Greek to his store of languages, and entered Oxford at the age of thirteen.

Naturally, skeptics were convinced that Bentham could not last long at that pace, but he proved them wrong by outlasting the skeptics themselves. He lived to the age of eighty-four, maintaining his remarkable faculties, including his mighty memory, throughout his long career. He specialized in reforms of law and government, introducing such terms as "utilitarian," "international," and "codification" to the English language. Literally living a century ahead of his time, he projected plans for the building of the Suez and Panama Canals, only to have them rejected like many other of his sound proposals, on the grounds that they would be impossible.

Another child prodigy destined for a long and distinguished career was Thomas Babington Macaulay, who was born in England in 1800. He became an avid reader at the age of three, with such a retentive memory for facts that at seven he wrote a compendium of universal history from antiquity to the year 1800. By the age of ten, he had added poems, hymns and ballads to his early literary achievements.

In his teens, Macaulay could recite the entire poem of Milton's *Paradise Lost* and it was claimed that he remembered everything he ever read. His knowledge was not merely stored in his memory; it was always at his command, as evidenced by his essays, which drew from the records of all ages and all countries. Before he was fifty, he had become one of England's leading statesmen; he then turned his chief efforts to producing successive volumes of a great *History of England* which he had nearly completed when he died in his sixtieth year.

The A I R formula for a mighty memory was amply illustrated by Macaulay's career, an illuminating sidelight being the fact that at college, he actually recoiled from mathematics, a direct contrast to the lightning calculators. Yet, he was utterly fascinated by Greek and Roman classics, into which most of the mathematical wizards never even delved.

To strike a mid-point between these two extremes, we should consider cases that are neither mathematical nor classical. Here are a few striking examples:

In the year 1800, John Thompson, then in his forties, was living in St. Giles Parish in London. To impress his neighbors, he drew an entire plan of the parish from memory, working from every corner shop, pump, or stable, and filling in from there. From that, he became known as "Corner Memory Thompson" and continued to update his descriptions of the neighborhood until he died at eighty-six. His formula: Attention + Interest + Repetition = A I R.

In the early 1840's, a child named Paul Morphy was allowed to sit by while his father, Alonzo Morphy, played chess with his Uncle Ernest, who was the champion of Louisiana. One day, the boy spoke up and criticized their play, which led to the amazing discovery that he knew the game better than they did. So, at the age of ten, Paul was pitted against all the chess experts in New Orleans and proceeded to defeat them in regular succession.

From then on, Paul Morphy traveled by A I R. He went to Europe and defeated all the chess masters that he met there. His *attention* had been drawn to chess; his *interest* was in chess; all chess moves to him, were a *repetition* of those that had gone before. As a result, Morphy was able to remember every move in every game that he had played throughout his remarkable career. But by the age of twenty-three, he had lost all interest in chess and he faded into obscurity. Too much concentration on one subject could have been the cause, including too much fame, acquired at too early an age.

That brings us to William John Bottell, the man who could remember anything and do nothing with it. Born in England in 1875, he spent his boyhood in London, where he ran errands and worked in a blacksmith shop. He was interested in everything he heard and tried to find the answer for whatever he didn't know. Hence, he wasn't limited to a neighborhood or a game like chess.

At the age of twenty-six, while working the night shift at a gas-works, Bottell dropped into a pub and became involved in a discussion of recent events to which he supplied all the answers. He was overheard by a theatrical agent, who signed him up as a music hall performer to answer any questions put by the audience. Billed under the name of "Datas," Bottell sprang to immediate fame and steadily increased his capability by checking the answers to any questions that he had to dodge, and adding them to his repertoire.

Wherever he went, Datas picked up local information and rapidly memorized it by the A I R formula. He gave it full *attention*, added the element of *interest* and *repeated* it until he had it fixed in his mind. With Datas, the great aim was to show how far memory could go; hence, his mind was already filled with links which formed a vast cross-index, often enabling him to hook up new facts through a process of multiple associations, both rapidly and efficiently.

How Such Remarkable Cases Link with You and Your Memory

It may seem a far cry from these remarkable cases in thinking back to the "horrible example" of Marcia Wilet, as described on page 23. Actually, the gap is not so wide as it seems, for, in a sense, we have circled back to the starting point. Lightning calculators and giant intellects may be beyond the range of average individuals, but the last three instances have a fundamental touch.

They associated things that were at hand or as they came along, literally finding it easier to remember certain things than to forget them. With Marcia, it was a matter of throwing some new fact into a file that was already helter-skelter, without benefit of effective linkage.

Marcia should have: (1) encouraged the young man to talk about his family and friends in order to tab his name properly. She should have (2) shown more interest in the shop that Peggy mentioned, instead of reverting to the charm bracelet. With Helen's new address, she could have (3) asked about the neighborhood and the house itself, in order to recall it. If she had asked (4) the name of Anne's baby or what name might be given it, she would have remembered whether it was a boy or girl. With the fudge recipe (5), Marcia had only to visualize the actions of mixing each ingredient in succession and she would have known when to add the butter.

All the links were there. It was simply a matter of connecting them by the A I R formula. The trouble was that Marcia was satisfied with snatches of information which she thought would fall in line, but didn't. Only slight tabs were needed, but she neglected them completely; so if you are making the same mistake, correct it. Keep A I R in mind as your basic tab, form others as you go along and your memory will show a marked improvement.

Actually, you have everything it takes to build a mighty memory. Among the fringe benefits are a waked-up mind that will appreciate its own potential along with faculties that may improve with age. A whole new vista opens up when you apply your memory to things that count and also find that you can recall immediate needs without floundering or groping mentally.

A good memory increases your self-confidence and will enable you to proceed with the expectation of success, whether you spell it $U¢¢E$$ or just SUCCESS. In short, recognition of your natural memory, plus ways to apply it, will produce the winning combination. That is the advantage gained from studying the remarkable cases cited and applying your formula in the right way.

Using Tested Tabs as Patterns
Toward Forming Your Own

Tested memory tabs like $U¢¢E$$ are often used to remember general subjects. Some fairly jump at you, while others serve as reminders of facts already learned. All are good to note and come in handy when needed. They also may give you ideas toward special tabs of your own. Here are some good examples:

To remember which way to turn the clock when changing from Standard Time to Daylight Time and vice versa:

When going anywhere, you *spring forward* and *fall back*.

Set the clock an hour *forward* in the *Spring*; and an hour *back* in the *Fall*.

In yachting parlance, "port" means "left," while "starboard" signifies "right." A red light is carried on the port side of a ship; a green light on the starboard. This is very confusing to land-lubbers when they first come aboard, but they can avoid that problem by simply putting the *short words* in one group; the *long words* in another, thus:

| LEFT | — | PORT | — | RED |
| RIGHT | — | STARBOARD | — | GREEN |

Here is an excellent device whereby a list of items may be remembered by means of an acrostic, or key-word formed from the initial letters:

To remember the four divisions of the British Isles, use the key-word: WISE.

WALES
IRELAND
SCOTLAND
ENGLAND

To remember the five Great Lakes, use the key-word: HOMES.

HURON
ONTARIO
MICHIGAN
ERIE
SUPERIOR

This system can be carried further by coining a sentence in which the first letter of each word can be used to form an acrostic, which becomes the key-word to related items. The countries composing Central America are easy to learn, but hard to remember, for if you forget how many there are, you are likely to leave out a few. Their location, too, is hard to remember; but the following tab takes care of that as well:

To remember the countries of Central America in continuous order from north to south, use the following key-sentence:

Big Game Hunters Eat Nice Cold Potatoes

Putting the capital letters into acrostic form, they become the key-word to:

BELIZE
GUATEMALA
HONDURAS
EL SALVADOR
NICARAGUA
COSTA RICA
PANAMA

Now that geography is carrying itself into outer space, remembering the planets in order, from the sun as center, is a matter of some importance. It can be done by the same system of turning a key-sentence into an acrostic:

Men Very Easily Make All Jobs Serve
Useful Needs Promptly

The planets corresponding to those capital letters are: Mercury, Venus, Earth, Mars, Asteroids, Jupiter, Saturn, Uranus, Neptune, Pluto.

Here is an old but still useful device for recalling the colors of the rainbow, in their regular order:

Think of the name: ROY G. BIV

Who is Roy G. Biv? Nobody, but an odd name like that is easily remembered and its letters form an acrostic that becomes a key-word to the colors:

RED
ORANGE
YELLOW
GREEN
BLUE
INDIGO
VIOLET

There are many of these "dodges" as such tabs are sometimes called. You will find them all useful, and if you form those of your own, so much the better, as they will be all the more easily remembered. But it is not always easy to line up just the right combination of names to make a good key-word. It would be nice, indeed, to have seven friends named Doris, Ellen, Fran, Irene, Nancy, Ruth and Sally, because by switching them about a bit, you could make the first letters spell FRIENDS. But what would you do with Bill, Bob, Charley, Jack, Joe, George and Tom?

The answer would be to find some other system, which you will in the chapters that follow.

* * * * * * * * * *

CHAPTER 2

Ordinary Senses
and Ordinary Knowledge
Build a Mighty Memory

In a simple intelligence test used by modern psychologists, a person is shown ten common objects and allowed to study them for a minute or two. Then, after a brief interval, the person is asked to call off all ten. These may be actual objects, or just pictures of them. Either way, the test is practically the same and it seems absurdly simple. Most people start to reel off the articles in rapid, confident style, only to hit a snag when they come to the last few.

Actually, the fixing of seven objects firmly in mind represents about an average memory span. Try it yourself with those depicted in Fig. 2-1, page 36, and you will appreciate the difficulty of going beyond that limit. According to one rating, seven is "average"; eight, "good"; nine, "very good"; and ten, "exceptional." Sometimes luck helps in hitting a high number; after getting to eight, a person may grope mentally for the last two and recall one or both, but more often, the result is apt to be a blank, particularly if a person is given a time limit, of say two or three minutes for the entire list.

One thing is certain with such a test. It proves how greatly a systematized memory is needed in everyday life. Often you may have to remember half a dozen things, without having pad and pencil handy, or even lacking the time to write them down. Again, something else may crop up, diverting your thoughts from whatever you originally had in mind, so that when you backtrack to it, you find that the things that seemed so easy to remember are now totally forgotten.

An Instant Aid to Memory
That You Can Use Right Now

Some people shy away from memory methods due to the mistaken notion that if they can't remember obvious things that are right in front of them, why should they complicate it further by trying to learn memory aids that will be even more easily forgotten? That, of course, is absurd, as no one would ever learn anything by adopting such an attitude. The simple answer is that memory, like every other subject, should be developed step by step.

We begin our study of mathematics with the simple premise that 2 plus 2 equals 4, and we continue on through advanced arithmetic and algebra. Similarly, as we learn words, we form them into phrases and sentences. But with memory, the faculty seems so natural, so inherent, that people tend to regard it as if it were a "sixth sense" or something wholly instinctive. They say, "I can't remember anything," much as they would admit to having weak eyes or being hard of hearing. Yet by that very token, they should realize that memory can be improved, just as eyesight can be helped by corrective lenses, or hearing by means of hearing aid devices.

So with memory, let's take the simple factor of memory span. Admitting that seven is the usual working limit, how would you go on from there? Assuming that you tried to remember ten objects and bogged down somewhere between seven and ten, how could you repeat the test (by using the ten objects shown in Figure 2-1) and remember all ten, right now?

Very simply. Start by remembering just five; then take five others and remember them. But since 5 plus 5 equals 10, how can that help the situation? It helps in this case, because you purposely pick the five objects in the top half of the page. Those are: a pencil, a bottle, a canary, a knife, a shoe. Since there are only five, you can remember them quite rapidly, calling them off to make sure.

Now look at the bottom half of the page. There you see a pad, which goes with a pencil, so you say, "Pencil and pad." Next, a glass, which goes with the bottle, so you say, "Bottle and glass." Next, a cage for the bird, so you say, "Bird in cage." Since a fork is needed with a knife, you say, "Knife and fork"; then finally, since a sock goes with a shoe, you say, "Shoe and sock." (Fig. 2-2, page 38.)

Still looking at the bottom five, call off the items: "Pad, glass, cage, fork, sock." All this can be done so rapidly, that you should still have time to repeat your pairs in reverse: "Sock with shoe"— "Fork and knife"—"Cage for bird"—"Glass with bottle"—"Pad and pencil."

That done, close the book and talk about something else for a few minutes. Then try to call off your first list of five objects, or even better, jot them down from memory. That shouldn't be hard at all, since there are only five, two less than the average seven. Once you have listed the first five, regardless of their order, the

Figure 2-1

second list falls right in line, since each item pairs up with its companion from the other group.

Although you are actually remembering ten objects, this pairing process really makes it easier than if you were simply trying to remember only five, because the reversal of the pairs serves as an added memory tag.

For example, if you ran through the top group a few times, then dropped it and didn't think about the list until the next day, you might say to yourself: "Pencil—bottle—canary—what was the next thing? A shoe—but that was the last one—there was something else before that—" That "something else" was a knife, but by some chance quirk you skipped over it; and there are times when a "lost" item just won't come to mind when you try to run through a list again.

But when you have paired the items with those of another group, as in the present case, you can run through the companion list for your verification. Let's suppose that you have trouble there, too, as you mentally check the list: "Pad—glass—let's see, what was next? A fork—a sock—but that only makes four. I've missed something in between." That "something" was a cage, which represents another memory lapse. But having two lists to go by, you simply revert to your pairing system and call them off alternately: "Pencil—pad. Bottle—glass. Canary—cage." There, you pause triumphantly, for you have found the missing item from the lower list; namely "cage." So you continue with the lower list, adding the paired item from the upper: "Fork—knife." Again one list has provided a memory jog for the other.

Using Your Imagination and Ingenuity in the Memory Pairing Process

This example has purposely been kept simple and brief, so as to stress the principle involved; but you can readily see that it could work with a much longer list. With twenty items, you would have two lists of ten, pairing up with each other; and though you can expect to miss one or two items in a list of ten, here the interlocking of the lists would again come to your aid.

There is just one problem with this pairing process. It works very beautifully and easily when the items themselves pair up as precisely as already described; but what if you don't have "naturals"

Figure 2-2

that go together, like pad and pencil, bottle and glass, and the rest as listed?

In that case, you will have to exercise some imagination and ingenuity toward forming pairs of your own choice. Pair any items that naturally link, as those already given; then find common points with others on the list. These can vary and they can even be far-fetched, as they are sometimes easier to recall when the linkage is somewhat odd. Take these two groups of seven, as an example:

> Table, glove, stone, milk, clock, coin, perfume
> Tree, coat, string, pillow, typewriter, ring, paint

- *Table* can be paired with *Tree*, because:
  Both begin with the letter "T" and are composed of wood.
- *Glove* can be paired with *Coat*, because:
  Both are articles of apparel and a glove will fit into a coat pocket.
- *Stone* can be paired with *String*, because:
  Both begin with "S-T" and a stone may be used to draw a string down into water, to moor something.
- *Milk* can be paired with *Pillow*, because:
  Both are white.
- *Clock* can be paired with *Typewriter*, because:
  Both make a ticking sound.
- *Coin* can be compared with *Ring*, because:
  Both are round and made of metal and a Chinese coin has a hole in the center like a ring.
- *Perfume* can be paired with *Paint*, because:
  Both are liquid and give off a distinctive odor.

Note that this personalized pairing process is actually a natural procedure, which can be improved with practice, as combinations once formed have a way of jumping to mind. Horse-and-buggy, Stars-and-stripes, Night-and-day, Ham-and-eggs, all have become part of the English language, as though they were single words in their own right. The combinations given in the first set of examples come close to being in that category, while those in the second set of examples simply represent a liberal extension of the rule.

In short, it is an easy jump from "stars and stripes" to "pencil and pad" and from there it should be equally easy to jump to "perfume and paint." Some of the jumps will become much longer if you use the pairing process regularly, but almost invariably you can find common points that will literally stick in your mind.

Using a Visualization Process to Extend Your Memory Span

We have seen how "pairing" can reduce two lists to the equivalent of only one; now, we come to an alternate device whereby a group of items can be reduced to lesser groups, with each becoming an item in itself, thus increasing the total sufficiently to make memorization virtually automatic. An example will make this clear on practically first sight; namely:

Suppose you want to remember the twelve objects shown in Figure 2-3, which can be listed in the alphabetical order: Baseball, Book, Bowl, Clock, Flag, Goblet, Hat, Necklace, Piggy-bank, Ruler, Scissors, Spool. To remember all twelve at a stretch could prove difficult, but it certainly would not be asking you too much to remember just three or four.

So you remember the objects as *three* groups, consisting of *four* items each. In forming each group, you visualize it as a picture, preferably an animated one, as the action will strengthen the pictorial effect and your memorization as well. Here is the suggested treatment for the present case (Figure 2-4, page 42):

> At the left, visualize the *baseball*, with the *ruler* resting across it, the six-inch mark being over the very top of the ball. The ruler keeps rocking like a see-saw because you think of the *clock* standing on it and the back and forth motion of the clock's pendulum is what causes the ruler to teeter. To make it all the more precarious, the *flag* is flying triumphantly from its pole on top of the clock, dipping one way and then the other as the rocking continues.
>
> At the center, you picture the *book*, lying on its side. On it stands the *goblet*, or at least it was standing there when you started, but now you imagine that someone or something has caused the book to open; and its cover, flipping upward, has tilted the goblet, so that its contents are pouring from it, in the form of loose pearls from the *necklace* and they are landing in the *hat* which is lying brim upward close beside the book.
>
> At the right is the *bowl*, which preferably should be pictured as inverted, thus serving as a pedestal for the *piggy-bank* which is standing with its nose tilted upward in order to balance the

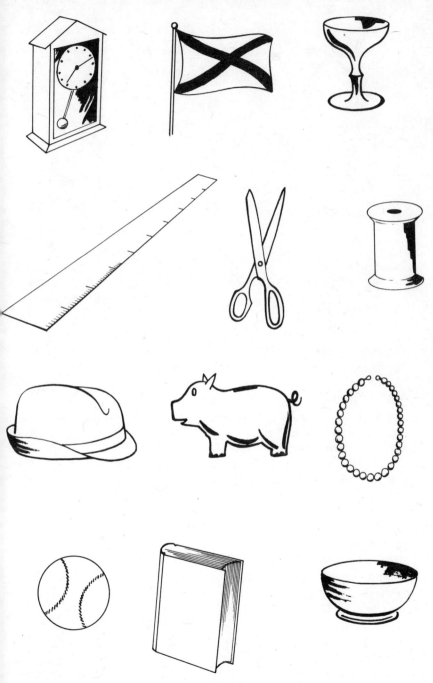

Figure 2-3

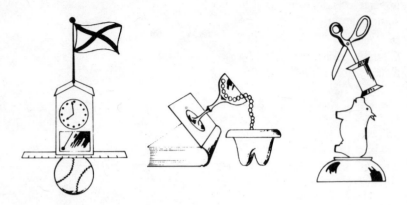

Figure 2-4

spool, which is wobbling at a crazy angle because it is counterbalanced by the *scissors,* which have one blade poked down into the spool and the other blade hanging outside.

Taking advantage of three of the objects that are spelled with the initial letter *B—baseball, book* and *bowl—*they were used as the *bases* of the three memory pictures, and that word also happens to begin with *B.* That, however, is purely arbitrary. Instead, one picture could begin with the *bowl,* the next with the *goblet* and the third with the *hat,* since each represents a *container* and its *contents* would consist of the three articles which you would decide to visualize in each. Such "tie-ins" are not really necessary, as after all, there are only three sets to remember, but any time you can use similar objects as "starters" for your pictures, so much the better.

What makes this memory device so natural is the way it conforms to our actual experience with many common objects. When you speak of a *house,* you really include a collection of other items, as *door, window, steps, porch, roof, chimney.* The word *tree* brings up the components of *roots, trunk, bark, branches, leaves, blossoms.* By simply picturing the outline of a house, you can add the items that go with it; the same with tree, or any object that has a quota of readily recognizable parts.

That same process is applied when you create the synthetic image of a baseball topped by a ruler, clock and flag. The baseball is the central object and the others become the appendages, thus making it a standard pattern, even though the choices were arbitrary. As such, it tends to stay in mind as long as needed—and sometimes longer.

Getting Acquainted with Your Ordinary Senses for Memorization

Basically, our recognition of the external world about us comes through one or more of our five senses: Sight, hearing, touch, taste, and smell. Dependent on these are "sensations" which serve as preliminaries to knowledge. Once sensations grow or combine into a meaningful experience, they are classed as "perceptions," whereby the mind becomes conscious of external objects.

However, sensations may be considered in two distinct groupings: Objective Sensations, which are excited by some object in the outside world and Subjective Sensations, which originate within the brain itself. Appropriately, almost from the start, the memory factor is involved and may often play a major part by the time the state of perception is attained. In this way, memory power may take on the nature of a "sixth sense," which, for convenience, may be termed "your ability at forming mental images" or simpler still, "your imagination."

In daily life, objective and subjective sensations are often closely related. You might see an object, like a lamp on display in a store window, and later you might think of a place in your home or office where the lamp could go nicely. Next, you would be visualizing it as already there. You might do this to such exactitude as to size, shape and color that once the lamp was bought and placed there, it would fit your image to perfection. That simply proves how the inclusion of special details can aid in the retention of an image, or even its projection. Both are big factors in memory. This applies to other senses as well as sight.

Since each sense plays its part in observations which are transferred to your "memory file," it is important to use those individual senses to full degree and purpose. Here, an important adjunct is the "cross-file," in which the findings from one sense amplify or verify the others. Over-dependence on a single sense may limit your memory file, just as limiting the activity or observational range of a single sense is the reason why memory may "fail" a person later.

Another important fact that should be recognized at the very outset of your planning for a better memory is this: In consulting your memory file, you often visualize things which you did not actually see; for example, the facial expression of a friend to whom you gave good news over the telephone. Similarly, you may have an auditory recollection of something you did not actually hear; such as reading a speech given by someone whose style of oratory is so familiar that you would remember it as spoken words. Or a friend might write to you or tell you about something which he touched, smelled, or tasted, making the description so vivid that you would think back to it as if you, personally, had experienced the sensation precisely as described.

There we see objective and subjective sensations working in alternating or interlocking fashion to increase the power of your memory. The more you test it along those lines, the stronger it will become, often automatically, with no extra effort on your part. Indeed, sometimes you will require less effort, for you will find that your memory-file of certain things will enable your imagination to fill in essential facts toward a completed whole.

Here are important pointers toward gaining full acquaintance with your ordinary senses in their relation to your memory.

Applying the Sense of Sight Toward Better Memory

Since sight is used more frequently than all the other senses combined, it is not surprising that many people rely on it alone when committing something to memory. The old saying, "Seeing is believing" has often been quoted to prove that sight is virtually infallible; and that is where people begin to over-trust this one form of perception. They look for what they want to see, to the exclusion of all else, and thereby overlook many things that may be quite as important.

So the first step is to learn to see more; that is, to notice more in any scene that you want to remember. You can test yourself on that score right now, in a very simple and direct way. Just shut your eyes and picture the scene about you; or, if it is more convenient, picture the scene in another room, or outside the front door. All you need is a scene that is readily available to go into your test immediately.

After visualizing the scene, open your eyes and write down a description of it, or simply check the items in it. With a room, this might run:

Big chair in one corner. Framed picture between two windows. Book-case in another corner. Top shelf has no books. Floor lamp beside book-case. Door to other room half-open. Table in far corner. Two phone directories resting on table, with telephone on top of them. Another window closed with curtains drawn to keep out sunlight.

That done, you check the room itself to see what you might have included without any added effort. For example, there might be a pillow in the big chair. Also curtains with the first two windows, but drawn so wide that you wouldn't ordinarily notice them. In noting that the top shelf was empty, you might have overlooked the fact that the bottom shelf is empty, too. There are three bulbs in the floor lamp and you notice now that a small chair is almost obscured by the partly opened door. The reason the telephone is on the directories is that the other half of the table is occupied by a small lamp. The local directory is underneath an out-of-town directory.

Now, if you shut your eyes and go over the same scene again, you will have no trouble including all these details. In fact, they will help you to remember the scene more clearly, because each to some degree is a portion or appendage of the main scene, thereby strengthening the overall image.

For example, you might skip the big chair completely, if you didn't happen to note and recall the pillow. Another look about the room might enable you to include the colors of the pillows and the curtains or the titles of some of the more important books in your next mental review. All such points contribute toward perfection of the mental picture and therefore etch it more deeply into your memory.

After trying this test with available scenes, you can extend it further by picturing fairly familiar places, such as a bus station, a restaurant, your favorite supermarket, an office where you go occasionally, or even some scene along a familiar highway. Recall these to mind as well as you can, make your list and take it along when you go to those places again. Check it for further details, and here again, you will be surprised by the speed and ease with which you can improve your observation and with it your memory.

Things of which you were totally unaware will add a new dimension to such scenes, enabling you to recall them much better.

There is another angle to this that many persons have found early in their steps toward memory improvement; that is, if you look directly at something and say coldly, "I will remember this as is," you are almost sure to miss some of the very details that will help you to recall it. Contrastingly, some chance incident or trifling matter may link up various details so that all are kept in mind.

As an example, you might be with a group of people whom you know, with everyone sitting about stuffily through the entire session. When you look back to that occasion, you will remember them only as so many bumps on a log and if you were asked, "Who was there?", you may find that you can't name more than half of them.

Now just let someone inject something funny or exciting into that same event, with everybody laughing, making comments of their own and kidding one another—the result will be that everything will come to life in your memory. Later, thinking back to the surprise and interlocking reactions, you will find that in a few minutes you can call off the names of everyone present. Just as the eye notes motion, so does memory retain it. Action itself supplies more details for the mind to remember.

There is another very valuable memory adjunct where sight is concerned. That is to see things as other people see them. That is why many witnesses are often brought before a jury. From their partial accounts, it is often possible to build a full picture. You can apply this in a practical way by comparing descriptions of a scene with other peoples' recollections of it. You are each apt to come up with individual details because of your varied interests.

Ride along the countryside and a fisherman will notice the streams, an engineer will watch for bridges, a builder will study houses, a geologist will look for rocks, and so on. By sharing their observations, you will broaden your own. Even if you don't recognize certain objects, by taking interest in them, you will raise a query in your mind that will help you to remember them. This is much better than ignoring things that seem of little consequence to you, but must have value or they would not appeal to other people. What's more, it brings us right back to the basic principle of AIR—Attention, Interest, Repetition—which forms the vital key to memory.

Checking Your "Everyday" Use of Sight as Applied to Memory

As another type of test, see how many of the following questions you can answer right now. All of them concern things that you observe so often in daily life that you should have no trouble with them. Yet you may be surprised to learn how many you will have to check to find out whether you are right or wrong!

(1) Whose portrait appears on the U.S. $5 bill?

(2) Whose appears on the $1 bill?

(3) Which is the top light on a traffic signal—red or green?

(4) Which way is the head of Lincoln facing on a penny: Left or right?

(5) To remove a light bulb from a socket, do you turn it clockwise (to right) or counterclockwise?

(6) If you saw the following letters on the top row of a typewriter keyboard: QWARTSU—which letters would be wrong?

(7) Which letter of the alphabet is missing from the average telephone dial?

(8) What number is often missing from a watch dial?

(9) What is the color of the cloth on most pool tables?

(10) Which is larger—a quarter or a nickel?

(11) Some pencils are round; others have flat surfaces. How many sides do the latter usually have?

(12) What is the shape of the standard highway STOP sign?

If any of these are things with which you are totally unfamiliar, skip them when giving your answers. Later, however, you should check them for the very reason stated under the previous heading; namely, that it is helpful toward memory building to keep the AIR formula constantly in mind and to apply it to facts that you should know because other people find them valuable.

Pictorial Test for Application of Sight to Memory

To apply the sense of sight toward memorization and gain

constant improvement thereby, you should pause whenever possible and study some outdoor scene. Shop windows make another target for such development; and photographs in magazines or paintings in art galleries can serve as proving grounds.

Applying the Sense of Hearing
Toward Better Memory

There are instances in which the sense of sight is supplanted by the sense of hearing. When that occurs, hearing takes over as the chief factor in memory. The shriek of a fire siren immediately reminds the volunteer fireman that he is needed at the firehouse and he responds to the call, unless he also remembers that the siren is tested every day at the noon hour.

Then, he would look at his watch to make sure that he didn't have to go, thus using sight as an adjunct to hearing. But if he happened to be where a clock was striking the hour, he could simply listen to the chimes and if they totalled twelve, that would settle it and the sense of hearing would predominate throughout.

Many situations could be cited where recognition of sound is of primary consequence; and in some cases, hearing may supplant sight altogether. That, of course, is true with blind people, who almost "see" through things they hear, or ascertain through some other sense. But most people who depend on sight are apt to miss some of the opportunities where hearing serves just as well or even better. Ordinarily, that would not seem to matter, since they already have a stronger factor at work; but put such people in a dark room or in a blackout and they will soon wish that they had learned to depend on hearing as well as sight.

You can learn to hear more just as you learned to see more (page 44) provided you choose certain surroundings where identifying sounds are available. Here is such a test:

It is early morning and you are in a house in the country. The windows are slightly raised but the shades are drawn to keep out the sunlight, hence you can not see outdoors. Nevertheless, you can visualize the following surroundings:

> Trees out front. Beyond them a road. Across the road is a farm. A stream runs past the house. Along it, people are fishing from small boats. Well down the stream is a railroad bridge that crosses it. In the other direction, well away from the stream, is a main high-

way. Beyond that is an airfield. Out in back, some
buildings are under construction. Farther off is a boy
scout camp.

To stress the memory factor, let us assume that you are visualizing this scene as it was when you were last there, say a few weeks
ago, just as you might visualize a room that you had seen. But here,
the impressions were auditory; namely:

- *Trees out front:* Twitter of birds above level of window.
- *Road beyond:* Occasional sound of a passing car.
- *Farm across way:* Rooster's crow and barnyard sounds.
- *Stream past house:* Chugging sounds from outboard motors
    following the stream.
- *People fishing:* Motors sound like small ones and they run
    shortly, then stop.
- *Railroad bridge:* Distant rumble of train crossing it.
- *Main highway:* Faint but steady sound of heavy traffic.
- *Airfield:* Planes passing low above house.
- *Building construction:* Sounds of hammering and sawing.
- *Boy scout camp:* Someone practicing a bugle call and having
    trouble with a few notes.

You would not have to hear all these sounds simultaneously
to visualize the entire scene. It could be pieced together, as they
occurred, just as new objects might be placed in a room, adding to
the mental picture of what you see there. That simply emphasizes
how hearing can supplant sight as a memory stimulus.

Using Hearing as a Supplement to Sight
in Building a Better Memory

Once you have cultivated the practice of trying to hear more
as well as see more, you will really broaden your path toward
memory development. You will find that generally, hearing can be
used to supplement sight, rather than to supplant it. This is like
looking at an object and seeing the extra things with it; but in this
case you add hearing as the principal "extra," which at times can
prove to be a vital factor.

As an obvious example, you might say you saw a creature with
a head that had pointed ears and sharp eyes, that it could run fast
on its legs and that it had a conspicuous tail. That might be a

cat, a rabbit, a squirrel or even a raccoon, but if you added that while you saw it run, you heard it bark, everyone would know that you had seen a dog. There, sight outnumbered hearing by four to one, where memory was concerned, but the one count was more important than the other four together.

Check back to the lamp seen in the store window (page 43). There, the sense of sight alone was involved. But in visualizing the spot where the lamp was to go, the purchaser logically would have added another point where sight figured; namely, whether the lamp had enough bulbs to light that portion of the room properly. That would mean picturing the room in terms of the lamp, as well as the lamp in terms of the room. That was an extension of "sight memory."

In contrast, take the case of a lady who saw a fine old clock in an antique shop. It was in good running order and had chimes that rang the half-hours as well as the hours. It was just the right size for the mantel over the fireplace in the small but attractive living room of her compact apartment. So she bought the clock and was delighted with it until that night, when it chimed so loudly that none of the family could sleep.

In buying the clock, she had thought of her living room in terms of "sight memory" only. If the clock had been too large for the mantel, she wouldn't have bought it. If she had applied "hearing memory" in the same way, she would have realized that the clock would be too loud for the room.

It may come as a surprise to present-day readers to learn that their sense of hearing has fallen off badly during the past few decades. It's not that there are so many new sounds to listen for, or that people's hearing may have been dulled to a degree by the increasing turmoil of modern life. It's true that we hear less sounds of nature, such as birds, frogs and crickets; but there is another answer; namely:

In the days of radio programs, listeners extended their sense of hearing to a fantastic degree. People talked about radio dramas and news events as though they had actually seen them, because the sounds that came over the air were designed to waken the memories of the listeners to a point where visualization took over. Conventional sounds were introduced, as footsteps denoting someone's approach or departure; chimes of a clock, to establish a meeting hour; and so on. As these became hackneyed, others supplanted them. Organ bridges were introduced and elaborated, to indicate a change of scene or the passage of time. Voice contrasts were emphasized, dozens of special sound effects were injected and in the case of newscasts, eye-witness reports were handled so graphically that the listener felt that he was there amid the action.

Women who followed the daily installments of "soap operas" practically lived other peoples' lives while going about their household duties. But with the influx of TV, all that ended. A radio drama produced today would be almost unintelligible to the present-day generation of "screen watchers" who have to see in order to hear. Just as the modern art of reading has developed to an extent where the mind pictures all that the eye devours from the printed page, so did the art of listening reach a high state in the days of radio.

The fading of radio is regrettable, but no more so than the passing of earlier eras. The point is, if you take a hint from the past and start studying neglected sound effects all on your own, your memory will be improved in due proportion.

Applying the Sense of Touch Toward Better Memory

Just as the sense of hearing is an important adjunct to that of sight, so is the sense of touch a great aid to hearing and, in fact, to sight as well. We have cited cases where hearing actually takes the place of sight—for example, recognizing the sound of a fire siren and acting accordingly. Similarly, touch may supplement or even supplant both hearing and sight.

Take the analogy of a darkened room or blackout where hearing was needed when sight was impossible. Under such situations, hearing too may be curtailed or even nullified if no sounds occur. In that case, touch takes over in full. We have all heard the old term, "groping in the dark," and anyone who has gone through such an experience will recognize how important touch can be.

Touch also has specialized functions, which are extremely useful in everyday life. One is the use of a dial phone, yet oddly, people depend upon sight to note the dial numbers; but actually, you can pick the holes in the dial and use it through touch alone. One reason this has been neglected is that few people go to the trouble of noting and remembering the exact positions of the letters on the standard phone dial, easy though that should be.

However, even that is unnecessary now that modern phone numbers are so frequently listed by numerals throughout. For example, a number like UN 5-8118 is now dialled as 865-8118.

Hence it is only necessary to run your finger counterclockwise around the dial to each figure in turn, which enables you to complete the call through touch alone, a great help in the dark. But touch as a memory device is even more remarkable when applied to the typewriter. The use of the aptly termed "touch system" with the standard keyboard has become such second nature to many persons that they type in complete words, more rapidly than they could write them out.

Yet if you ask some of these experts to call off the order of the letters on the keyboard in the order they appear there, they won't be able to do it. They know the alphabet in regular order from A to Z, but the keyboard letters simply jump to their finger-tips in response to the linkage of memory with touch, with no conscious effort on the typist's part. This ability is often defined as "motor memory," yet it could be more inclusive. Many things with which we are familiar may be noted at a glance through sight; or sounds may be checked automatically, as when a radio operator reads a coded message. These are akin to typing, tying shoe-laces and many more complex uses of the sense of touch when it has reached the state of motor memory.

To further this function and thereby apply the sense of touch toward better memory, it is a good plan to try doing minor actions automatically or even in the dark, while putting your mind to other things. In driving a car, you must be alert for things you see and hear, yet all the while, you are handling the controls by applying touch and linking it with your other senses.

Applying the Sense of Smell Toward Better Memory

The sense of smell plays a constant part in memory development and there are times where its training has proven vital. Take the case of the two policemen in a New York patrol car who were so trained to detect the smell of gas, that when they noted it too strongly while covering their route, they wasted no time whatever.

They knocked at every door and evacuated an entire neighborhood, taking the whole burden on themselves, rather than waste time in waiting for orders. It was good they did, for they had the area cleared just before the gas mains blew and the fires that followed would have taken many lives, but for the alertness of the patrolmen.

Linking smell with the other senses is an important memory adjunct, as it may provide just the needed difference in some essential matter. The smell of food tells when it is properly cooked; a burning smell warns of a short-circuit and so on. But the sense of smell can go much further. The waft of an exotic perfume can bring back a flood of treasured memories. A whole story might be written hinging upon the aroma of a fine cigar.

Applying the Sense of Taste Toward Better Memory

There are many cases where taste becomes important to memory, or depends upon memory, but these are usually more specialized. Many memories are induced by bitter or sweet tastes; and wine tasters make a profession of such distinctions. Tastes of various foods often bring back recollections of almost-forgotten experiences or surroundings, all adding to the memory cross-file.

One curious example was that of a man who loved the smell of crisp bacon, because it awakened vistas of sparkling lakes, virgin forests, lofty mountains, indeed nature in its greatest grandeur; but he never wanted to eat the bacon. The reason was that years before he had gone on a camping trip in the Canadian wilds and the party had run out of all supplies but bacon. So meal after meal, he had associated its smell with unspoiled surroundings that came back in a flash; but his taste for bacon itself had been totally spoiled.

This shows how closely the senses of smell and taste are interrelated and indeed, they can often be used interchangeably as memory jogs. To illustrate how even a single sense other than sight can be used in an entire sequence, take this example involving the sense of taste alone. There are six states in New England. To remember them, most people would use a map in order to fix their names in mind at the outset. But it can be done quite as readily as follows:

Think of a tasty dinner beginning with a bowl of Rhode Island clam chowder. Follow that with a broiled Maine lobster, with Boston baked beans—symbolizing Massachusetts—as a side dish. For dessert, picture a shortcake composed of fresh New Hampshire blueberries, loaded with rich Vermont maple syrup, sprinkled liberally with Connecticut nutmeg.

That may give you indigestion, but if so, it will help you to remember the six New England states—Rhode Island, Maine, Massachusetts, New Hampshire, Vermont, Connecticut—all the better. New York, technically speaking, is not part of New England, but if you want to remember it along with those states, just think of topping off the meal with a glass of New York State cider, which is about as good as any, and which applies to these memory links as well.

*   *   *   *   *   *   *   *   *   *

CHAPTER 3

Exercise Your Imagination:
The Simple Link Method
of Memory

In testing instant aids to memory, as described in the previous chapter, you will find that you advanced in easy steps toward a better way of remembering objects. The "pairing" method is almost automatic when two objects obviously belong together; and you have seen how easy it is to find certain points in common by which objects can be paired. Grouping objects to form mental figures is simply an extension of the same device, thus increasing the range of instant memory.

Having gone that far, you are ready to analyze the "pairing" system and turn it into a "linking" method. As a start, you can move from pairs to triplets by putting three related objects together; for example, instead of merely pairing a fork and knife, resting on a dinner table, you think of a fork, knife and spoon. With the game of baseball, don't just think of a player swinging a bat and hitting a ball; add a mental picture of the ball being caught by another player's glove. Similarly with golf, you can visualize a club hitting a ball and then add the ball rolling into a hole.

An example of further linkage, involving several items, would be to start from an electric outlet near the floor, find a plug lying nearby and insert it into the outlet, reach for a lamp switch and turn it, thus lighting a bulb, enabling you to open a phone book and look up a number. Note that here the sense of touch is utilized up until the light comes on; then the sense of sight takes over.

By way of variation, suppose that you wanted to turn on an electric fan instead of a light, but that you are still operating in the dark; in fact, you might have first pulled out the light cord in order to plug in the fan. In that case, plugging in, following the wire, turning the switch, would all be due to a sense of touch; then hearing would take over with the whirr of the fan telling you that it was in operation; finally, touch would resume when you felt the breeze from the fan, enabling you to turn it in the proper direction.

Using Your Imagination to Extend Memory Links to Everyday Life

The items already given have natural connections, to the point where they could represent motor memory, which in itself is auto-

matic. If night after night, you plugged into an outlet to turn on a
light or start an electric fan, it would become so automatic that
seemingly no memory would be involved. But memory is involved;
that is the important factor. If you recognize that, you will be able
to extend the same process into everyday needs. Through imagination, you can forge memory links into a chain of your own making,
more solid than anyone else could provide.

This is illustrated in the following example.

Items to be remembered: (1) A horse. (2) A house. (3) A
table. (4) A motel. (5) A speed-boat. (6) A paper-clip. (7) An
airport. (8) A glass of water. (9) A microphone. (10) A cat.

Now to link them.

Picture a *horse* walking into a *house*. Naturally, the surroundings are limited, particularly because a large *table* fills the center
of the living room. So to give it enough space, you think of it in the
lobby of a huge *motel* where people come from their cars and
immediately take off in a *speed-boat* up the river only to be blocked
by a wall of *paper-clips*. The only way to surmount that is to jump
to an *airport*, where the first thing you need is a *glass of water* in
order to tell people of your problem over a *microphone*. But hardly
has your voice become clear, before a *cat* begins to wail louder than
you can talk, so you put the cat on the back of a *horse* which
gallops away happily, with the cat waving back to you.

Not only have you forged your memory links into a chain, but
it is an *endless* chain with the last link leading into the first one,
so that you can pick it up at any link along the line. That is using
your imagination in a practical way and you can apply it to any
sequence of ideas that may occur to you, provided that you exercise
your imagination to whatever degree that is required.

Actually, you have paired these objects in succession, one to
another, one to another, so that your links represent a continuity
of pairs. In the pairing process—as described in Chapter 2—
a deliberate effort was made to keep the pairs natural; that is, the
obvious associations like "fork and knife" or "pad and pencil" were
stretched to form such pairs as "table and tree" or "glove and coat."
But in the simple linkage method, you just take items as they come
and though you still are pairing them, you do it any way you want.
If two things are very much alike, you naturally pair them, as
before; but if they are totally unlike, you take advantage of that,
too.

In fact, the more incongruous the links, the better they may
be, once you have brought imagination to the fore. Oddities jump

to mind all the more quickly. But in either case, whether the links are obvious or ridiculous, you should always strengthen them with minor associations—which in their turn can be either logical or imaginative—and whenever possible, your visualization should include supplementary impressions from the various senses.

In the example given, you can imagine the clatter of the horse's hoofs as he comes into the house. You can picture him bringing his front feet up onto the table with the same *click-clack* sound. That is promptly drowned by the roar of motors and you find yourself at the motel watching people rush from cars into speed-boats which go zooming away still louder. Then you are in the speed-boat, smelling the fumes of the gasoline and suddenly hearing and feeling the *cruuuunnnnch* of the boat's bow as it knifes through a wall of paper-clips. You can feel yourself precipitated into the airport where the roar of planes is still louder, and you find yourself drinking something tasteless which therefore must be water. You hear yourself talking hoarsely into the mike, only to hear the cat's louder *meow*, which in turn is drowned by the clatter of hoofs as the cat goes riding away on the horse.

Other associations could be the fact that a *horse* does not belong in a *house*, yet if you change the letter "R" to "U" one word becomes the other; that *table* and *motel* both end with an "L" sound; that *speed-boat* and *paper-clip* each have the same number of letters with a hyphen in the same place; and that both are made of metal. So is a *microphone* and if you picture it as a floor mike, with the *cat* climbing up its rod, you add incongruity as a supplementary association, because a cat can't dig its claws into metal.

Finally, in checking over a series of such links, the fact that they form interlocking pairs enables you to go backward as well as forward. So any time you tap into the chain, you have the choice of two pairs. Thus any slight lapse or confusion of associations can be overcome by going the opposite way, or tapping in somewhere else along the chain.

Putting Action and Practicality into the Simple Link System

Once you have tested yourself on random objects and have developed your own pet ways of linking them, you can proceed to put action and practicality into your memory process. The simplest form of practicality is to use items that you have a good reason for remembering, such as a shopping list or certain things that you must do, yet might ordinarily forget.

Of course, you can write those down, but there are times when pencil and paper are not handy, and there are also times when you may start out blithely and forget to take along the list that you prepared so carefully. Often, such lists are the hardest things in the world to remember, for the very reason that you are apt to write each item at random and then forget it, simply because you have relieved your mind by putting it on the list.

So instead of relieving your mind, try exercising it; and thereby strengthen your memory, just as physical exercises will strengthen your muscles. You have nothing to lose and a lot to gain, if you keep your purposes in mind rather than on paper, as witness the case of Harold Wright, who put action into memory links, as follows:

Late one night, Harold began thinking of the things he had to do at the office the next morning. First and most important, was to send a check for his insurance. Next, he was to buy some circus tickets for his niece and nephew. There were contracts to be mailed to Harold's lawyer and he had to phone a man named Joe Barton, who had forgotten to pay some back rent on an old garage. Tomorrow was Harold's day for his service club luncheon, and after that he was to look at portable swimming pools and pick up a watch that he had left at the jeweler's for repairs. He was to meet a client at the bus terminal at six o'clock and take him to dinner at the country club, but instead of driving straight home, he was to stop for his wife at the local bowling alley, as her bowling league was scheduled for tomorrow night.

Here is how Harold linked those actions into a continuous series of pairs that formed an endless memory chain. He started with a simple memory jog, a pen that he used for writing checks and signing letters, which bore the name of his insurance company. That triggered the entire list composed of: (1) Insurance. (2) Circus tickets. (3) Lawyer's contracts. (4) Back rent. (5) Lunch. (6) Swimming pool. (7) Watch. (8) Bus terminal. (9) Country club. (10) Bowling alley.

First, Harold thought of signing the *insurance check*, with his pen in hand as a reminder. But instead of picturing himself putting it in an envelope to mail it, he mentally inserted the *circus tickets* instead. Then, to continue his whimsy, he addressed the envelope to his lawyer and pictured him receiving it and finding circus tickets instead of contracts. He could even hear his lawyer saying, "How stupid can Harold get! Why, he's as absent-minded as his friend Joe Barton, who keeps promising to pay his back rent, but never does!"

Now, with Jim Barton in mind, it occurred to Harold that a good way to collect the back rent would be to invite Jim to the service club luncheon and mention it then. As for the luncheon, if tomorrow proved to be a hot day, the room would be warm, so Harold pictured the group diving into a portable swimming pool, himself among them. They were bringing up prizes from the pool and Harold's was a watch, still running, despite the water. But to make sure, Harold decided mentally to check it by the clock in the bus terminal which was always on the dot.

So Harold timed it for exactly six o'clock and who stepped from a bus but his client, wearing a golfer's outfit, to remind Harold that they were going to dinner at the country club. There, during an imaginary dinner that was to be, they watched golfers swinging their clubs, so Harold decided to tee off for himself. But instead of hitting a golf ball, he pictured a bowling ball, coming down the bowling alley and smashing his club to smithereens. But he still had his pen, so he brought it out and used it to add up his wife's bowling score.

Note that although there was some leeway in pairing up the items in this list, they were chronological, taken in the order in which they were to occur the next day. Thus at any time during that day, Harold was able to check backward or forward on the sequence he had imagined and thereby note what he had already done and what he still had to do. This system is so simple and effective that anyone can try it on their own, with immediate results.

Applying the Simple Link Method
Toward Remembering Essential Facts

In Chapter 1, you were introduced to the use of "dodges" as a means of recalling facts, provided you already knew them so well that a simple combination of letters, or a key-word, could suffice as a memory jog. One example in that chapter was the use of the name ROY G. BIV as a "dodge" to recall the colors of the rainbow in correct order according to their capital letters: Red, Orange, Yellow, Green, Blue, Indigo, Violet.

That was followed by the comment that you would later find other systems that would fulfill the same purpose. In keeping with that statement, here is a way to utilize the "simple link method" to recall the rainbow's colors in order:

Start by thinking of a total blackness, which the sun is to banish. You have the sun in mind, because it is the primary source of the rainbow, which includes all the colors of the spectrum. Night, as represented by the blackness, is ended when the first tints of dawn streak the sky, which thereby becomes *red*. Next, the sun itself rises above the horizon, appearing as a bright *orange* orb. Toward noon, it has become a vivid *yellow*, so when the sun is directly above, the only way to rest your eyes is to look at the *green* grass and foliage of the earth about you. But by mid-afternoon, you can look straight up and view the *blue* sky; and by the time the sun is setting, the sky has deepened to *indigo*, which later resolves itself into *violet* of twilight. After that, the blackness of another night, to be dispelled by the next day's dawn.

This method has the advantage of enabling you to recall the actual colors, rather than just their names, yet it still places them in their proper order.

Historical data can also be pegged by the same method. As an example, take the highlights in the career of George Washington, which can be listed as follows:

(1) As a boy, he supposedly chopped down his father's favorite cherry tree; then admitted it, rather than tell a lie.

(2) In his youth, he became a surveyor and made many trips into the Virginia wilderness.

(3) He accompanied Braddock's ill-fated expedition against the French and saved many British soldiers from massacre.

(4) When war began with England, a dozen years later, Washington was appointed commander-in-chief of the American army.

(5) After bringing the war to a victorious conclusion, Washington was elected first President of the United States.

(6) The city of Washington was named after George Washington and there a great monument was erected in his honor.

(7) Every Spring, thousands of visitors flock to Washington to view the magnificent cherry blossoms on hundreds of trees that have been planted there.

It is not only an easy matter to visualize all these items as vivid pictures, but also they can be given action that carries each into the next, by the continued pairing process:

For (1) you picture a boy chopping down a cherry tree and keep watching it as it falls. In your visualization, include a surveyor's transit, beneath the falling tree. You can even let the transit flatten, as you go into your next scene:

For (2) you see the same boy, grown older, setting up the transit in the middle of a forest. He is sighting on a rod held by another surveyor. Now concentrate upon the rod alone. Imagine it turning into an Indian with upraised tomahawk. The action continues:

With (3) you see other Indians springing up beside the first one. They start surging upon soldiers in red coats, chopping them down. Next, from behind surrounding trees, you see the youthful surveyor, now a man in full uniform, leading a charge of riflemen in buckskin, routing the Indians. Picture the man in uniform upon a horse, because:

In (4) he is riding a horse through welcoming throngs of soldiers, all clad in uniforms of blue and buff. Other men on horses meet him. They exchange salutes. This is Washington's meeting with other generals of the Continental Army. They dismount and begin exchanging hand-shakes beneath the overhanging boughs of trees on a village green.

Then (5) is concentrated on the same man, Washington, still surrounded by a welcoming group, but in civilian clothes of the period, as he ascends steps between two trees into a hall where he takes the oath of office, the civilian group accompanying him. And then:

In (6) you see our modern congressmen, coming from the capitol in Washington, as they would after some important session. Beyond are tree-lined streets and in the distance the Washington Monument, which you should picture in full stature of 555 feet, 5.5 inches. Drifting downward and spreading your field of vision, you see:

As (7) a magnificent stretch of cherry trees in full bloom, with all the pinkish colors or shades that you can envision, with thousands of modern citizens agape as they view nature's wonderland, with one exception: A little boy is sneaking up past an unwary policeman, armed with a little hatchet, ready to hack, hack, hack at the nearest cherry tree and hew it down, down, down.

That completes the circuit. You are back to George Washington as the typical American, as he was then and may be now.

Whether the story of the cherry tree is fact or fiction does not matter; it has become traditional and therefore must be given due consideration, whether right or wrong. Beginning with the boy chopping the cherry tree, the two themes, boy and tree, are carried through the whole continuity. The boy, of course, grows up; the trees change to suit the different scenes, but Picture 1 is that of a boy chopping a cherry tree, while Picture 7 is that of a cherry tree waiting for a boy to chop it. Thus the boy in 7 becomes the boy in 1, making an endless chain.

Always try to include some overall theme in your mental pictures, even though the actual pairing links may wander afar. This is not absolutely necessary; in fact, there are times when it is difficult to introduce such a theme, so don't over-strain your imagination on that score. But any added associations are always helpful.

Injecting Humor into Memory Chains

Since anything that is odd, exaggerated, or incongruous is a help toward forming memory links, it follows that any funny situation or a play upon words will also prove valuable when injected into such chains. When puns are used, it doesn't matter how bad they may be; in fact, the worse they are, the better, because there again, incongruity enters as a memory aid.

Take this example: Picture a scene from the Gay Nineties, where there is a young man, all "spruced up" in white flannel trousers, striped blazer, whites shoes, straw hat and wearing the old college tie. He is speaking pleadingly to a demure damsel in Gibson Girl costume, who is seated in a hammock, beneath some evergreen trees. In brief, the scene, plus the young man's statement, runs thus:

Young man, spruced up, says to girl seated in hammock:
"For you I'll pine—and bawl some, too."

Now go through the two lines and change certain words to others that have a similar sound, as far as necessary, stressing all that are in italics:

Young man, spruce(d) up, says to girl cedar(ed) in hemlock:
"Fir yew I'll pine—and balsam, too."

That bit of nonsense is very easy to remember, particularly

when mispronounced; and in mispronouncing it, you are naming the seven common types of evergreen trees. A nice way to remember them and have a laugh at the same time.

Less useful, but more laughable is the following sequence, which illustrates the simple link method to perfection, although it is just a nonsensical riddle that someone concocted soon after World War II, and which is still good today:

> Question: Why are fire-trucks always red?
> Fire-trucks are red because magazines are read, too.
> And two times three are six,
> And twice six is twelve.
> Twelve inches is a ruler,
> And there was a ruler of England named Queen Mary.
> But Queen Mary was also the name of a liner,
> And a liner crosses the ocean.
> The ocean is filled with fish—
> And all fish have fins.
> But the Finns fought the Russians—
> And the Russians are known as Reds.
> Since fire-trucks are always rushin' to fires,
>
> Answer: That's why fire-trucks are red.

Read that over a few times, mentally emphasizing the linking words,and you will have no trouble remembering it, as it forms an excellent endless chain. If you like riddles, you can repeat it to your friends and soon you will find that you can reel it off quite rapidly, with never a miss. So the little time taken to memorize it will prove worthwhile, not just because you have learned to recite a whimsical riddle, but for a much bigger reason; namely:

You Can Literally Link the Simple "Link" Method to Your Personal Needs

So far, the link method has been traced through such phases as remembering objects, things to do, colors, history, trees and finally a complex riddle. Those actually form a chain of their own, so far as developing memory is concerned, and unquestionably one or more of those links has been of direct interest to you. If you try them all, you may even find that those that seemed most trivial may loom to special importance.

Why?

Because they can open new memory vistas that you may not have recognized before, either because they seemed too common-place or presented obstacles that appeared too difficult. If you are already fairly good at remembering a list of items or things that you have to do, you probably have the makings of a memory system all your own, although you haven't recognized it as such. Or possibly you are aware of it, without realizing that it is far better than you suppose.

Therefore, if you apply some phase of the link system, you may find to your surprise that you have been using it right along, though perhaps in a modified way. So once you have learned its real possibilities, you can play it up to much greater advantage. Cultivate it and you will find that the little things that escaped you may become even larger than those you once thought were big, because you managed to remember them without trouble.

Where facts are concerned—historical or otherwise—purposeful application of the link method may double or even triple what you have thus far regarded as your normal limit or capacity. You have been remembering facts either because you *want* to remember them or feel that you *must* remember them. Therefore, you have been following the A I R formula on your own; for if you hadn't, you would not be getting the results you have.

To get more results, check back on how you have applied the A I R formula and see how you can increase its efficiency. Suppose that certain historical facts have immediately captured your attention. That so rouses your interest that you promptly peg those facts through repetition, thus completing the A I R process. That leaves you free to direct your attention elsewhere and go after something else on the same basis. As a result, you may amass a large array of facts that are too disconnected or superficial to be of any value.

The proper course is to give more *attention* to the basic facts, thus rousing your *interest* in additional data, thus giving you that much more to clinch for all time through *repetition*. This, of course, raises the time-worn question: Won't it be too difficult to remember all the additional data? The answer is: Not at all. In fact, it will be easier. You will still be utilizing repetition, but instead of becoming cut-and-dried, it will get sharper with each trial because you are constantly introducing some new element, which demands attention and therefore rouses fresh interest, leading to further repetition. In short, you are keeping A I R in circulation.

As a perfect example, consider your present circle of acquaintances. Assume that you have three friends: Joe, Steve and Jerry. You're going on a fishing trip, but Joe can't make it, so Steve brings a fellow named Fred. He fits in with the group so well that later you introduce him to Joe. It turns out they both know a chap named Charley, so he is invited on a trip. You meet up with a friend of Charley's named Hank and he becomes a member of the crowd.

You now have six friends instead of only three. One day you go on a trip with Fred, Charley and Hank. Does that mean that you have forgotten Joe, Steve and Jerry? Far from it. From them you learn that Fred saw Joe a few days ago, that Charley is going to meet Steve at a convention in Miami, and that Hank is engaged to Jerry's sister. So by increasing your circle of acquaintances, you have kept in closer touch with all of them.

Utilizing the A I R Formula to Supply Key-Links in Memory Chains

Reverting briefly to history, the more you learn about certain noted personages, the more they seem like friends; therefore, the same rules apply. You should look for new data to link it up with facts you already have. One criticism of history, as it is often taught, is the way it is confined to individual nations, as American history, French history or Russian history. By studying these in relation to one another, cross-links can be formed. These would include Washington's attitude toward the French Revolution. They would tie in events in France and Mexico with those of the American Civil War, rounding them into a more understandable whole.

Where humor is concerned, you often hear someone say, "I just can't remember jokes. I start to tell one and I leave out something important. Then I get to the finish too soon and spoil it all. Nobody thinks it's funny, so I guess I just can't tell a joke."

Here, the A I R formula is usually humped in the middle. When the person first heard the joke, he failed to give it due attention. What roused his interest was the climax, when everybody laughed. So in repeating it to himself, he concentrated on that. Thus in telling the joke later, he lost out in the early stages, simply because he lacked the necessary links or they were too weak to stand the strain.

That is why the riddle of the red fire-trucks, as quoted earlier, is such a good example of a memory chain. Each link leads to the next, and all are essential to the story. To tell it at all, it must be told right. Apply the same process to any story—humorous or serious—treating each step as a vital factor, giving it proper emphasis, and you will see for yourself how well the system works. Just remember that the saying, "A chain is only as strong as its weakest link," applies to the rules of memory as much as the laws of physics.

A past master of this art was Jacques Romano, who died in 1962 at the age of ninety-eight, and whose remarkable memory served him throughout all those years. He was noted for his ability to speak many foreign languages, but he made no claim to any amazing power. Instead, he willingly revealed his secret as the simple link method, applied as follows:

Romano found that he needed only about one hundred twenty-five basic words to make himself understood in a new language. By learning ten of those words a day, repeating them over and over to gain the right pronunciation, he acquired his basic vocabulary in two weeks' time. Using those words as key-links to others, he branched out with interlocking chains that steadily increased his vocabulary to fluent proportions.

As further proof of the efficacy of the simple link method, Romano frequently gave talks to specialized groups of bankers, brokers, engineers, lawyers, or others, using their own profession as his theme. Invariably, he won their admiration—and sometimes their amazement—by the wealth of little-known facts he told them regarding the business they knew best; their own.

What Romano did was to brief himself on a working knowledge of his subject—like the basic vocabulary of a new language —and then form links composed of unusual off-trail features, many being minor points that most of his listeners had overlooked or neglected; or which might even be new developments, not yet generally known. Naturally, by acquiring one language, Romano was better equipped to try another, and similarly, once he had delved deeply into a technical subject, he could keep his notes and use them as a starting point toward digging deeper as well as a refresher when he talked to another group of the same sort.

The main point is that Romano's process was unquestionably based on the simple link system, in contrast to some of the freakish memories mentioned in the first chapter. Hence, anyone can follow the same pattern and gain results, by giving due regard to the forging of the needed links. It is probable that Romano strengthened his ability by utilizing other and more advanced methods; you, too, will not only have that privilege, but you will possess the necessary "know-how" after you have delved into the chapters that follow.

So for the present, keep working to expand your basic memory by coupling fact with fact, and then go on from there. Results will definitely be forthcoming, and let's hope that you will keep improving them until the age of ninety-eight.

*   *   *   *   *   *   *   *   *   *

CHAPTER 4

Memory Aids in Your Own Home or Office: The Topical Method

Professor Lucian Napier, who taught classical languages at an Eastern college several decades ago, was noted for having the worst memory on the campus. He was a man who began each day in an automatic fashion from which he never departed, but once beyond that, he was totally lost. His set routine ran like this:

Awakened by an alarm clock at seven o'clock, he went downstairs to the kitchen, and:

(1) Took a coffee percolator from a cupboard and filled it with coffee and water.

(2) Put the percolator on the stove and turned on the gas.

(3) Went to the living room while the coffee was perking and lighted a fire in the fireplace.

(4) Went back to the kitchen, poured the coffee, and took a cup to his wife in her upstairs bedroom.

(5) Went down to his study and sipped his coffee while reading classics in their original Greek or Latin, as a warmup for the day's teaching.

(6) Answered his wife's call that breakfast was ready and had breakfast with her in the dining room.

(7) Went to the shed and brought in a box-load of wood for the living room fire.

(8) Went to the front hall, took his hat and coat from a rack.

(9) Went out through the vestibule where he stopped to put on gaiters and take an umbrella if needed.

(10) Went down the front steps and started to the campus.

There, Professor Napier followed a more general routine. He taught his first class, went to the post office, then to the administration building, up the hill to teach another class, then back home for lunch. But he could not keep track of anything in between, and "Nappy," as the students called him, became the prime example of an "absent-minded professor."

At the post office, he would become absorbed in the mail and forget an appointment with the college president. If he stopped to talk to someone, he would forget that he was to stop at the market and bring home something for dinner. Every morning, Nappy would read over a list of things to do, but when he absent-mindedly left the toast burning during breakfast—as he usually did!—he was apt to drop the list under the table or forget it entirely. Even when he took it with him, he was sure to lose it or misplace it; and worse, he would occasionally find an old list in a neglected pocket and use it by mistake.

One day, the whole situation changed. Professor Napier had a list of nearly a dozen things to do. He read it over at breakfast, but after he left, his wife found it in the pocket of a dressing gown that he had been wearing. She tried frantically to reach him at some of the places listed and found that he had already kept his appointments. She was sure that he would miss his meeting with the college president, for that was his worst weakness. But when she called the president's office, who answered but her husband, to assure her that he had arrived there on the dot.

Never had there been such a complete turnabout; not merely that day, but from then on. In many minor ways, Professor Napier continued to be happily absent-minded, but with everything that was vital, his memory proved infallible. Other members of the faculty, as well as students, began wondering about the professor's ability to remember the important things he had to do. At last, after smiling off inquiries for weeks, he revealed his deep secret.

That day of the great change, the classic which Professor Napier picked from his shelf happened to be Cicero's *De Oratore*, which dealt with the advantages of artificial memory, as used by Cicero himself around the year 60 B.C. In that work, Cicero discussed the advantages of linking *places* with *images*, so that the recollection of one would immediately conjure up the other. In rehearsing his orations, Cicero customarily went from one room to another; that is, from place to place, as he introduced each new phase, or image, of his subject.

Then, when the time came to deliver his oration, he simply visualized his own home, room by room, and repeated exactly what he had said there. In short, he went from place to place, and the proof of this has survived today, when a speaker says: "In the first place—" or "In the second place—" meaning that he is switching from one point to another.

Professor Napier, reading this, realized suddenly how he already had a fixed routine resembling Cicero's. He had ten definite *places,* or actions, that started off his day—as already listed—which he could recall at any time. All he had to do was link each action with an *image* that would stay fixed for that day. At any time, he could refer back to the early morning routine that he knew so well, and that would be it.

It really was. Looking over the list that was lying on his desk beside Cicero's *De Oratore,* he decided to picture each item in terms of his own procedure; namely:

(1) He was to pick up some books at the college bookstore. So he thought of them being in the cupboard with the coffee pot on top of them.

(2) He was to buy some bill-heads at a stationery shop to make out a bill for a lecture and mail it from the post office. So he thought of those bill-heads lying on the stove, to be brushed away before he put the coffee pot there.

(3) He was to pick up some examination papers at the administration building. So he pictured himself stuffing those exam papers into the living room fireplace and burning them completely, which some of his students would have greatly appreciated.

(4) Next, he was to do some research at the college library, so he pictured himself looking for books around the bedroom while his wife was drinking coffee.

(5) Then, he was to meet the college president, which would be perfect in his own study, where they wouldn't be disturbed, rather than in the administrator's office, where interruptions were constant.

(6) He was to buy a new umbrella because he had left the old one somewhere, so he thought of himself eating breakfast with the umbrella spread above the table.

(7) At the same store, he was to order a set of teacups for his wife, so he pictured them lying in the wood-box.

(8) He was to stop at the dean's office for a report on new students, so he thought of it hanging on the hat-rack.

(9) He was to invite the dean and his wife to Sunday dinner, so he imagined meeting them in the vestibule.

(10) He was to come back by the market and order a turkey for that same dinner, so he pictured a big turkey strutting on the front steps.

The whole routine worked to perfection, and the next day

the professor concentrated on a new list so intently that the old one was wiped out and supplanted, just like writing on a blackboard. So, after a lapse of two thousand years, a college professor in the United States of America was able to take a memory device direct from ancient Rome and use it to advantage, day by day.

Applying Cicero's System to Your Own Daily Affairs

You, too, can apply this same system just as promptly and effectively as the professor did. He followed Cicero's scheme exactly, by moving from room to room, but you don't even have to go that far. Picture ten places as they might be viewed in a single room. For example, a living room, where, looking in from the front door, you see:

(1) A big arm-chair in the corner to your left.

(2) A television set against the left wall.

(3) A window, in the same wall, opening onto a porch.

(4) A book-case in the far corner.

(5) A desk against the rear wall.

(6) A doorway to a hall beyond.

(7) A couch in the far corner on the right.

(8) A telephone table by the wall on the right.

(9) A straight-backed chair farther to the front.

(10) A folded card table in the near corner at the right.

Having fixed those ten objects as your places, you take the day's list of things to serve as images. For example:

(1) Ask your neighbor's son to mow your lawn.

(2) Cash a check at the bank.

(3) Buy a new leash for your dog.

(4) Buy a bottle of shoe polish.

(5) Buy a present for a new baby.

(6) Have lunch with an old school chum.

(7) Buy an airplane ticket at the travel bureau.

(8) Pick up the laundry on the way home.

(9) Fill the gasoline tank at the local service station.

(10) Get dressed for a dinner-dance at the country club.

Before starting out, you would either visualize the living room, or better still, look around the room, putting *images* in actual *places*, in the exact order that you want to remember them. Here, another element asserts itself quite strongly; that of *incongruity*. The very limitation of the *places* in relation to the wide variety of the *images*, may force you to picture combinations which are distorted or absurd; and these—as you will learn by experience—are all the better as memory links because of their incongruity.

In the present instance, there are excellent chances for exaggeration, with *action* woven into the imaginary scenes, along the following pattern:

For (1) you can visualize a power mower parked in the armchair, with its motor roaring away. Next to it (2) you see the television tuned to a prize-winning contest, with money actually fluttering from the TV screen. (3) A huge, snarling dog is trying to leap in through the window, only to be yanked back by a leash. (4) Picture yourself in the far corner, carefully applying black shoe polish to all the books in the book-case, while (5) a baby is lying on the desk, squalling at full blast.

Continuing on (6) you see your school chum beckoning frantically from the hall beyond the doorway, while (7) is an airline pilot, seated on the corner couch, operating imaginary controls. Next (8) you find yourself hunting hopelessly for the telephone because its table is buried under a pile of laundry, while (9) the straight chair is occupied by a service station attendant, holding the nozzle of a hose, ready to fill your gas tank. Finally (10) when you look for the folding card table, you find that it has been set up and that a couple of your friends are dancing on it.

Considered in the form and order given, the ten items can be memorized almost automatically. In fact, it would be more difficult to forget them than to remember them, once you begin picturing the basic objects in rotation, letting the imaginary scenes spring to mind just as you envisioned them for future reference.

Strengthening Your Memory Links
Through Supplementary Associations

In using the "Topical Method" as this "place plus image" is termed, the proper course is to use a scene with which you are already familiar. Take a room that you know well and utilize it in the manner described, adding any logical objects—say a waste-basket, a shelf, or an ash-stand—if needed, to complete a set of ten places. But once fully fixed, keep it for all future use. Your chosen room—like the professor's morning routine, must fall in line automatically, so that you make your mental trip around it without hesitation. The more familiar the places, the surer the images, when you come to recall them.

The link in each case is association. In the example just given: (1) Arm-chair with power mower. (2) TV with cash. (3) Window with dog-leash; and so on. But those links, if too slight or simple, are apt to slip the mind. An outright effort to implant them firmly has two bad features: It may take too much time; and the link may become too strong, so that when the system is used with a new list of items, you may flash back to the former image.

That is why incongruity is important. It brings in action, which in turn produces supplementary associations as strengtheners. To be specific: (1) The power mower being in the arm-chair is the main association; the fact that it is running is the supplementary association that keeps it in mind. Keep the "buzzzzzz" of the mower in mind.

Then: (2) The cash program on the TV links with money to be obtained at the bank. That could be strengthened by visualizing the TV screen as a teller's window at the bank—your bank! —where the money is coming from. You might even think of the bank teller watching a TV program while you are waiting for him to cash your check. Such a supplementary association will really stick.

With: (3) The bigger and more powerful the dog in your image, the smaller you can make the leash, until you really wonder why the leash doesn't snap. That reminds you that you are buying the leash for your own dog, who isn't that big or ferocious. Indeed, the smaller your dog, the more incongruous it becomes and therefore the better the association.

Continuing on through: Any supplementary association that springs to mind will make the overall association all the more clear. That, in turn, makes the erasure all the more effective, once the picture has fulfilled its purpose. Being dependent on lesser links, rather than one big one, it will fall apart like the links themselves and leave the mental slate clear for a new memory train.

Extending Your Range of Remembered Items

In using objects as places and items as images, you are by no means limited to a single room. You can move mentally about the house, from room to room, as Cicero did; and each room can have its own series of ten places upon which images can be imposed. We have taken a living room as an example; but a kitchen would be equally effective. Its arrangement might run: (1) Cupboard. (2) Dishwasher. (3) Sink. (4) Refrigerator. (5) Back door. (6) Shelves. (7) Range. (8) Door to Dining Room. (9) Freezer. (10) Breakfast nook.

All such places can readily accommodate images, and they offer some very funny or ridiculous associations, which are all the more helpful. Exaggerations always are effective, particularly when they become fantastic. Thus: (1) Automobile tires bouncing from the kitchen cupboard would remind you to buy snow tires for the coming winter. (2) An elephant filling its trunk with water from the dish washer would mean that you had promised to take your nephew to the zoo. (3) Books floating in the kitchen sink would remind you to take some books back to the library; and so on.

A bedroom, an office, a workshop, even a garage, can be used as memory settings. By having such alternates fixed in mind, you can extend a list of memorized items to 20, 30, 40 or even 50, by simply moving on to the next room. There are also times when you may retain a list that is already "set," as with the living room list given earlier; yet you may be suddenly confronted with other things to be remembered independently. That is when you simply move into another room.

Actual rooms are not necessary. Floor plans can be used instead and are often better because you can alter them and furnish them as you choose. If you need a new couch in the study, it is a good idea to include one as one of the places, as that in itself will remind you to buy the couch, without any help from a corresponding image.

Just make sure that any imaginary rooms and their contents are as fixed as real ones, so as to keep the places intact. Douglas Kimber, a contractor who was continually building suburban homes in upstate New York, used this system by planning rooms that he felt were ideal, then using them for memory links. This went on for several years, and he began talking about his "rooms" as though they actually existed. As business improved, the time came when Mr. Kimber could afford to build a "dream house" and he incorporated those very rooms in it, exactly as he had visualized them so many, many times. He is still using his topical memory system, but with real rooms instead of their imaginary prototypes.

Extending the Topical Method to Broader Scenes

The examples given show that memorization through the Topical Method is a stimulus to individual initiative, both in the picturization of places and the superimposing of images. It is strongly recommended because progress in the science of Mnemonics is like riding a bicycle, driving a car, or developing any other skill wherein coordination and recognition are vital factors. Memory is needed to improve those skills, and by the same token, memory can be used to improve memory itself.

Just as you have increased your memory span by adding more rooms with their fixed furnishings, so can you extend the process to public buildings or places which offer a more varied assortment of places on which to implant images. A good example is a bus station, viewed from the entrance, as follows: (1) A lunch counter. (2) Dining tables. (3) Baggage lockers. (4) Ticket windows. (5) Clock. (6) News-stand. (7) Gates to busses. (8) Waiting room. (9) Doorway to taxi-stand. (10) Telephones.

These lend themselves to more varied pictures on a larger scale than those formed with the "one room" method; hence, some persons will prefer this system. The best plan is try out each and decide for yourself. Use a bus station, railway depot, or airport with which you are familiar, altering the locale slightly or adding a few details if need be. Just be sure to establish it as a well-fixed setting.

A hotel lobby offers a good locale, such as: (1) Drug store. (2) Flower shop. (3) News-stand. (4) Lounge. (5) Registration desk. (6) Porter's room. (7) Elevator. (8) Entrance to dining room. (9) Stairway. (10) Barber shop.

Again, this is arbitrary, depending upon the hotel lobby with which you are familiar. However, it is possible to envision a progressive scene of a more or less standardized type, which will present a regular sequence of places where images can literally be enacted as they occur. Appropriately, the "theater sequence" is an out-standing example:

Start with (1) a typical theater lobby with its display boards advertising the show. Being interested, you stop at (2) the box-office and buy a ticket, which (3) you give to the ticket-taker at the door. Inside, you (4) go up the stairs to the balcony, where you (5) meet an usher who conducts you (6) down the aisle to a front-row seat. From there (7) you watch the orchestra come into the pit, and after the overture (8) the curtain rises and the show begins. At the finish (9) you go backstage to the star's dressing room and from there (10) you go out by the stage door.

Now, suppose that you have the following list of things to do: (1) Pick up a watch that has been repaired. (2) Buy a hammer at the hardware store. (3) Buy a bag of potatoes. (4) Call your lawyer's office. (5) Pick up some pictures at the photographer's. (6) Mail the pictures by registered mail. (7) Buy some magazines and (8) a box of cigars. Then (9) stop to watch a Little League ball game and finally (10) go for a swim.

Note how these *images* can imprint themselves upon the *places* much in the fashion of a motion picture reel.

Imagine yourself viewing (1) the *lobby display* and finding that instead of advertising a show it tells about (1) a sale of *watches*.

You go to (2) the *box-office* to buy a ticket, but the window is closed, so you start hitting it with (2) a *hammer* which happens to be lying handy.

Having obtained a ticket, you (3) offer it to the *ticket-taker*, but he ignores it as he is busy dumping (3) a *bag of potatoes* into the ticket chopper.

As you start (4) up the *stairs* to the balcony you (4) meet your *lawyer* coming down and he says to call his office.

Instead of meeting (5) an *usher* you run into (5) your *photographer*, who hands you the packet of pictures.

When you reach (6) your *front-row seat*, it is blocked by (6) a grilled window that says *Registered Mail*, so you push the package in there.

While you are (7) watching the *orchestra*, its members lay aside their instruments and (7) begin reading *magazines*.

As the (8) *curtain rises*, you see a dozen actors (8) all smoking *cigars* and clouding up the scene.

Backstage, as (9) you knock at the *dressing room door*, it flies open and you are overwhelmed by (9) a team of *Little Leaguers*, all swinging baseball bats.

To escape them, you dash for (10) the *stage door* and as it opens, you dive through it (10) into the deep end of a *swimming pool*.

After "acting out" this sequence a few times, you will recall it automatically and can use it without fail by simply picturing the *places* used in the routine and letting the *images* link with them. Any new sequence, once enacted, will obliterate the old, as with the usual Topical System. This type of memory association was a favorite with Bert Kalmar, the noted song writer, who spent much of his time in theatrical circles and was recognized as an expert in certain specialized fields of memory.

The Neighborhood System and Its Elaborations

Just as a larger building can supplant the single rooms of a house as a locale for the Topical Method, so can the sequence be carried out of doors, through an immediate neighborhood and even into the great wide-open spaces. Some memory experts have specialized in this type of work, and in the early 1800's, a man in London earned himself the title of "Corner Memory" Thompson, because he could call off every detail of an entire parish simply by recalling each corner shop and using it as a focal point from which he visualized the immediate surroundings.

Nor was that system new in its time. Actually, it dated back to the Roman author Quintilian, who elaborated Cicero's comments on memory a century after they were introduced. Quintilian's scheme was to imagine himself strolling among the buildings of ancient Rome, using them as *places* for the *images* he wanted to remember; and even visualizing writing and pictures on certain walls as keys to supplementary recollections.

Today, in order to remember a variety of objects, it is best to take a neighborhood which itself is varied. A main street, on which shops are too much alike, should be avoided. Similarly, a suburban area consisting entirely of homes, would not furnish sufficient individuality of places. It is better to take a "mental walk" through an "in between" neighborhood, where you might pass in succession: (1) A garage. (2) A vacant lot. (3) A fire station. (4) A lunch wagon. (5) A drug store. (6) A schoolyard. (7) A post-office. (8) An apartment house. (9) A garage. (10) A church.

These would not necessarily have to come together. They could be treated much like individual landmarks, ignoring buildings of lesser importance, or reserving those for secondary purposes, always using the primary *places* to recall your listed *images*, your aim being to become a modern Quintilian rather than another Corner Memory Thompson.

Going farther afield, you can picture yourself starting out in a car or a bus from (1) the center of a *small town* and (2) going over a *bridge* and passing (3) a large *shopping center*, shortly before (4) a new *hospital*. Following that is (5) an intersection with a *traffic light* and beyond that (6) a *service station*. Next (7) a modern *motel* and after that (8) a small *duck pond* until you see (9) a turnoff with a *sign* pointing to a turnpike and (10) finally the *toll-booth* where you stop to pick up a ticket.

With both the "mental walk" and the "mental ride," you can go from one neighborhood or one stretch of highway to another, extending your list of ten places to twenty, thirty, forty or fifty, all suitable for the planting of images. As with the rooms of a house, these should be kept in logical sequence, so that actually you are using one to five individual lists, rather than one big one.

The more you use your own imagination or follow your own inclinations, the better, as you will find that it helps make images stick. Different types of lists can even be used in sequence, as: (1) The living room with ten objects as places. (2) A trip through the house with ten rooms of places. (3) The walk through the neighborhood. (4) The bus ride to the turnpike. (5) Arrival at the theater and the sequence from lobby through to stage door.

Steps Toward Simplification of Topical Memory Methods

Two factors stand out in every memory system: One is the device itself; the other is its application. As these vary, so do the results gained from the methods themselves. From a practical standpoint, it is a question of whether the burden is chiefly on the method or on the person employing it. A perfect balance of those factors is sometimes desirable, but not always so. A greater aim is to keep the device adequate, without allowing it to become cumbersome; otherwise, it may defeat itself. Also, the purpose to which the person applies the system should be considered in determining its adequacy.

Finally, individual ability is important. As you progress in the use of the Topical Method—as well as others—you will find that you not only can use your natural memory to new advantage, you will also be able to assume some of the burdens borne by the device. That is because you will have gained or displayed aptitude in system usage.

This brings us to the bed-rock that forms a stumbling block for many people, where memory methods are involved. They feel that since they will have to go to exhaustive lengths to develop a solid system, it would be better to depend upon ordinary memory. They argue thus: If you can't remember simple facts, why try to remember something harder?

A good point indeed, but one that is easily answered. The mere fact that their ordinary memory is not sufficient, proves that it needs a booster. That is where the system enters, and like every good booster, it should add enough spark, gusto, "oomph" or what-have-you to enable the natural memory to function to the full.

This will be understood very clearly by a brief recapitulation: Going back to Cicero, who initiated it all, we find that he had only a trifling need of a memory system. His orations were so well planned, so detailed, that his main worry was that some slight mishap might divert him from his well-planned flow of logic. Cicero needed a system to keep his own natural memory within bounds.

All through the centuries that followed, other aspirants in the field of Mnemonics tried to expand on Cicero's original findings, little realizing that his system was 90% natural and 10% artificial. The fact that he fostered and furthered the 10% magnified it to undue proportions, as if his orations depended upon it, whereas the opposite was really the case.

Hence, Quintilian and a whole succession of mnemotechnicians who carried memory training from ancient times on through the middle ages, were actually putting the gears in reverse. Their emphasis was all on *places*, rather than the *images* which the person already had in mind and merely wanted to reinvoke. Some of these memory masters wove astrology into the picture, with the signs of the zodiac as places. One man, Giulio Camillo, devised an elaborate plan for a Memory Theater, while another, Boncompagno da Signa, produced an even more fanciful system, utilizing locations supposedly found in Heaven and Hell.

A great beauty of Cicero's system was its suitability for expansion, even though Cicero never carried it that far. Therefore, reverting to the case cited at the start of this chapter, namely, how Professor Napier took a passage directly from Cicero's *De Oratore* and applied it to his own problem, we find that he was following the direct pattern of Cicero's successors. The great difference was that Cicero hoped to add some touches of perfection to his almost infallible memory; whereas, Professor Napier was striving to rid himself of an utterly infallible forgetfulness, as others had through the centuries.

What Cicero originally prescribed as a mild tonic was turned into strong medicine by his numerous successors. It is a good plan, therefore, to revert to Cicero's technique and assume some of the burden whenever possible, rather than keep throwing more and more of it onto method. The original plan was to think of a single *place* and let it develop a dozen *images*, like prints in a photographer's dark room. The modern way, in contrast, is to plant a dozen *places* in a single room and hook a separate *image* on to each.

This is fine for a start, particularly for persons with minds less volatile than Cicero's. It brings immediate results, which in turn creates confidence. By expanding from room to room, building to building, scene to scene, you have increased your memory span, all in familiar terms, making it all the stronger, but still no faster. So the next step is reduce some of the early impedimenta if possible.

With your "living room" sequence, you will soon find that instead of moving *place* by *place*—arm-chair, TV and so on—and putting items from a list into them, you can start with the items as *images* and drop them into *place*. Think of buying a new hat and tossing it in the arm-chair, or bringing home some flowers and setting them on the TV.

The more motion you put into the *images*, the less they will depend upon the *places* to bring them to mind. The Theater Sequence is a good example, as its continuity has a natural flow. It therefore forms a stepping-stone to:

The Link-Place System
of Remembering up to 50 Items

In the Topical Method, the places may be likened to a framework on which images may be fixed for later recollection. That analogy provided a highly practical aspect; namely, an imaginary frame composed of nine squares in which objects could be pictured in numerical rotation. From that a person could move on to another frame, starting with a tenth space on top and nine squares beneath; then on to another.

By utilizing the Chain System (as described in Chapter 3) it was possible to link such objects in regular order, running the sequence far beyond the limit of an ordinary chain by using the Topical Method to identify each object with its own particular square, the number of the square serving as the place, and the object becoming the image. This reduced the requirements to the simplest of elements; numbered places that fell automatically into line, with self-linking images; an ideal combination.

This "Link-Place System" proved cumbersome at first, and as it was simplified, certain improvements were needed to make it really practical. Today, in its fully developed form, as will now be described, anyone who has mastered the basic principles of both the Chain System and the Topical Method should gain surprising results almost at the first trial. Here is the "Link-Place" procedure.

First, visualize a huge, square-walled room, with no windows. You have just entered a door in the front wall and have shut it behind you, so that the front wall is practically as solid as the others. Overhead is a circular dome, which by its shape reminds you of the figure 0. The bright light reveals nine squares forming three cross-rows that cover the entire floor and are numbered thus:

$$1 \quad 2 \quad 3$$
$$6 \quad 5 \quad 4$$
$$7 \quad 8 \quad 9$$

In these squares, you are to visualize the first nine items that you want to remember, linking them as you do. You then move mentally to the center of the floor and face to the right. On the ceiling just above the right wall you imagine a broad space bearing the number 10. On the right wall itself, you see another nine-square framework; so the whole arrangement stands:

10
11 12 13
16 15 14
17 18 19

Again face to the right and on the ceiling visualize a broad space with the number 20. On the wall beneath are nine more squares, so it appears thus:

20
21 22 23
26 25 24
27 28 29

Another right face toward the wall on the original left, with 30 above it, and squares on the wall itself:

30
31 32 33
36 35 34
37 38 39

Face right toward the rear wall and visualize:

40
41 42 43
46 45 44
47 48 49

From there, jump to the ceiling and use the dome for space 50, if you need it. All during the procedure, you keep *placing* your *images* or items, but in a *well-linked* manner, which can best be appreciated through an actual example. Therefore, we have taken the same ten items that were used in the "Theater Sequence" (page 78) so as to offer a comparison.

Those items were: (1) A watch. (2) A hammer. (3) A bag of potatoes. (4) Your lawyer's office. (5) A photographer's pictures. (6) A registered packet of pictures. (7) Some magazines. (8) A box of cigars. (9) A Little League ball game. (10) A swimming pool.

A typical picturization follows:

In *Square 1*, you visualize a huge *watch*, then add some feature that will carry appropriately into the next square. Here you employ an auditory effect, the ticking of the watch, because it can be translated into:

Square 2, the tick-tick-tick of the watch becomes the beat of the hammer which occupies the square and continues its beat as it moves visually into:

Square 3, where you picture the hammer hitting potatoes one after another and driving them downward. This is a very important point, as it explains why the middle row of squares is shown in reversed rotation. The only link between squares 3 and 4 is downward and it proves very helpful, because:

Square 4 shows those potatoes dropping on your lawyer's desk until they threaten to hide him completely. To avoid that, the potatoes must be shunted somewhere, so you picture them rolling into:

Square 5 where a lot of nice photographic prints—as well as the photographer!—are also about to be overwhelmed by the potato deluge. So you—or some unseen hand—snatches the pictures from such fate and moves them to:

Square 6, where a nice packet is dropped neatly into a very special box which says REGISTERED MAIL. So your mind moves happily downward to:

Square 7, where you are horrified to see your precious package being lost in a pile of magazines which pile up to such proportions that you have to dump them into the nearest outlet, namely:

Square 8, where what comes out but a huge box of cigars, which doesn't even pause, but continues on and dumps its contents into:

Square 9, where of all people, you see a whole team of Little Leaguers snatching up and lighting them, until clouds of smoke obscure the scene. That rising cloud continues right up the corner to the ceiling, where you follow it as you mentally turn to the right and see it spread along the entire ceiling, until it dissipates and shows:

Space 10, which proves to be a huge swimming-pool, just about ready to overflow—and don't think it won't!—upon the unfortunate squares just below.

How you go on from there depends upon the items that follow. If you intend to buy a stove, it would go nicely in Square 11, where the outpour from the swimming pool would totally extinguish it. In contrast, if you were buying a cabin cruiser, the whole swimming pool would not supply enough water to launch it. Whatever the case, you continue your links, square by square, as far as you want. Even if you reach Number 50, you can still go beyond, simply by picturing another square-walled room as your basis.

Summed up, the great feature of the Link-Place System can be told in a single word: *Imagination*. With that, we are ready to proceed further into the field of Memory.

* * * * * * * * * *

CHAPTER 5

Get Rid of Absent-Mindedness—
and Everybody Will Trust You!

Perhaps the greatest feature of any good memory system is the fact that the more often you use it, the better it becomes. The reason for this is very simple; since every memory train depends upon association, the more you follow a given pattern, the more you strengthen it. In short, you use memory to stimulate memory.

This is particularly true of the "topical method" given in the previous chapter, which is where we go into such detail regarding its ultimate development into the 50-item "link-place system" that anyone can build gradually and effectively. You will find the same thing true of more elaborate systems as we come to them, with each serving its own special purposes.

But before proceeding with those, let me stress an important function which belongs to all. That is the matter of "memory jogs" which not only are used to remember trifles, but may often serve to "trigger" a particular chain sequence which you have systematically memorized. These are doubly important, because without them you are apt to become absent-minded regarding the simple things of everyday life, and there is nothing more disturbing than that when you are striving to increase your memory span.

Hence, at this point it is better to backtrack in a sense, showing how the simplest devices can be applied individually or collectively toward immediate memorization.

Using Memory Jogs as an Impromptu Topical System

Simplest of all memory jogs is the old, old notion of placing a tied string around your finger as a reminder of something important. This is still a working device, and in modern times can be simplified by slipping a rubber band on the finger, just tightly enough to keep you aware of its presence.

People who relied on this alone sometimes forgot what the string was for, and old-time cartoons used to depict an absent-minded individual with his thumbs and fingers all looped with different colored strings, wondering what any of them meant. But that does not detract from the device itself. It simply proves how far wrong a good idea can go, when foolishly applied or over-strained.

The "string reminder" is always good, if you give it the A I R treatment. Give due *attention* to something you intend to do, show *interest* in doing it and fix it in mind through *repetition* before slipping on the string, and you won't have to use the string at all. Instead, almost anything else can serve as a reminder.

At night, if you want to remember something that must be done in the morning, simply tie a knot in a handkerchief, sock, or stocking. When you encounter the knot the next morning, you will remember what it meant, and that will set off a chain reaction of further recollections, provided you linked them properly initially.

Another good memory jog is to link something that you want to remember with something that you are sure to find, wherever you happen to be. Suppose that you customarily wear a hat. If you intend to go somewhere—say to a bank to cash a check—simply place some item with the hat to remind you of that purpose. In this case, a pen would be appropriate. In picking up your hat, you would find the pen, which would be an immediate guide to your next mission.

Such a reminder would be even more pointed if you placed your check book with your hat. Or, if you had to mail an important letter, you could drop the letter itself in your hat. But there is one mistake that must definitely be avoided; never try to link two totally unrelated objects in this fashion, for you may forget them both.

As a horrible example, take the case of a salesman who received an unexpected bonus in the form of a sizable check. That night, in his motel room, he kept forgetting where he had put it— in his wallet, his brief case, his suit-case, the glove compartment of his car and so on. Finally, just so he would remember it, he threw the check in the waste-basket and went to sleep, confident that in the morning, that was the one thing he would remember.

Instead, it was the one thing he forgot, until the next afternoon when he had driven fifty miles out of town. He had to call the motel, begging them to look through the trash pile while he was racing back. Luckily, they found the check, so all it cost him was a hundred miles of unnecessary driving and an hour of utter worry, but it could have been much worse.

If he had been trying to remember *ten items*, utilizing a topical system—as described on page 73—in which he depended on ten fixed objects, one of which could have been a waste-basket, the very incongruity of a check in the waste-basket would have registered itself in his memory. But as it was, it was much like throwing one end of a rope to a drowning man without holding on to the other end. So don't make that mistake with memory jogs. Stay with the "string on the finger"—or its equivalent.

Turning the Primitive Form of Count to Good Account

The "string on finger" stems from the "finger count," which is perhaps the earliest known form of memory device. This is evidenced by the Roman system of enumeration: *I* for *1*, *II* for *2*, *III* for *3*, *IIII* for *4* (and still used on clocks, though *IV* came into later use), and finally V for *5*. These numerals represent the raising of the fingers, one by one, (I, II, III, IIII) with the V standing for all five in spread-out form, only the thumb and little finger being needed. The numerical X can be pictured as two V's, one upright (V) and the other inverted (Λ) beneath it, thus signifying *10* Though this is not its actual derivation, it serves as another memory jog.

Ever since the time when Cicero mentally moved from "place to place" in delivering his orations (see page 71), many speakers have driven home their "points" by pointing to one finger after another. An old-time lecturer would declare: "There are three good reasons why such-and-such is so"—and he would enumerate them by using his right forefinger to tap the thumb, forefinger and second finger of his left hand.

Then, he would add: "But on the other hand, there are these three problems"—and he would use his left forefinger to tap the thumb, forefinger and second finger of his right hand. All six of these taps served as memory jogs, not just for the speaker, but for his listeners as well; for later, they would almost invariably remember witnessing the counting process.

There are times when this primitive count is still good, but only when it is tied in with something practical, which makes each "jog" ring a bell. Take the days of the week: You can count them on the fingers of the left hand: "Sunday—Monday—Tuesday —Wednesday—Thursday"—and then switch the count to the right thumb and forefinger for "Friday—Saturday."

Now that, in itself, is hardly necessary, as you already know the days of the week by heart. But suppose someone should tell you over the phone, "I'll drop by to see you next Tuesday—will that be soon enough?" You could then say to yourself: "Let's see. Today is Thursday"—and with that, you would tap your left thumb and begin the mental count: "Friday—Saturday—Sunday—Monday—Tuesday"—ending on the left little finger.

Then, you might say, across the telephone: "No, that's five days off. I really should see you sooner. How about next Monday?" So you see that such counting has its purposes; and you often may find other practical ways to utilize it, such as adding up the number of people you have invited to a picnic or a bridge party. You can also count off weeks, months or even years—backward or forward —by raising fingers, one by one, when you are trying to remember some important event, past or future.

The Calendar Count—A Perfect Type of Memory Jog

Just as you can count off days of the week, so can you enumerate the months of the year by name. But here, since there are twelve, you need two extra fingers. Lacking those, you can use your knuckles instead, in the following manner:

Close your left fist and turn it downward. Now, with your right forefinger, tap the knuckle at the base of your left little finger and say to yourself: "January." Now tap the hollow between that knuckle and the next, mentally saying, "February." Next, tap the knuckle of the left third finger, repeating, "March." Continue thus, hollow, knuckle, hollow and finally, the knuckle at the base of the left forefinger, repeating, "April, May, June, July."

Your count then stands:

Knuckles:	January		March		May		July
Hollows:		February		April		June	

Now close the right hand into a downward fist. With the left forefinger, tap the knuckle at the base of the right forefinger; then the hollow next to it; then the base of the right second finger; then the next hollow; then the base of the right third finger, repeating, "August, September, October, November, December," completing the year.

This additional count stands:

Knuckles: August   October   December
Hollows: September   November

Now, if someone refers to the "fifth month" of the year, a quick knuckle count will bring you to it, establishing it as May. Or the tenth month, by continuing the count, would be October, the entire line-up running as follows:

Knuckles: Jan. March May   July   Aug.   Oct.   Dec.
Hollows: Feb.   April   June   Sept. Nov.

It's simple enough to count from month to month, but that is not all. With this device at your finger-tips, you need never worry about which are "long" months and which are "short." Each "knuckle" month, being high, is a thirty-one-day month. Each "hollow" month, being low, has just thirty days, except February, with only twenty-eight days, which can be easily remembered in its own right. So you will never again date a check September 31, if you utilize this system.

This illustrates very clearly how simple jogs can be put to practical use toward better memory. Often, you may come across some similar device which is of value to you; or you may be able to improvise a few of your own when you need them. Always be sure to peg those for future reference. They will help you to shake off absent-mindedness, the thing nobody likes.

Reverting back to jogs of the "string on the finger" type, here is a very good one:

If you intend to drive somewhere in a car and have to take something along, say a book to be returned to the library; or if you have to stop somewhere, say to pick up a friend, all you have to do is put your car keys in the *wrong pocket*. Then, when you are getting into the car itself, you will find yourself looking for the keys, which will automatically tell you to go back into the house and get the book, or to go out of your way to pick up your friend, whichever the immediate case may be.

A similar result can be obtained by putting your money or your wallet in the wrong pocket, thinking of it in terms of some particular task that you must perform before returning home. As soon as you buy something while you are out, the jog will supply the proper reminder.

Pocketing Things to Remember
by the Pocket Topical Method

From the simple "pocket jogs" just mentioned, you can build a complete topical method for remembering up to ten or a dozen items in what is practically an impromptu fashion. Instead of places, you use pockets in which you mentally put reminders of the things you want to do. There are ten pockets in most men's suits, so you visualize them as follows:

  (1) Left trouser pocket.

  (2) Right trouser pocket.

  (3) Left hip pocket.

  (4) Right hip pocket.

  (5) Watch pocket (*may be imaginary*).

  (6) Left coat pocket.

  (7) Right coat pocket.

  (8) Change pocket (*within right coat pocket*).

  (9) Left breast pocket.

(10) Right inside pocket.

Assume that you are starting the morning with these things to do before leaving for the office:

  (1) Look in the mail-box for any letters.

  (2) If there are any checks, take them along for deposit.

  (3) Be ready to leave by eight o'clock.

  (4) But before you leave, call your friend Tom.

  (5) Give Tom your friend Joe's new address.

  (6) Pour a bowl of milk for the cat.

  (7) Replace the burned-out bulb in the front hall, so you can turn on the light when you come home.

  (8) Take along the umbrella that you promised to return to someone at the office.

That is enough for this particular list. You may have thought of some of these things the night before, during the night, or immediately after waking in the morning. Whatever the case, you form the following mental pictures:

(1) You are reaching in your left trouser pocket and bringing out a handful of letters. (2) Going to your right trouser pocket, you find your bank book there. (3) You hear a muffled ringing sound and reaching into your left hip pocket, you bring out an alarm clock and find that it is set at 8 o'clock. (4) As if that weren't enough, there's another ting-a-ling from your right hip pocket, where you find a telephone of all things. (5) You reach into your watch pocket and find a folded slip of paper bearing Joe's address. (6) Deep in your left coat pocket, you find something cold, which grows into a big bottle of milk. (7) In your right coat pocket, you find something round and hot, an electric light bulb. (8) In the little change pocket, you discover a teeny-weeny doll's parasol, which expands into a full-sized umbrella as you draw it out. (9) You thrust your hand into your left breast pocket and find a handkerchief already stuffed there.

That's all. Not only is it all, it is enough. If you can imagine such incongruous things, you will have no trouble remembering them, so try it. Check the list of "things to do" against "pocket pictures" with the corresponding numbers and you will see how readily the links can be forged; that is, up to the final image, number 9, where you find the left breast pocket stuffed with a handkerchief.

Actually, it is the simplest of the lot. The handkerchief serves as a "stopper," telling you that the list has been completed. If there were only five things to remember, you would have mentally stuffed the handkerchief in your left coat pocket (number 6). With nine items, you would put it in your right inside coat pocket (number 10). With ten items to remember, you wouldn't need the handkerchief at all.

It should be noted that this list can be carried to twelve links instead of only ten, by adding two shirt pockets, left and right. In the days when vests were customarily worn, the list was usually extended from ten to fifteen by counting five vest pockets: (11) Lower left. (12) Lower right. (13) Upper left. (14) Upper right. (15) Inside vest.

These are still as good as ever if you want to use them. You don't have to wear a vest; all you need to do is visualize one. The great feature of the "Pocket Topical Method" is the fact it is so natural. You just imagine yourself reaching into a handy pocket and out comes the answer.

Applying the Feminine Touch
to the Pocket Topical Method

As the perfect substitute for the pockets of a man's suit, a woman can picture a handbag with two outside compartments, left and right, for numbers 1 and 2; then an interior divided into two compartments, left and right, for 3 and 4; and at the right, a special inside pocket, as 5. With that, she can also picture a larger tote bag, also having outside compartments, left and right, for 6 and 7; inside sections, separated by a divider, 8 and 9; also an inside pocket at the right, as 10.

The procedure is exactly the same as with the "Pocket Topical Method" previously described. Instead of the handbag or the tote bag, a woman can visualize a "utility bag" with a special array of pockets. Some of these bags are even termed "organizers" because they are so fitted with pockets and compartments that they can fulfill all sorts of purposes. Anyone who has such a bag or who has seen one, can utilize it mentally for "pocket topical" purposes; or it is quite easy to make up your own idea of a bag with ten sections or compartments. Even a purse can be added as an adjunct to the bag, lying loose inside it, and the purse itself can be subdivided.

Here, part of the fun is the picturing or arranging of the "mental bag" which you intend to use in your memory system. If it is of your own creation, so much the better, as it is easier to remember anything in which your own personal likes may have played a part. There are persons who have become memory experts in their own right largely because they personalized almost everything they tried to remember. The closer you are to any system, the more effective it becomes.

In utilizing such methods as the "pocket" or the "pocketbook" system, one point should be noted. They are somewhat restricted where large articles are concerned, since some people find it difficult to picture such items in pocket-sized terms. As you progress and your skill develops, you should find this all for the better, as incongruity helps to build imaginative pictures, such as drawing an umbrella from a coin pocket. So it is wise to go on with them, as tests will prove that they are among the best.

However, it is often easier in the early stages of memory training to picture items on a large scale, even expanding small things; and also, it is very easy to visualize yourself as being literally surrounded by such things. So instead of reaching inward to find what's in the pockets of your handbag, you spread outward to see what's around you. This swing to the opposite extreme may well be termed:

Putting Yourself in the Driver's Seat Where Memory Is Concerned

In this extension of the topical system, the very automobile that you are driving can serve you as the basis for remembering required objects, which you can actually picture and add as you drive along. You do not even have to drive the car; you can simply imagine yourself in it, seated at the wheel. Whether it is stopped or in motion does not matter, but you should picture yourself in the driver's seat not only to make it all the more graphic, but because you belong there.

From there, you take various portions of the car as the "places" for your topical system, as follows:

(1) The front bumper.

(2) The fender above the left front light.

(3) The center of the hood.

(4) The fender above the right front light.

(5) The steering wheel and dashboard in front of you.

(6) The seat at your right.

(7) The back seat.

(8) The trunk at the rear of the car.

(9) A carrier on top of the car.

(10) A trailer behind the car.

To show how a variety of objects can be memorized through this device, let us suppose that you have finished an actual motor trip through Maine and that you have taken note of the principal products of that state. The ten chief items on your list run alphabetically:

Apples, Blueberries, Canoes, Clams, Fish, Granite,
Lobsters, Lumber, Moccasins, Potatoes

To remember those, you simply imagine yourself bringing
home samples in your car. Your mental picturization could run
thus:

Hanging from your *front bumper* (1) are several pairs of fancy
moccasins. On the *left fender* (2) some big *lobsters* are hanging on
with their powerful claws. The top of the *hood* (3) is literally
sagging downward under the weight of a huge block of *granite*.
On the *right fender* (4) a sack of *potatoes* is bouncing up and
down, gradually scattering its contents. The *steering wheel* (5) is
hard to grip because *clams* are attached to it and dropping onto
the dashboard. You are keeping your hand toward the *seat at the
right* (6) to ward off boxes of *blueberries* that are constantly
toppling your way. The *back seat* (7) is piled high with *apples*.
The *rear trunk* (8) is filled with water from which *fish* are leaping
madly. The *top carrier* (9) is stacked with enough *lumber* to build
a house. On the *trailer* (10) you are bringing home a *canoe*.

Visualize yourself driving through a toll-gate on the Maine
Turnpike loaded with that conglomeration; then think of yourself
coming across the New Hampshire line with that same load, where
the state police stop you and order you to remove the objects one
by one, which you do. It will all be so graphic, yet so ridiculous,
that you may find it more difficult to forget that crazy carload than
to remember it.

Don't blame the New Hampshire state police for telling you
to unload, because this helps you remember everything you brought
from Maine. Now they tell you to load up the truck with New
Hampshire products instead. Form your own list of those and
picture yourself driving clear across New Hampshire by way of the
White Mountains, worrying about the new load all the way. Then,
at the Vermont line, unload the New Hampshire products and take
on a Vermont load instead.

By the time you are through with your mythical car trip, you
will have no trouble remembering the products of all three states—
and more, if you want to travel farther. But you don't have to limit
yourself to such items while you are in the imaginary driver's seat.
You can remember a list of friends by perching them all over your
car—though they might not be so friendly if they knew it!—and

you can remember the wild animals that you saw at the zoo, or whatever else your fancy dictates.

Extending the Topical System by Aiming for Memory Targets

Often, you can extend the Topical Memory System to specific targets, making it all the more effective. Suppose you are to attend an important meeting and have some equally important points to remember. Instead of keying those points to objects in your living room (as described on page 73) or with your automobile, as just detailed, try linking them to the meeting place itself, provided, of course, that you are already familiar with it.

That's better than using your own home, as Cicero did, because you don't have to think back. The furnishings of the office, conference room, hotel dining room, or wherever the meeting is being held, serve the same purpose and you find yourself bringing up certain points at the very time and place where they should be discussed.

That is why actors go into their parts, the moment they walk on stage, or lecturers take up their theme, once they are faced by an audience. The surroundings, the lights, the very atmosphere, are all familiar and thereby render memory almost infallible. That is why skilled comedians are so quick with impromptu remarks or gag-lines. Anything they say or do links to some past recollection from a similar time and place.

Rehearsals, too, forge recollections. Hence by projecting your mind ahead to a scene-to-be, you are almost certain to recall things, once you are actually there. But those things must be "placed," and the stronger you apply the A I R formula and jingle those memory links, the better the results will be.

One noted fiction writer used to apply "tags" to every character he introduced in his stories. Those tags were descriptive statements, such as "the rangy man," or "a catlike smile," or "a silly giggle." This writer's advice to other writers was, "Wave those tags!" because they furnished memory links for readers, who never lost interest in the story or its characters.

As a sure cure for absent-mindedness, you can aim for memory targets in your own immediate surroundings, which is a good step toward developing any memory system that you may take up later. A good example was the case of Mr. Watkins, who could not remember where he put anything around his office. He was constantly screaming at his secretary, wanting to know where she had hidden his check book, or his reading glasses, or the letters he'd just signed, and sometimes even things like his golf bag.

It would turn out that he'd left his check book at home, or that he himself had mailed the letters, or something of that sort, with one exception: Mr. Watkins had a fine old briar pipe, which he liked to smoke about once a week. Whenever he demanded, "Where's my pipe?" his secretary would calmly respond, "Have you looked in the back of the top drawer on the right, where you always put it?"

Mr. Watkins would look there and find it, for the simple reason that he valued that pipe so highly that whenever he finished smoking it, he would put it exactly where it belonged. That was the ray of hope from which he gradually and eventually managed to emerge from his absent-minded coma. He began putting away other articles individually, just as he did his pipe, associating them with the places where they belonged, until the process became automatic.

That became a personalized memory system, the sort that will work for everyone. With that established, there is no limit to the development of other methods, as the following chapters will prove.

*　*　*　*　*　*　*　*　*　*

CHAPTER 6

Alphabet Action
Makes Memory Might!

A business man named Randall had moved to a new location and was having trouble with his telephone. He had been given a new number, 726-3255, and his customers were getting it mixed up with 726-2355. In fact, Mr. Randall himself had a tendency to put the "2" before the "3" when he gave it to customers over the phone. So he thought that perhaps he should have it changed again, before mailing out cards to all his customers.

The trouble was, another number might be even worse. Brooding thus, Mr. Randall found himself longing for the days when you used the first three letters in the name of an exchange, then four figures, like W-I-N-6800 for WINston 6800. Anybody could remember a first syllable and four figures to follow; but seven figures in a row, like 726-2355—no, there he had it wrong again! —a number like 726-3255, was just too much to keep in mind.

Why couldn't it begin with letters? Studying the phone dial, Mr. Randall began to spell it out: R for 7, A for 2, N for 6, D for that troublesome 3, A for the equally troublesome 2, and two L's for 55. He didn't realize that he had gone beyond the first three letters, until he stared at what he had written, his own name, Randall! So Mr. Randall sent out cards to his customers, saying:

For Prompt Results

Just Dial

RANDALL

It would be wonderful indeed, if everybody's name had just the right number of letters to spell out their phone numbers, like Randall's did. But there are not enough names and there are too many telephones. That, however, does not alter the basic factor on which this type of memory jog depends; namely, that words of seven letters can be noted and remembered at a glance; whereas, a number of seven figures has to be noted carefully and then represents the limit of the average memory span.

Words can be broken into syllables, phrases and initials. Sometimes if they are spelled oddly, or even if they are not real words, they can be all the more easily remembered. If they can be linked in any way to the name of a person or business, they can serve just as well as if they spelled out a name exactly.

Tabbing Telephone Numbers and Addresses for Ready Reference

Before going into examples of these "jog words," let's take a look at the typical telephone dial. It has numbers from 1 to 0, but there are letters only with figures 2 to 9 inclusive, three letters for each figure. That makes 24 letters in all, hence two letters of the alphabet—Q and Z—do not appear upon the dial. So we term Number 1 as the letter "I" and with it, we place the letter "Q." This is easily remembered by the abbreviation "IQ" which in psychology stands for "Intelligence Quotient." We term the figure 0 as the letter "O" and to it, we assign the letter "Z" which stands for "Zero." Together, they spell "OZ," which is also easy to remember.

Keeping these two points in mind, the figures and letters of the standard phone dial will then run:

1—(I-Q)	6—M-N-O
2—A-B-C	7—P-R-S
3—D-E-F	8—T-U-V
4—G-H-I	9—W-X-Y
5—J-K-L	0—(O-Z)

The letters in parentheses (I-Q) and (O-Z) are those that you supply mentally for "1" and "0", respectively. You do not have to remember the other combinations, as you can see them on the dial when forming your code-words. Note: "1" is never in the first two figures; nor "0" in the first three figures of a phone number, so up to those points you can represent the figure "4" with "I" on the dial; and the figure "6" with "O." This helps give you vowels toward your "key-word." The "I" and "O" for "4" and "6", respectively, are not to be used for the last four digits of a number.

Now for some good examples:

(1) A family who had a pet cat of which they were very fond:

    Phone Number: 6 8 7 - 5 1 8 1
    Key Phrase: O U R-K I T I (Kitty)

(2) A kindly old gentleman who exaggerated things:

    Phone Number: 6 5 7-3 1 2 7
    Key Phrase: O K'S-F I B S

(3) A storekeeper who was always out of stock of whatever you asked for:

Phone Number: 2 7 9-5 0 7 8
Key Phrase: C R Y-L O S T

(4) A friend who always complained about things:

Phone Number: 4 8 5-1 2 5 7
Key Phrase: I T-K I C K S

Those so far given are fairly obvious. Here were some that required a somewhat specialized treatment:

(5)   Phone Number: 5 2 8-9 5 8 9
        Key Words: K A T Y-L U X

Simply an imaginary name that was associated with the person who had that number, to form a memory link.

(6) Phone Number: 5 4 6-4 0 0 0
    Key Word: L I N G O

The word "lingo" is slang for "talk," an excellent link for a phone number. The fact that it is cut short (with only five letters) means that the last figure is to be repeated twice.

(7) Phone Number: 7 4 7-8 2 9 9
    Key Word: S I R V A Y

The wrong way to spell "survey" but easy to remember. Being one letter short, the final figure "9" is repeated.

(8) Phone Number: 4 3 7-6 8 7 2
    Key Letters: G E R M U.S.A.

The word "germ" plus the abbreviation "U.S.A." is an easy combination to link with someone.

(9) Phone Number: 2 6 5-9 1 2 4
    Key Word: A N K W I C H

Simply a "coined word" but pronounceable and therefore much easier to remember than the number.

(10)   Phone Number: 4 3 7-1 7 9 3
        Key Words: H E R-I S-W E

It doesn't quite make sense, but it's easy to remember as if it did; perhaps easier!

Naturally, all phone numbers are not as amenable to word

formation as those that have been listed. You may run into allowable combinations, like 825-3642 = TALENGA; or 681-9610 = OVIX-MIO or even 889-8774 = TUX-URSH. But when you meet up with 485-6914 = GULMWIG; or 434-8126 = HE-IT-I-AM; or 767-4119 = POP-GI-IX, you may find it easier to remember the numbers themselves.

However, all this is good preliminary training before taking up more elaborate methods of remembering any list of numbers, up to twenty-six figures and more, if need be.

Extending A-B-C to A-B-Z Through Use of a Pictorial Alphabet

To say that the following system is as simple as A-B-C is absolutely true. In fact, it is as simple as the Mother Goose alphabet, which ran: "A" was an Apple-pie; "B" Bit it; "C" Cut it and so on. Only with this system, we start with an Apple, not an Apple-pie, and we forge the links with the succeeding letters much more strongly than in the nursery jingle.

Also, it has been specially arranged so that you can test it out immediately after reading it, with its special applications at your finger-tips as well.

The first step is to visualize each letter of the alphabet in the form of an object beginning with that letter, choosing objects that will form a logical, running chain. Hence the list that follows, though arbitrary, is advisable, since it has been designed for that purpose. It will be treated as our "standard" list throughout, so references can be made to it. Later, you can make substitutions if you want, or even devise your own list.

Proceeding through the alphabet from A to Z, you begin by picturing an:

APPLE, which is hanging from a branch, where a—
BIRD, which is pecking at it, flies away when a—
CAT comes stalking toward it, only to be chased by a—
DOG, which then runs toward an—
ELEVATOR, which opens suddenly and lets a—

FAMILY step out. With them they have a—

GOAT, which starts butting into things, until a—

HORSE chases it into an Oriental temple and knocks over an—

IDOL, which falls upon a large metal—

JAR, which is carried away on the tail of a—

KITE, which gets tangled in a tree, among the—

LEAVES, from which a—

MONKEY emerges and starts gathering—

NESTS, which in turn are snatched by an—

OCTOPUS, which in turn is attacked by a—

PORCUPINE that finally throws its—

QUILLS through the air toward a large—

ROCK, which is snatched up by a—

SAILOR, who rolls it like a bowling-ball toward some—

TEN-PINS, which fall away, revealing a huge, outspread—

UMBRELLA, which rises to disclose a ship manned by fierce—

VIKINGS, who chase after a—

WHALE, driving it onto a beach where a—

XYLOPHONE is standing and being played by a—

YOGI, who is seated on the back of a—

ZEBRA, which suddenly becomes frantic when an—

APPLE falls and hits it on the head.

This completes the circuit from A to Z and back to A again, giving you twenty-six linked objects, forming an endless chain as described in Chapter 3. Here, however, the chain is doubly strong, because it is *alphabetical*, as well as *pictorial*. As with any memory chain, you can tap in at any point, but with this one, you have the added advantage of recalling the exact position due to the initial letter of the link.

You can think of "H" and immediately have "Horse"; and in going back to "G," the picture of a butting "Goat" will come to mind; or you can go ahead to "I" and see an "Idol" toppling from the horse's kicks. But the usual procedure is to start by running straight through the alphabet from A to Z, using your pictorial list as a *permanent* alphabetical chain for purposes now to be described.

Expanding the Alphabetical-Pictorial Chain into a Numerical Memory System

We are still dealing with numbers. Remember? You do, because this book itself is geared to the "link system" where one phase leads to another; and all can be backtracked. To expand your "A-Z" links into the figures "1" to "0" inclusive, you proceed, beginning with APPLES:

For the figure "1," visualize one large apple as the main object. That is easy, since one apple is your original impression. But the larger you picture it, the more strongly will it represent "1."

For the figure "2," picture two apples, being balanced in a scale; or simply side by side.

For the figure "3," think of a triangle. At each point, an apple. Whether the triangle is inverted or upright does not matter.

For the figure "4," put an apple at each corner of a square. If you prefer a diamond, picture it that way, like a baseball field.

For the figure "5," hitch your wagon to a star. One, two, three, four, five points, with an apple dangling from each. Think of them shining brightly, like a star.

For the figure "6," picture a pyramid. One apple at the top, two in the row below, three below that, adding up to $1 + 2 + 3 = 6$.

For the figure "7," think of one thing only: Luck. That's what number seven means. So you're lucky to have seven apples. It's that simple, as you will see.

For the figure "8," picture a cube. It has eight corners, with an apple on each; doubly solid, like two squares; one above the other; $4 + 4 = 8$ apples.

For the figure "9," you go "all out." Just picture a multitude of apples, literally pouring down from the sky, burying everything in sight.

For the figure "0," blot it out. Picture an utter blank, a blackout. Just think that it never happened. You may be surprised to find out how easy that is.

So now, you are ready to remember a number, let us say, composed of thirteen figures, like "4276490103585," which is far beyond the normal memory span. Here is how you would picture it.

Figure-by-Figure Visualization
Produces Alphabetical Results

First break down the number:

4-2-7-6-4-9-0-1-0-3-5-8-5

Then picture each figure in alphabetical terms, thus:

You see *four apples*, forming a perfect square.

Two birds are sitting side by side, each ready to peck a pair of apples.

Think of *lucky* (7) *cats*, creeping up the tree to capture those foolish birds.

However, *six dogs* are forming a pyramid to reach those climbing cats.

In the background, *four elevators* are waiting. Or you can picture just one elevator, but with its dial at Floor *Four*. In either case, a door pops open.

Out surges a *huge family*, so many that you can't count them, which signifies *nine*.

But there is *no goat*. Everybody is looking for it, yet nobody can find it. That stands for zero. In fact:

Even the *big horse* that you now picture is puzzled because it has nothing to chase. You see it running around *alone*, meaning *one*.

Hopefully, the horse runs into the Oriental temple, but there is *no idol* there. The pedestal on which it belongs is *empty*, unoccupied, for zero.

However, three ornate metal *jars* are standing on the floor, forming a perfect *triangle* for *three*. The jugs start to rise in air:

You then see that they are attached to tails of *kites*, but there are two extra kites, both free, making *five* in all, which are flying in star formation. In fact, they can be flying up toward a star in the sky.

Then, suddenly, the kites are trapped within a huge, hollow cube composed of tree *leaves*, its corners representing *eight*.

Now, *monkeys* are jumping into sight, using tree limbs as a trapeze. They wind up in a star formation, denoting the figure *five*.

Since the sequence has only thirteen figures, you end it there. If you take each impression slowly, getting it fixed in mind before going on with the next, you will find that you can call off the row of numbers, forward, backward or at intervals, simply by visualizing the multiple images you have formed.

The beauty of this system is that you can test it out immediately, before you have actually learned your A to Z key-list. Write down the number on a slip of paper, then read through the instructions on page 107. Then turn back to the list on page 105 and visualize the figures as you read it, writing them on another slip, as you go from "A" for "Apples" through "M" for "Monkeys." After that, compare the slips and see how close you came.

Actually, you should hit 100% on almost the first try. If not, note the weak links in your chain, strengthen them by concentrating on them; then go through the figures again. Once you have them all correct, write out another row of thirteen figures, and picture them as representing letters "N" for "Nests" through "Z" for "Zebras." Those can then be checked off the same way.

With this system, you can peg a phone number of ten figures (including the area code) and tack on the person's street address and zip code as a follow-up. If you want to remember that Australia has an area of 2,967,902 square miles with an estimated population of 11,651,340, use "A" through "G" for one; "H" through "O" for the other. If you want to deduct the statistics for the island of Tasmania, which is included under Australia, translate its area of 26,383 square miles into pictures "P" through "T" and its population of 373,684 into letters "U" through "Z."

Social security numbers, closing figures on the stock exchange, total votes in a presidential election, the racing revenues for a given year, and many other statistics can be memorized with ease and accuracy, once you have familiarized yourself with this system. Normally, however, it should be used only to retain certain figures temporarily, because when you form mental pictures of another number, the new one wipes out the old, like cleaning a slate.

You can keep a special number, say social security, firmly pegged by repeating it over and over, at the same time linking each picture with the thing itself, in this case a social security card, using it like a background for your visualization. Another course is to use a different picture alphabet.

Interlocking Alphabet Action with Simple Linkage to Recall a Group of Objects

We have already noted how a series of objects can be recalled by linking them pictorially. The "A to Z" system goes beyond that, as the alphabet itself provides the basic linkage. So once you have your A to Z pictures fixed in mind, it is quite possible to take a sequence of unrelated items and link them individually to the alphabetical key-words.

As an example, here is a list of your key-words "A" to "R," along with a random assortment of objects:

(1) Apple—Piano	(10) Jar—Book
(2) Bird—Envelope	(11) Kite—Wallet
(3) Cat—Garage	(12) Leaves—Bottle
(4) Dog—Telescope	(13) Monkey—Fork
(5) Elevator—Lawn Mower	(14) Nest—Dice
(6) Family—Card Table	(15) Octopus—TV Set
(7) Goat—Broom	(16) Porcupine—Bag
(8) Horse—Mail Box	(17) Quills—Flag
(9) Idol—Teapot	(18) Rock—Bucket

Simple links can be formed by picturing (1) an APPLE lying on a PIANO; (2) a BIRD flying from a large ENVELOPE; (3) a CAT sitting outside of a GARAGE and so on. By going over the pictures a few times, it is generally easy to recall the corresponding objects from these associations. If any seem weak, you can strengthen the picture, say by having the cat sitting on top of a car in the garage. However, if you want to keep the list in mind for a day or two, or even longer, you may have trouble pairing some of the items, since each depends on a single association.

In that case, you can link each list and also interlock them. You have already linked your A-B-C of "Apple" pecked by a "Bird" which is chased by a "Cat." Hook "Piano," "Envelope" and "Garage" into their proper places and keep going on from there.

For example, you can picture:

(1) APPLES pouring over a PIANO, completely covering it until (2) a BIRD emerges from the pile carrying an ENVELOPE in its beak. It flies to (3) a GARAGE and delivers the message to a sleepy CAT, which is so surprised that it fails to notice (4) a DOG that is studying it through a TELE-SCOPE from outside the door of (5) an ELEVA-TOR from which a power LAWN MOWER roars out, revealing (6) a happy FAMILY seated about a CARD TABLE. The game is broken up when (7) a GOAT jumps on the table and takes off on a

BROOM, like a witch. The flying goat lands on (8) a MAIL BOX from which a HORSE is eating some oats. The horse runs off with (9) a TEAPOT bouncing up and down on its back, finally falling off and smashing against an IDOL, which tips over (10) a large JAR from which a BOOK falls out and spreads itself into the shape of (11) a KITE which flies high with a WALLET dangling from its tail. The wallet falls into (12) a BOTTLE which rolls beneath a pile of LEAVES, where (13) a MONKEY starts digging with a FORK and uncovers (14) a NEST containing a pair of DICE. In moves the long tentacle of (15) an OCTOPUS, which grabs the dice and rolls them on top of a TV SET from which (16) a PORCUPINE jumps out and lands in a large burlap BAG, from which it projects (17) its long QUILLS which rip a FLAG from its staff. The flag falls onto (18) a ROCK, which becomes dislodged and rolls into a BUCKET.

Further items can be added to the list, up to a total of twenty-six, using the same interlocking process throughout. If it takes extra time to form suitable composite pictures, so much the better, as once formed, their images are apt to be sharper. That, of course, is valuable toward retaining the interlocked impressions over a prolonged period.

*   *   *   *   *   *   *   *   *   *

CHAPTER 7

Pictures, Letters and Numbers Together Bring Amazing Memory Results!

Writers on memory improvement constantly tell their readers that there is no such thing as a bad memory. For this, they have been criticized, even by their fellow-writers on the same subject, who claim that they are merely trying to instill confidence in persons who really do have bad memories. But such is not so.

If anyone ever says to you, "I have a bad memory," just ask that person to prove it. In response, such people will come up with instance after instance of how they forgot something dreadfully important and have suffered horribly ever since. By the time they are through, they will have remembered and recounted more data than you could perhaps ever hope to get from a Grade A Memory Expert. The only difference is, they remember all the things they have forgotten. He simply remembers and lets it go at that.

The person who says, "I have a bad memory," invariably has a good memory. His real trouble is a deficiency in one or more of three other departments. Either he fails to give *attention* to the things he wants to remember; or he loses *interest* in those things while he is trying to remember them; or he neglects the *repetition* that is needed to keep those things in mind. He probably never heard of the A I R formula, let alone tried to follow it.

The result is, he generally remembers more than he would ordinarily, but none of it is organized. Therefore, none of it really registers, because all of it is scattered. Oddly, the people who feel deficient in memory invariably blame it on something else, saying, "I am a poor speller," or "I just can't understand mathematics," or "Somehow, I can't learn languages," or "History is my weakness."

Actually, anyone can spell well if they give spelling due *attention*. Mathematics is something that can be mastered if given proper *interest*. Languages and history both depend upon *repetition* which can not be neglected. So failure in any of those departments is invariably due to lack of A I R, which in itself spells Memory.

Since association is a prime mover where memory is concerned, it should be constantly employed toward memory improvement. But like everything else, associations have their limitations and it is often necessary to rise above them. For example, consider a person who is fond of a few catch phrases or knows a few good jokes. Such a person is always making new friends, then gradually losing them and wondering why.

What's needed here is some fresh A I R. This is truly a case of "too little and too late." Too little *attention* was given to things that were going on, otherwise this person would have had more sayings or jokes to choose from. He was lacking in *interest*, too, both his own and that of other people, or he would have become bored with his scanty repertoire before they did. All he really relied on was *repetition*, which in itself can become deadly.

It is just as fatal to depend on *interest* only, with almost total disregard for *attention* and *repetition*. That can be termed putting "I" ahead of all else. Collectors and hobbyists frequently fall into this category and they, too, complain that they have bad memories except in their chosen domain. There, they may exhibit an encyclopedic knowledge, so the truth is that they are just indifferent to about everything else.

Where *attention* is the dominant factor, you find people who are always taking up something new and dropping it just as quickly. Since they never gain enough *interest* to use it, they never reach the stage where *repetition* will help. In fact, it may hinder, because whatever they repeat is apt to be garbled, since they never got it right to start with. Here, again, they think that faulty memory is to blame, entirely overlooking the fact that you can't possibly remember something you don't really know.

Extending Memory Power by Expanding the A I R Formula

So far, we have learned how memory can be improved by using ordinary senses and ordinary knowledge to build a memory file which your "sixth sense"—our name for your imagination— can activate far beyond normal expectations. You have seen that the act of grouping, linking, and visualizing thought impressions becomes a memory builder. From there on, your mental file has taken on actuality through alphabetical and numerical treatment. Now, you can take time to cross-index it.

This involves stimulating your imagination in itself, by testing it through alternate procedures. In going through a memory sequence, you may find weak links or faded impressions. But the more you practice any system, the more effective it becomes, so don't blame the system if you encounter loop-holes. Just blame your imagination and give it a different workout, through other ways of pegging ten items in a row.

In that way, you can extend memory power by expanding the A I R formula. You may find a better way to gain *attention*, rouse *interest* and encourage *repetition*. If you do, you will find yourself walking on A I R. If you don't, you can go back to the old way and strengthen it because you like it better. But what is most likely, you will realize that one not only supplements the other; it implements it as well.

Study the following devices and you will see why.

The Ten Picture Method: Retaining Figures Visually

While the "A to Z" System is ideal for memorizing long numbers, there are times when you may want to remember a short number quickly, or mentally note several important items. Here is a method suited to such purposes, but it is really more than a supplementary device. It is worthwhile in its own right, and it is a very natural way of developing the imaginative faculty so valuable in memory training.

You simply take the ten figures from 1 to 0 and picture them as objects in their own right while listing them as follows:

1: SPEAR:		Upright, pointed, resembling the figure 1.
2: GOOSE:		Long, curved neck, like the upper portion of the figure 2, with body as base of that figure.
3: PITCHFORK:		With three prongs pointed sideways like the figure 3. Can be pictured in smaller size if desired.
4: SAILBOAT:		Headed toward the right, so that its sail represents the figure 4.
5: SPREAD HAND:		This represents the Roman numeral V, the equivalent of the figure 5. Thumb and fingers being five in all adds that much emphasis.
6: SNAKE:		Coiled, with head raised as if to strike, this makes a good figure 6.
7: SEMAPHORE:		Either a railway signal, or simply an outstretched arm signifying "Stop." Looks like a figure 7.

8: HOURGLASS: A perfect figure 8, though somewhat angular rather than rounded.

9: SNAIL: Picture this creature heading down a steep hill in order to gain speed, with its shell up toward the right and it makes a good figure 9.

0: DISH: Round, like the figure 0.

Once these images are fixed in mind, you can put them into action, so to speak. To you, SPEAR = ONE, so with that being established, you can imagine a spear being thrown or lying on the ground. Similarly, though GOOSE = TWO, it does not have to be restricted to the graceful pose resembling that figure. The goose can be waddling, honking, flying, or whatever else you want, provided that to you it always means two.

The same rule applies to the other figures and due to this flexible treatment, you can readily visualize a row of such symbols, giving them a running sequence like a cartoon strip, thus keeping them in order. For example:

Suppose you want to remember the number 425-065. You picture a *sailboat* (for 4) but have it veer about, so it is heading to the left instead of the right. Behind it swims a *goose* (for 2). A *hand* dips down (for 5) and picks up a *dish* (for 0), revealing a coiled *snake* (for 6) that rears up to strike, so the *hand* (for 5) moves quickly away.

This is a good way to remember license numbers, as you can repeat them numerically and then pictorially, until you have your sequence fully established. That's where imagination enters and with a little practice, you will find that you can build it step by step. Where the same figure appears twice in succession, you can treat it as a double symbol, according to a set routine. For example:

In remembering the phone number 338-8554, you could picture two pitchforks crossed (for 3 and 3) followed by two hourglasses, side by side, one with the sand at the top, the other at the bottom (for 8 and 8). Next, two hands clasped (for 5 and 5), followed by a sailboat (for 4) which can be sailing toward the right, since no more figures are to follow.

Note how a few touches emphasize the "doubles." With a single "8," you would picture an hourglass with the sand equal in the top and bottom sections. For three 8's in a row, you could visualize one with sand in the bottom, the next in the top, the third in the bottom. With all such cases, it is best to use your own imagination in the final picturization; then the impressions are even surer to stay with you.

Applying the Ten Picture Method Toward Remembering Ten Articles—and More

Once you have the numerical pictures solidly fixed in mind, you can use them to remember a series of articles, just as with the various systems already described, particularly the "A to Z." Here is a specimen series of ten:

Numerical Keys   To be Remembered

(1) A SPEAR with its point jabbed through a DOLLAR BILL

(2) A GOOSE complacently seated upon an AIR-CONDI-TIONER

(3) A PITCHFORK with one prong poking the button of a DOOR-BELL

(4) A SAILBOAT of toy size, sinking under the weight of a large DICTIONARY

(5) A HAND recoiling from a snapping MOUSETRAP

(6) A SNAKE coiled around and around a FLOOR-LAMP

(7) A SEMAPHORE supporting the handle of a PITCHER

(8) An HOURGLASS with its sand trickling into a SUITCASE

(9) A SNAIL poking itself down into an open POCKETBOOK

(10) A DISH on which a knife is carving a TYPEWRITER

For "10" you could simply depict a dish with a typewriter resting on it. However, a knife with the dish is better, because side by side, they represent the number "10." Thus KNIFE + DISH = TEN rather than merely the figure "0." If your series runs to more than ten, you can use some more composite numbers, such as:

(11) GATEPOSTS:	Tall and simple, with an open space between, these make a nice "11."
(12) CLOCK:	Picture this as having both hands pointing up to the number "12."
(13) BROKEN "B":	A huge letter "B" breaking apart to form the number "13."

"B" for the bad luck that goes
with "13."

(14) TWO MASTER: A sailboat headed east (to the
right) but with two masts in-
stead of only one. No sail on
the mast at the stern, for figure
"1," but the foremast has a sail
for figure "4." Together they
make "14."

(15) FINGER AND HAND: The forefinger of the right
hand, representing "1," point-
ing to the open left hand meaning "5." Together: "15."

You are quite free to concoct more than these, if you feel
that the series should go higher, but ordinarily, ten to fifteen should
be enough. In remembering articles from 11 to 15 inclusive, treat
them like those from 1 to 10. By linking the remembered items—
Dollar bill, Air-conditioner, Door-bell, and so on, you can
strengthen this series just as you did with other methods. But
there's no need to link the key-pictures, Spear, Goose, Pitchfork,
for since they represent the figures "1," "2," "3" and up, they are
already linked!

Applying Catch Phrases Toward Remembering
Historical Dates and Other Data

The farther you progress with well-established memory
methods, the more you recognize the value of lesser devices as well.
These "dodges" as they are sometimes styled, are often overlooked,
largely because they seem too trivial, or because they have to be
tested to prove their possibilities. Often, they serve best as adjuncts,
or as cross-files, in connection with a more elaborate system.

The telephone dial device at the start of Chapter 6 stands as a
case in point. There, you learned a quick, sure way of pegging any
numbers that proved adaptable to the device, giving you a chance
to run up quite a helpful list. However, whenever you found it
difficult to change numbers into words, you were advised not to
overstrain the device, but to use a sure-fire system like the "A to Z."

Now here, the same rule applies. Instead of short key-words,
catch phrases will be used to identify specific dates, statistics or
whatever else will lend itself to such treatment, by the neat expe-

dient of identifying each figure by a word containing the exact number of letters as the figure itself, running from 1 to 10, with the 10 standing for zero.

A few samples will show how this device works:

(1) To remember the date of the Battle of Hastings (in 1066) when William the Conqueror overcame Harold and became King William I of England:

I, CONQUERING, KILLED HAROLD
1   0   6   6

(2) To remember the date of the Declaration of Independence, in the year 1776:

A COUNTRY CREATED ITSELF
1   7   7   6

(3) The Battle of Gettysburg fought in 1863:

A TERRIBLE BATTLE WON
1   8   6   3

(4) Accession of Queen Victoria to the throne of England in 1837:

A PRINCESS WAS CROWNED
1   8   3   7

(5) The Spanish-American War in 1898:

A REPUBLIC THREATENS MONARCHY
1   8   9   8

(6) Landing of the Pilgrims (1620) in Massachusetts:

A NATION IS INSTITUTED
1   6   2   0

In contrast to historical dates, the areas of states and countries can be checked against appropriate sentences.

(1) The state of Maine, 33,215 square miles:

BIG FUN IN A CANOE
3   3   2 1   5

(2) The state of Florida, 58,560 square miles:

MIAMI VISITORS OFTEN TRAVEL EVERYWHERE
5   8   5   6   0

(3) The Republic of Cuba, 44,218 square miles:

CUBA WILL BE A REPUBLIC
4   4   2 1   8

(4) The island of Ceylon, where good tea comes from, with its area of 25,332 square miles:

TO ENJOY TEA, SIP IT
2   5   3   3   2

(5) The area of New Zealand, 103,736 square miles:

A PROSPEROUS AND VALIANT NEW NATION
1   0   3   7   3   6

These are admittedly special cases, but you will find many more if you look for them. Whenever you are confronted by something numerical that you simply must peg properly, try this device. If it works nicely, utilize it; otherwise try some other memory method. It is particularly good with short numbers like street addresses. If you have to remember quite a lot of them, tying in with a simple picture never leaves room for doubt.

Here are a few samples:

(1) Street address to be remembered: 1449.

The person remembering it pictured himself leaving the house, then rushing back to it. Key-phrase:

I WENT BACK HURRIEDLY
1   4   4   9

(2) Street address to be remembered: 3615.

This gave people a lot of trouble, as they were always confusing it with 3516. They tried to recall which side of the street had odd numbers, which side even; that proved a problem, too. Then someone coined the key-phrase:

ODD NUMBER I THINK
3   6   1   5

(3) Street address to be remembered: 14467.

This place was far out in the suburbs at the end of a bus line. Someone appropriately keyed it:

A VERY LONG TIRING JOURNEY
1   4   4   6   7

Develop an Actual Audio-Visual Memory Through the Homophonic Method

We have seen how well the "Ten Picture Memory Method" (page 116) can serve as an adjunct or a separate system in remembering ten numbers, its beauty being that it won't conflict with any other method. Here is another device of the same ilk, the "Homophonic Method" which is quite as good as the "Ten Picture Method," particularly because they won't conflict with each other.

The intriguing feature of the "Homophonic Method" is that you start with *sounds* and translate them into *figures* (1 to 10 or 0) so that the result is truly audio-visual and therefore not just easy to remember, but almost impossible to forget. Here is the list, with comments that will serve as helpful jogs:

(1) WAND stands for ONE. The word "wand" without the final "d" sounds like "one," W-A-N-(D) and a *wand* looks like the *figure* "1."

(2) TUBE stands for TWO. The word "tube" sounds like "two," T-U-(B-E) and a *tube* has *two* ends.

(3) TREE stands for THREE. When slurred, "tree" sounds like "three." T-H-(R)-E-E, and a trunk with two branches represents "3" visually.

(4) FORT stands for FOUR. Without the "t," the word "fort" becomes "four," or its equivalent, "for," F-O-R-(T), and a *fort* has *four* walls.

(5) FIFE stands for FIVE. Very appropriate, as "five" is often pronounced "fife" over the telephone; and a *fife* is played with *five* fingers.

(6) STICKS stands for SIX. Leave out the "t" and "sticks" will be "six," S-(T)-I-X. There is also a jingle that goes: "Four, five, *six*, pick up *sticks*."

(7) HEAVEN stands for SEVEN. Pronounce the phrase, "It's heaven," and it sounds like, "It's seven." Drop a few letters and spell: (I)-(T)-S-(H)-E-(A)-V-E-N. Seven is a *lucky* number and people are lucky if they get to *heaven!*

(8) WEIGHT stands for EIGHT. Just leave off the first letter "w" and you have it: (W)-E-I-G-H-T.

(9) MINE stands for NINE. Switch the first letter, "m" for the one that sounds most like it, "n" and "MINE" = "NINE." During the California gold rush, MINERS were called "forty-NINERS."

(10) TENT stands for TEN. Leave out the final "t" and there it is: T-E-N-(T). To picture it as zero ("0"—instead of "10"), take away the *tent pole*, which resembles the *figure* "1," and the tent collapses into *nothing*, becoming "0."

To remember items by this method, use the regular procedure of picturing them along with your audio-visual keys. Thus you could imagine: (1) A CAT waving a WAND. (2) A LIGHT BULB shining in a TUBE. (3) A FISH climbing a TREE. (4) The MOON shining on a FORT. (5) A ROSE-BUSH sprouting from a FIFE. (6) A LAMB picking up STICKS. (7) GLASSES being worn by angels in HEAVEN. (8) An EGG being crushed by a WEIGHT. (9) A FOOTBALL bounding down into the shaft of a MINE. (10) POP-CORN showering down upon a TENT.

The audio-visual key-list can be extended by additional pronunciation symbols, such as: (11) ELFIN, or a group of elves, for ELEVEN. (12) SHELVES, or a big shelf, for TWELVE. (13) THIRSTING, or a bubbling spring, for THIRTEEN. (14) FROSTING, or a fancy birthday cake, for FOURTEEN. (15) FISTING, or gloved hands punching a bag, for FIFTEEN.

These, it will be noted, are much more strained than the simple "1" to "10" list, but for persons who intend to use such symbols frequently, that is sometimes an adjunct, as stretches of the imagination stimulate memory chains. Hence, if anyone wants to carry the list into the twenties or beyond, they will do best to coin their own "sound symbols."

*   *   *   *   *   *   *   *   *   *

CHAPTER 8

Using a Ten-Letter
Figure Code to Build Profit
and Power with the
100-Word Super-System

So far, we have seen how all memory methods are a phase of an instinctive process in which the A I R formula predominates. Anything to which you give due *attention* can be remembered if you show *interest* in remembering it and clinch it through *repetition* as long as you need to remember it. This, as we have also seen, hinges on the natural process of associating various items with one another, in groups, or by links, or through definite mental pictures.

The methods given include mentally placing objects in known locations belonging to our daily life; or picturing them in a mental framework specially designed to bring them back to mind. From this stemmed the use of various devices, all of familiar types, as extensions of the natural memory process. These include the alphabet, which most people regard as natural, but which is actually artificial, since the order of the letters is purely arbitrary and has become "second nature" to most persons only because they learned it early and have repeated it often.

That also applies to word formation; hence, by extending A-B-C to A-B-Z, as described in Chapter 6, we truly developed a system, rather than a mere method. Numbers, too, have their individual features which serve as natural memory jogs, as evidenced by the three memory methods discussed in the previous chapter. There again, we merely touched on artificial systems and their possibilities; now, we are ready to consider them on a fully developed basis.

It is a long recognized fact that special codes, once memorized, can prove of vast value in various forms of communication. Sailors, using signal flags with the semaphore code, can transmit and receive messages with the speed of the spoken word. Everyone is familiar with the dot-dot-dot—dash-dash—of the telegraph key, although only persons trained in its use are able to recognize the messages that come over the wire or the air, so rapidly are they spelled out.

Also, there is shorthand, which to the average person represents nothing more than an unintelligible scrawl, yet which enables anyone skilled in such practice to jot down statements as fast as they hear them. Every code of that type not only is worth learning, but must be learned by all persons whose work depends upon such forms of communication. At first trial, these codes seem difficult, because it takes study and long practice to acquire the necessary facility to employ them regularly and efficiently.

That is the reason why comparatively few persons learn such systems unless they have to use them, yet nearly everyone recognizes that there are times when they might prove of value in everyday life. That rule applies to memory, but much more emphatically; hence, it would be helpful indeed if memory could be systematized and reduced to codified form. Actually, it can be, and the process is more easily acquired than any of the cases just cited; because here, you use memory itself to memorize the code which helps you remember other things.

Even better, you will meet with no complications when learning the memory code. Speed is not necessary, so you have plenty of time to think over the process not only while practicing it, but when utilizing it. What is more, you are already two steps on your way, because this system depends upon two codes with which you are already familiar: The alphabet, which in itself is a lettered code; and the figures 1 to 9, which is a numerical code, with zero as an added symbol.

It is through knowledge of letters and figures that Morse code, semaphore signals and shorthand can all be learned and used fluently; but with those, other factors must be added. With the Figure Alphabet or Phonetic Numeral Code as it is also known, letters and figures can be transcribed directly into a code, making the whole procedure very easy. This system, incidentally, dates back long before telegraphy and shorthand were invented; hence, it has stood the test of time and has become the basis for many effective elaborations.

Though the term "Figure Alphabet" is the one commonly given to this system, you do not have to remember the entire alphabet in terms of figures; rather, you think of figures in relation to sounds represented by certain letters, which spring automatically to mind, so the term "Phonetic Numeral Code" is more truly applicable and reduces the process to ten simple "keys," as follows:

Taking "0" or "naught" as a primary example, we observe that it is termed a "cipher," a word beginning with a sound like "S"; and that it is also known as "zero" which begins with the similar sound of "Z." Therefore, in our phonetic code:

"0"   represents the sound of "S" or "Z," remembered by the words "cipher" and "zero."

"1"   represents T, also the similar sounds of TH or D, remembered because "t" has a single downstroke.

"2"   represents "N," as the letter "n" has two downstrokes.

"3"   represents "M," as the letter "m" has three downstrokes.

"4"   represents "R," remembered because "r" is the last of the four letters forming the word "four."

"5"   represents "L," as "5" is the first half of "50" which is signified by the letter "L" in Roman numerals.

"6"   represents "J," also the similar sounds of soft "G," "CH" and "SH," remembered because the script "j" looks like "6" in reverse.

"7"   represents "K," also the similar sounds of hard "C," hard "G" and "Q," as "7" looks like a key.

"8"   represents "F," also the similar sounds of "PH" or "V," as "f" in written form has two loops like "8"; and you can also think of "F" in *FATE* (pronounced "f"—"eight").

"9"   represents "P," also the similar sound of "B," remembered because "P" looks like "9" in reverse.

The fact that some of these links are a bit far-fetched makes them all the easier to remember, once they have been properly pegged. Note especially that all these basic sounds, S, T, N, M, R, L, J, K, F, P, are consonants, each distinctly pronounceable in its own right. The vowels A, E, I, O, U, Y and such letters as H and W, serve strictly as fillers, enabling you to form words in which the figure values stand for numbers.

As an example: To you, the number "352" is the equivalent of the letters "M," "L," "N." From these it is easy to form the word "MeLoN," so your code word is MELON and by simply picturing a melon on the porch of a house, you can remember its address as 352. Take a longer address like 7684 and you can use the letters "C" (hard), "TCH" (phonetically "CH"), "F," "R." From these, you can form two words, "CaTCH" "FiRe" or "CATCH FIRE," so you could think of that house burning up.

Dates are readily remembered by the figure alphabet. The year that Columbus discovered America, 1492, becomes T, R, P, N, which easily forms the word "TaRPoN," or "TARPON," a kind of fish that Columbus and his crew probably saw as they approached their destination. With modern dates, you really don't need the first figure, as it is invariably a "1," so you could remember the year when George Washington was born as 732 (instead of 1732) giving the letters "K," "M," "N." Those form the word "KiMoNo," or "KIMONO," so picture George Washington wearing a kimono and you will have it pegged.

Longer numbers generally require catch phrases or full sentences to be remembered by this method. For example:

47850292 = 4, 7, 8, 5, 0, 2, 9, 2 = R, K, F, L, S, N, P, N.
This becomes: RICKY   FEELS   NO   PAIN
                        4 7   8   50 2   9   2

That fell into line neatly but others are more strained:
62533712 = 6, 2, 5, 3, 3, 7, 1, 2 = CH, N, L, M, M, K, T, N.
This becomes: CHINA   LAMA   MAKE   A   TUNE
                        6   2   5 3   3 7   1   2

Or this one:
56092148 = 5, 6, 0, 9, 2, 1, 4, 8 = L, SH, S, P, N, T, R, GH.
This becomes: LUSH   SOUP   NOT   ROUGH
                        5   6   0   9   2   1   4   8

This method can be used to remember telephone numbers, which usually have seven figures, or ten, if the area code is included. But unless a very appropriate sentence can be formed, as FINE FRIENDS (FiNe FRieNDS) for 929-4210, you will have no lasting link. Therefore, in most cases, it serves only as a temporary device where phone numbers are concerned. However, there are other ways of applying the figure alphabet toward this purpose, as will be described later.

By practicing word and sentence formation with the figure alphabet, you will become familiar with its use and soon words will fall in line almost automatically. Always remember that you are dealing strictly with phonetics and must act accordingly, but this will be more of a help than a hindrance.

For example, all double letters are treated as singles, so that "PeNNy" is simply "P-N" or 92; and "MiSSiSSiPPi" would reduce to "M-S-S-P" or the number 3009. The "J" sound for the figure "6" would apply with a word like "eDGe"; whereas, a letter like "X" would break up into "K" and "S." The word "exquisite" would read phonetically as eKS-Kw-iZ-iT, thus representing the number 70701. We have already noted how "CK" is treated as a single letter "K," while "GH" can become "F," as in "rough." With a word like "through," the pronunciation would be "thru," so there, the "GH" would not count at all.

Be careful with a word like "LooPhoLe," which would be "L-P-L," or 595; and *not* "L-PH-L," or 585, with the "PH" serving as an "F." With "aCCident," the two "C's" would represent "K" (7) and "C" (0), but in the word "aCCord," the double "C" would be treated as a single "K." With "aRT," you would have both "R" (4) and "T" (1), but with all words ending in "ing," it is best to treat the "NG" as a simple "G" for "7." The same would apply to "ink" which could be treated as "inK." However, "iNNiNG" would be "N-G," representing 27. You can even form your own rules in some instances, but keep them consistent to avoid confusion.

Forming a Ten-Word Key List from the Figure Alphabet

It is quite a simple matter to form a "key list" of single-consonant words to represent the figures 1 to 9, in picture form, but there are so many possible words to choose from, that it is a good plan to limit the list to words of a specific type, so that they themselves can be pegged permanently and will help keep the figure alphabet in mind. The best of such devices is to use the same letter as the start of each word; then fit in each code letter to form a key-word.

Perhaps the best of starter letters is "H," so we link it to the letter "S" to form the key for zero, thus:

0 is represented by the word HOUSE (HouSe).

So when you want to think of nothing, just think of an old empty house, in which you can picture any object that you want, thus forming a visual link. From there, your list runs:

1 is the word HAT (HaT)

2 is the word HEN (HeN)

3 is the word HAM (HaM)

4 is the word HARE (HaRe)

5 is the word HILL (HiLL)

6 is the word HEDGE (HeDGe)

7 is the word HOOK (HooK)

8 is the word HOOF (HooF)

9 is the word HOOP (HooP)

Once this list is memorized, you can remember nine items by simply associating them with the key objects. To run the list to ten, drop the "H" and start with the phonetic equivalent of "1" (as D) and add a letter for "0" (as soft C) to form the key for ten, as:

10 is represented by the word DICE (DiCe).

This list is easy to remember, and by using it frequently, it will always be fresh in mind. However, you can peg it still more firmly, if you wish, by linking the words of the list itself, somewhat as follows:

Picture yourself leaving a HOUSE (0) wearing a HAT (1) and as you take off the hat, out jumps a HEN (2) that flies to a large HAM (3) which is lying nearby. That frightens a HARE (4) which runs up a HILL (5) that is topped by a HEDGE (6) where a huge HOOK (7) comes down and lifts a mule's HOOF (8) that kicks a HOOP (9) which rolls away. As the hoop wobbles and flattens, it forms a circle around a pair of large DICE (10).

Since these form a running chain, they will not conflict with any items that you may associate with the individual numbers of the key-list. Take a list of ten objects in any order, say: book, typewriter, yardstick, telephone, stove, clock, tire, playing cards, flower pot, paint. Then form mental pictures with your key-list:

1: A HAT being crushed by a heavy BOOK.

2: A HEN pecking at the keys of a TYPEWRITER.

3: A HAM so large it takes a YARDSTICK to measure it.

4: A HARE calmly talking over a TELEPHONE.

5: A HILL with a STOVE bouncing all the way down.

6: A HEDGE with the face of a CLOCK showing from it.

7: A HOOK lifting an automobile TIRE.

8: A HOOF kicking and scattering a pack of PLAYING CARDS.

9: A HOOP rolling up against a FLOWER POT and knocking it over.

10: A pair of DICE stuck in a pool of PAINT.

This follows the same pattern as various lists described in

previous chapters, but the figure alphabet goes much farther than any of those. By forming two letter pictures, as with DICE (DiCe) for 10, you can continue a list clear up to 99 (with a three letter combination for 100) as shown on this and the opposite page.

There is no need to memorize this list all at once. After becoming familiar with the "H" list from 1 to 10, try the "D" list beginning with DEED (DeeD) for 11. You can picture your pair of DICE (DiCe) for 10, rolling across a title DEED (11) which is lying on the DOWN (12) of a soft pillow which falls into a stream and becomes a DAM (13) over which a DEER (14) walks. The deer is startled by a large DOLL (15) which is holding a DISH (16) filled with food which a hungry DOG (17) begins to eat until a DOVE (18) flies up and pecks at a package from which DOPE (19) pours in the form of a powder. You can link that with NEWS (20) by having the package spread open and become a newspaper with big headlines.

Later, you can lead in with NEWS (20) and memorize the "N" list from 21 through 29, using the same linking process and finishing with MOUSE (30). Each of these groups of ten can be used as an individual list in its own right; that is, if you want to remember a mere ten items, you don't have to begin always with "H" for HAT, as 1; instead, you can start with "M" for MAT at 31, but treat it as number one.

KEY-LIST OF 100 WORDS

0—HOUSE

1—HAT	15—DOLL	29—KNOB	42—RAIN	56—LASH
2—HEN	16—DISH		43—RAM	57—LOCK
3—HAM	17—DOG	30—MOUSE	44—ROWER	58—LEAF
4—HARE	18—DOVE	31—MAT	45—RAIL	59—LIP
5—HILL	19—DOPE	32—MOON	46—ROACH	
6—HEDGE		33—MOM	47—ROCK	60—JUICE
7—HOOK	20—NEWS	34—MARE	48—ROOF	61—JET
8—HOOF	21—NUT	35—MAIL	49—ROPE	62—JEAN
9—HOOP	22—NUN	36—MATCH		63—JAM
	23—NAME	37—MUG	50—LACE	64—JAR
10—DICE	24—NERO	38—MUFF	51—LADY	65—JAIL
11—DEED	25—NAIL	39—MAP	52—LAWN	66—JUDGE
12—DOWN	26—NICHE		53—LOOM	67—JACK
13—DAM	27—NECK	40—RICE	54—LYRE	68—JOVE
14—DEER	28—KNIFE	41—ROAD	55—LILY	69—JEEP

70—GOOSE	77—GIG	83—FOAM	90—BUS	97—BOOK
71—GATE	78—GAFF	84—FIRE	91—BOOT	98—BEEF
72—GUN	79—GOB	85—FILE	92—BONE	99—BABE
73—GUM		86—FISH	93—BEAM	
74—GEAR	80—FEZ	87—FIG	94—BEAR	
75—GALE	81—FOOT	88—FIFE	95—BELL	
76—GASH	82—FAN	89—FOB	96—BADGE	

100—DAISIES

Supplementary List

00—SAUCE	05—SEAL
01—SEAT	06—SASH
02—SUN	07—SKI
03—SEAM	08—SAFE
04—SEER	09—SOAP

By the time you have pegged the R's, you will have a list of 50 items and by going on from there, you will wind up with 100. Thus it becomes quite feasible to remember up to one hundred items and many persons have done this largely as a "stunt" to show how remarkably a memory can be developed. This can be put to many more practical uses, as later chapters will show; but for the present, it will be treated with reference to its basic function; that of remembering numbers themselves, so indelibly that they can be retained as long as desired or required.

It would be easy to team up pictures from the basic "H" list and thus form numbers of two figures. To picture a huge HAT (1) on top of a HOUSE (0) would represent 10. Two HATS (1 and 1) together, would be 11. A HEN (2) flying over a HEDGE (6) would be 26. A HOOK (7) lifting a HAM (3) would be 73. The important thing is to be sure of which comes first; and that can generally be done by picturing one as larger than the other, or else placing the first above the second in forming the mental picture. But to add a third figure is almost certain to create confusion.

With the 100-word list, that problem is eliminated. You can go to three or four figures, by teaming a one-figure "H" word with any two-figure word; or by putting two two-figure words together. As examples: A HEDGE (6) growing over a fence RAIL (45) would represent the number 645; while a NAME (23) scrawled on a placard above a GOOSE (70) would stand for 2370.

To render this effective, you actually need a supplementary

list for two-figure numbers beginning with "0," as follows:

> 00 is the word SAUCE (SauCe)
> 01 is the word SEAT (SeaT)
> 02 is the word SUN (SuN)
> 03 is the word SEAM (SeaM)
> 04 is the word SEER (SeeR)
> 05 is the word SEAL (SeaL)
> 06 is the word SASH (SaSH)
> 07 is the word SKI (SKi)
> 08 is the word SAFE (SaFe)
> 09 is the word SOAP (SoaP)

With this "S" list, you can form numbers like 4709 which would be visualized as a ROCK (47) falling on a small cake of SOAP (09); or a MAP (39) being dipped in some SAUCE (00) for 3900. Thus whenever you have an "H" picture, you will know that it starts a three-figure number: Example: A HOOK (7) swinging in a GALE (75) for 775; while any "S" picture will represent the last two figures of a four-figure number, as with ROCK (47) and SOAP (09) for 4709.

That makes it unnecessary to think in terms of "large" and "small" or "above" and "below," where the "H" and "S" lists are concerned. They can be pictured together, as a HAM (3) being dried under a burning SUN (02) which represents 302, with no chance for a mix-up. However, you will still have to be careful with other combinations, those in which no "H" or "S" words are involved.

Take the number 2980. There you could picture a KNOB (29), fallen from a door and lying on a FEZ (80). In contrast, for 8029, you could think of a FEZ (80) actually hanging on a KNOB (29) and obscuring it. As another example, for 8185, you could visualize a FOOT (81) stamping on a FILE (85) or file-cabinet; but with 8581, the FILE (85) would be dropping with a hard thump on somebody's FOOT (81).

Once you have practiced this art of imagery, you will be able to remember any number up to 10,000, simply through forming action pictures from the list that you have learned. The highest number on the regular list would be 9999 which you would remember by a pair of twin BABIES (99 and 99), while 10,000 can be formed from a crop of DAISIES (100) floating in SAUCE (00), taken from the "S" list.

Extending Numerical Memory
into the Millions by Using Paired Lists

The system just described can be carried much farther by utilizing two *lists*; one for the *first pair* of figures, the other for the *second pair*. The problem here is that if two standard lists are used, each dependent on the figure alphabet, they are apt to become mixed. Suppose that with your present list from 31 to 35, you had a similar list running concurrently, like this:

31, MAT; 32, MOON; 33, MOM; 34, MARE; 35, MAIL
31, MEAT; 32, MEN; 33, MUMMY; 34, MAYOR; 35, MEAL

Since both revert to the same source, they are practically interchangeable and if you try to separate them by thinking which comes first, you are apt to mix them all the more. It is obvious, therefore, that there should be some way of instantly identifying words from the companion list to differentiate them from the original.

Since association is the vital key to memory, there is a logical and effective way of doing this. Use the original list, as given, dependent on the figure alphabet; then from it form a list of associated objects, giving no phonetic significance whatever to the items composing the companion list.

Suppose we start with HOUSE for 0, as in the phonetic list. To be kept tidy, a house needs a maid. So we take MAID as the "paired word" that signifies 0 on the companion list.

Going on from there:

	Original List			Companion List
1:	Picture a	HAT	resting on a	HEAD
2:	Think of a	HEN	flying to a	ROOST
3:	Recall that a	HAM	comes from a	PIG
4:	Visualize a	HARE	with big, long	EARS
5:	In winter a	HILL	is covered with	SNOW
6:	To trim a	HEDGE	you always use	SHEARS
7:	In a fire a	HOOK	goes along with a	LADDER
8:	A horse's	HOOF	is shod with a	HORSESHOE
9:	A wooden	HOOP	is girded around a	BARREL

Going into the next bracket, running from 10 to 20, you can start with the simple fact that:

10:   In gambling casinos, DICE are rolled in a CAGE.

There is no need to continue these associations in detail, as all are fairly obvious in the "paired list" on this page and 137 following, which is augmented by a supplementary "pairing" for the "S" list, representing 00, 01, 02, etc.

PAIRED LIST

0–HOUSE	—MAID	33–MOM	—APRON
1–HAT	—HEAD	34–MARE	—BLINDERS
2–HEN	—ROOST	35–MAIL	—BAG
3–HAM	—PIG	36–MATCH	—BOX
4–HARE	—EARS	37–MUG	—BAR
5–HILL	—SNOW	38–MUFF	—EARPHONES
6–HEDGE	—SHEARS	39–MAP	—TREASURE
7–HOOK	—LADDER		
8–HOOF	—HORSESHOE	40–RICE	—CHOPSTICKS
9–HOOP	—BARREL	41–ROAD	—BRIDGE
		42–RAIN	—UMBRELLA
10–DICE	—CAGE	43–RAM	—FENCE
11–DEED	—PEN	44–ROWER	—MOTORBOAT
12–DOWN	—BED	45–RAIL	—AXE
13–DAM	—BEAVER	46–ROACH	—BOMB
14–DEER	—ANTLERS	47–ROCK	—CHISEL
15–DOLL	—DRESS	48–ROOF	—ANTENNA
16–DISH	—CUP	49–ROPE	—NOOSE
17–DOG	—KENNEL		
18–DOVE	—RIBBON	50–LACE	—BONNET
19–DOPE	—POISON	51–LADY	—CASTLE
		52–LAWN	—NOZZLE
20–NEWS	—TELEGRAM	53–LOOM	—MILL
21–NUT	—WRENCH	54–LYRE	—GUITAR
22–NUN	—CROSS	55–LILY	—WOODEN SHOES
23–NAME	—MONOGRAM	56–LASH	—JOCKEY
24–NERO	—CROWN	57–LOCK	—HANDCUFF
25–NAIL	—HAMMER	58–LEAF	—BRANCH
26–NICHE	—SHELF	59–LIP	—TONGUE
27–NECK	—NECKLACE		
28–KNIFE	—GRINDSTONE	60–JUICE	—TOMATOES
29–KNOB	—DOOR	61–JET	—AIRPORT
		62–JEAN	—JUG
30–MOUSE	—TRAP	63–JAM	—BUTTER
31–MAT	—GALOSHES	64–JAR	—PICKLE
32–MOON	—ROCKET	65–JAIL	—TURRET

66–JUDGE	—SCALES	83–FOAM	—RAZOR
67–JACK	—AUTO	84–FIRE	—EXTINGUISHER
68–JOVE	—TEMPLE	85–FILE	—TYPEWRITER
69–JEEP	—GAS PUMP	86–FISH	—FRYPAN
		87–FIG	—FRUIT CAKE
70–GOOSE	—TURKEY	88–FIFE	—DRUM
71–GATE	—HINGES	89–FOB	—WATCH
72–GUN	—BULLET		
73–GUM	—TEETH	90–BUS	—TICKET
74–GEAR	—SWITCH	91–BOOT	—SHOE TREE
75–GALE	—FLAG	92–BONE	—SKULL
76–GASH	—BANDAGE	93–BEAM	—LAMP
77–GIG	—FEED BAG	94–BEAR	—HONEYCOMB
78–GAFF	—BOOTS	95–BELL	—STEEPLE
79–GOB	—BOAT	96–BADGE	—POLICEMAN
		97–BOOK	—BOOKEND
80–FEZ	—MOUSTACHE	98–BEEF	—HAMBURGER
81–FOOT	—CORN	99–BABE	—BOTTLE
82–FAN	—THERMOMETER		

SUPPLEMENTARY PAIRED LIST

00–SAUCE	—PAN	05–SEAL	—ICEBERG
01–SEAT	—PILLOW	06–SASH	—MEDAL
02–SUN	—SUNGLASSES	07–SKI	—SKI POLE
03–SEAM	—NEEDLE	08–SAFE	—TORCH
04–SEER	—WAND	09–SOAP	—BATH TUB

Actually, once you have really pegged your original list, forming the companion list is virtually automatic because you are using the very principle of association for which the system was designed. Instead of remembering a list of 100 objects temporarily, as you will be doing right along, your companion list becomes a permanent one, thanks to its natural linkage and its frequent employment.

In numerical memory, any number up to 10,000 can be remembered instantly by forming a composite picture representing the first two figures from the original list and the second two from the companion list, without worrying about their order. Here are some quick examples:

For 2138 a NUT (21) being tightened on a pair of EARPHONES (38). No danger of confusing it with 3821, for that would be a woman's MUFF (38) containing a metal WRENCH (21).

For 5516, a LILY (55) growing from a cup (16). In contrast, 1655 would be a large DISH (16) containing a WOODEN SHOE (55).

For 1896, a DOVE (18) flying around an annoyed POLICE-MAN (96). Quite different from 9618, which would be a BADGE (96) hanging from a RIBBON (18).

Since these pairings automatically declare their order, we can drop the paired "H" list temporarily and use the "S" list through-out. Thus, 476 would be regarded as 0476, depicted by a SEER (04) applying a BANDAGE (76). As for 911, that would be 0911, with someone writing on a cake of SOAP (09) with a PEN (11).

Such use of the paired "S" list makes it possible to hold the original "H" list in reserve for numbers from 10,000 to 100,000. Just use your original "H" to form the first figure of any such number. For example: 53,412 would be a HILL (5) with a MARE (34) sitting on a BED (12); while 99,095 would be a HOOP (9) sailing from a BUS (90) and encircling a STEEPLE (95).

Reverting to the Original List to Add Another Pair of Figures

Thanks to the twofold listing, any five-figure number can be pegged by visualizing the components of a single scene. Now, by appending another object from the original list, you can add two more figures, raising the total to seven. This added object can be pictured as a sort of target or an afterthought; indeed, it can be any-thing that ties in with the main picture, yet still retains enough in-dividuality that marks it as a separate item.

This is particularly good for remembering telephone numbers, which usually consist of seven figures, as:

A HOOF (8) kicking into sea FOAM (83) and sending a pair of *SCALES* (66) into a huge container filled with SAUCE (00). This pegs the number 883–6600.

A HAM (3) being drawn from a MUFF (38) and being hit by a *BULLET* (72) and tossed to a hungry BEAR (94). This pegs the number 338–7294.

A HOOP (9) rolling along a LAWN (52) and bouncing into a *MOTORBOAT* (44) which takes off and nearly runs down a swimming SEAL (05). This pegs the number 952–4405.

Note that in each case the *italicized* item comes from the

companion list, thus separating the items from the original list, thereby establishing which of those two comes first.

Using the Amplified List
to Remember Population Figures

The "seven figure" setup just established can be used to remember the population figures of large cities. Take these:

New York City, 7,781,984

Picture a tremendous HOOK (7) which lifts a huge spar or GAFF (78) which dumps a gaseous POISON (19) from a canvas onto a FIRE (84) which is promptly extinguished.

Chicago, 3,550,404

Think of a large HAM (3) beside a tall, blooming LILY (55) with a mystic WAND (04) poking up above it, and being taken by a SEER (04) in wizard's costume.

Los Angeles, 2,479,015

Here, a HEN (2) is seated on a ROCK (47) offering a TICKET (90) to a DOLL (15) made up like a movie actress.

Philadelphia, 2,002,512

Again, a HEN (2) is stirring a SAUCE (00) with a HAMMER (25) and then shaking DOWN (12) into it from a pillow.

Memorizing Important Business Data
Through the Figure Alphabet

Brief experiment with the figure alphabet will show you that it can be used for many purposes beyond fixing long numerical sequences in mind. One striking example is that of setting up a day's appointment schedule. Assume that:

At 9:30, you have an important conference; at 11:13 you must definitely make a very special long distance call; at 12:45 you have a business lunch that must be over by 2:30, when you are due back at the office to meet an out-of-town customer. Today, you must stay late because a friend is arriving on a plane at 6:40; and after dinner, you are going to a movie where the second show starts at 9:35.

From your dual list, you can picture yourself rolling a HOOP (9) after a MOUSE (30) which is running into the conference room. You think of using the telephone to talk about a DEED (11) for a DAM (13). For lunch, you imagine yourself attacking the DOWN (12) of a soft pillow with an AXE (45). Back at the office, you picture a HEN (2) caught in a TRAP (30). At the airport, you think of looking over a HEDGE (6) and receiving a shower of RICE (40). Finally, you imagine yourself rolling a HOOP (9) through a pile of MAIL (35) to get to the movie theater.

Note that the "minute" figures were taken from either list, because there was no chance of confusion where the "hour" was a single figure (as 9:30), and even where it had two figures (as 11:15) there was really little chance of trouble. You can use this device to remember train or bus schedules throughout the day. Instead of working from a standard list, you can form new pictures linking with the figure alphabet. For example, to recall 1:35, a TOE(Toe) (1) kicking a MULE(MuLe) (35) would serve as well as a regular listing (MAIL) and perhaps better, because it would be applied in that one case alone.

This is especially true in remembering price lists, which many salesmen as well as buyers, have to do. Here are some examples, culled from a special clearance sale:

A small gas range priced at $128, would give HEAT (heaT) 1, ENOUGH (eNouGH) 28 for cooking.

An automatic double-oven gas range at $278 raised the query, "Any coffee?" ANY (aNy) 2, COFFEE (CoFFee) 78.

A small electric freezer furnished the mental picture of a pot of TEA (Tea) (1) being taken from it by a GNOME (GNoMe) (23). Price $123.

A larger freezer with the same tea being taken out by the head of the family: TEA (Tea) (1) and PAPA (PaPa) (99). Price $199.

A still larger freezer that the salesman pictured standing in an old INN (iNN) (2) with a MOB (MoB) (39) around it. Price $239.

A set of furniture at such a bargain that the salesman began by saying, "We're silly to offer this at so low a price." His opening words, WE'RE (we'Re) (4), SILLY (SiLLy) (05) gave the code. Price $405.

From these samples, you can form your own examples, using almost any price list or anything else wherein numbers need to be remembered. The more you practice this system, the better it will work and you can then apply this memory device to other purposes, as will be detailed in later chapters.

* * * * * * * * * *

CHAPTER 9

How to Remember Names:
First Step in Better
Personal Relations

In every memory method so far described, two factors have combined to activate the all-important A I R formula of Attention, Interest and Repetition. First, *Device*, which has increased in ingenuity during the successive methods; second, *Visualization*, which has incorporated imagination and carried it to a highly exaggerated scale.

The term "visualization," it should be noted, has been used in its broadest sense, not being limited to sight alone, but incorporating imagery of sound, touch, taste or smell. Mental reproductions of words, either written or spoken, have also been recommended as memory jogs. So, beginning with the link method, with its simple pairing of objects or words, and continuing through more advanced systems, up to the highly developed figure alphabet, the same general procedure has been followed.

All of these systems have one feature in common, in that they provide pegs or hooks, by which various facts or items can be remembered temporarily or over a prolonged period. The best way to decide which method is most suited to some given purpose is through actual experiment, which by now, you may very well have proved to your own satisfaction. Quite obviously, the simpler systems are satisfactory for ordinary purposes; whereas, figures, statistics and long lists can only be handled through a more powerful process, such as the figure alphabet. But there is a great advantage in trying them all and switching from one to another, whenever feasible. By so doing, you will increase your adaptability, thereby stimulating the imagination and exaggeration so helpful to these memory methods.

This is particularly important where you encounter memory situations which off-hand seem beyond the reach of the methods which you have so assiduously studied. In such cases, you must improvise a system, so to speak, by applying the rules in reverse, or in some special way. Here, the outstanding example is that of remembering names and faces, which many people—especially those whose occupations depend upon it—regard as the crux of all memory work.

Utilizing Names as a Primary Factor
in Remembering People

It has become customary to speak of "names and faces," because the two are so interrelated that for a long while the usual practice was to link them almost from the very start of the memorization process. But the more modern procedure is to begin with names and develop devices for pegging them solidly, before introducing the factor of facial memory. There was a time when most introductions took place face to face, and practically all business was conducted in the same manner; but all that has changed, except in special instances or comparatively limited fields.

Today, many contacts are made by telephone, through agents or through references to various departments, where the turnover in personnel is so frequent that you may often find it expedient to forget a name a few weeks after you have memorized it in order to make way for another. Formerly, many contacts were good to keep for future reference; but in this day of mergers, branch offices, diversification and changes of trend, the new is constantly supplanting the old. All this makes memorization of names all the more important, in order to keep up with the trend; but it must be suited to immediate, rather than long-range needs.

Along with the names of people with whom you may deal but never see, there are names you read about, or which are associated with various products or enterprises that are more or less familiar. Just to be up on current affairs, you must recognize dozens of new names as fast as they crop up; and yet be ready to supplant them with others once they have gone out of vogue.

This in no way negates the tried-and-true memory processes that have long been used with names and faces. On the contrary, they are more valuable today than ever, because they represent the fundamental law of *association* on which all memory hinges. However, they should be handled in a more volatile manner than formerly, often by using lesser links as tabs, rather than relying upon a single association, no matter how strong it may seem at the time.

Centering on names at the outset, with faces to follow, it can be said that today's great keynote in such memorization · is the factor of *preparation*. If you merely expected to hear about or meet a few new people each day, all in a given field, as with a salesman making a regular route, no special preparation would be needed. But to be attuned to the constant changes in today's world, it is wise to be governed accordingly where memory is concerned.

Broadening Your Own Personal Interests Through Memory Power

If your own interests are widespread, you will find immediate links where many names are involved. That is why, as preliminary preparation, you should apply yourself to a study of names and their connections in as many fields as feasible.

Assuming that you like grand opera, keep posted on the names of today's singers and compare them with those of the past. Do the same with movie stars, fiction writers and athletes. If you are watching a football game on TV, don't think of the players in terms of the numbers on their uniforms. Think of their names, as represented by the numbers. Do the same with characters in stories that you read. Dwell on their names long enough to fix them in mind. If you forget them later, it may be their fault, not yours, for if they are properly portrayed, they should make a lasting impression.

At the same time, you should not strain with this type of mental exercise. Your aim is to cultivate memory for names; not to force it. By broadening your outlook, you will actually develop an ability at linking names with daily interests, provided you keep both in mind. In looking through a newspaper, for example, don't just note the headings that interest you and dismiss them with a mere glance. Read enough of the text that follows to establish the who, what, when, where and why that form the vital elements of every news story. With headings that seem of less interest, delve at least far enough to find out who is involved; and you may be surprised by the way seemingly unrelated facts link up.

In discussing business matters as well as social affairs, keep personal relations to the fore. Chance mention of someone you have almost forgotten may revive old memory links and at the same time supply new ones due to fresh factors involved. In short, make memory a habit where people are concerned.

How Your Mental Filing System Can Deliver Personal Information

It is very easy to form a filing system from A to Z, into which anything from memos, to letters, to contracts can be dropped with ease. But suppose that you are confronted with a batch of scattered papers that have no relationship to one another—what then? The answer is simple:

You must put the wheels into reverse. Instead of depending upon the files to receive the items, you let the items themselves create the files. It is like gathering a lot of loose papers and sorting them into groups, then deciding where they should go. To do that, you should have experience in orderly arrangement, as covered in the previous chapters. Now, it is just a case of gathering the loose threads and arranging them in the same way.

To start, we have the new factor: *Preparation*. That is followed by the elements already emphasized: *Attention, Interest* and *Repetition*, which fall in line as follows:

> Preparation
> Attention
> Interest
> Repetition

Spell the capital letters downward and they produce the word PAIR. That was the basis of the simple linking system, and it can be applied to names quite as effectively. Part of your preparation consists of forming classifications for names which spring to mind automatically. Then, by giving due *attention* to a new name, taking an *interest* in the person, which may include recognizing his own interests as well, and finally *repeating* the procedure several times, or at intervals, you can invariably complete the pairing operation.

Each time you do, you will be adding a tab to your memory file, and with many names, you do not have to stop with a single tab. Instead, you can pair it two or three ways; or even more, if you pair up things with which the person is associated. How far this can or should be carried will soon be noted through a study of the system itself, which shows how readily you can turn those tabs into an actual cross-reference index.

Suggested Classifications for Your
Cross-Reference Name File

In the early days of name memorization, some memorizers began with the simplest of pairing devices, putting all names into one of two classes: (a) names that mean something, and (b) names that don't. But the process soon outgrew that primitive concept. It was quite obvious that names with meanings could be subdivided into categories of their own; and that those without definitive meanings could be artificially supplied with some type of significance.

Here is an expanded list of such classifications, covering practically all the needed phases. The list is arbitrary, in that some classes could be grouped together, or for that matter, subdivided further. In fact, you can form your own list if you prefer; and in any event, there is no need to memorize the list itself. By simply using it for reference, the various groupings will become so familiar that they will be interwoven or may be used interchangeably.

(1)	Occupational Names.	(7)	Nicknames.
(2)	Descriptive Names.	(8)	First Names.
(3)	Names of Things.	(9)	Personal Linkage.
(4)	Names of Places.	(10)	Actual Connections.
(5)	Famous Names.	(11)	Imaginary Connections.
(6)	Names of Products.	(12)	Pictorial Sequence.
	(Trade Names)		(The Rebus Method)

After taking each of these in turn, to note the different points involved, study the examples of names that follow them, showing how individual names may be classified under varied heads. After that, you can form similar memory tabs for names of your own choice.

1: Occupational Names—The Original Memory Tabs

Dating from antiquity and carrying right up to the present, the use of occupational terms as forms of names is as much in vogue as ever and perhaps even more so. With the development of small communities, it was often enough to refer to the proprietor of an inn as the innkeeper, the owner of a mill as the miller, the town physician as the doctor, and so on.

It is surprising how strongly this has not only survived but expanded in modern life. People speak of the local postmaster, or druggist, or schoolteacher, as if they were unique, so their names become secondary. On a broader scale, they refer to the bus driver, the bank teller or the stewardess, by occupation, rather than by name.

In contrast, many occupational terms have come down as family names that no longer relate to the persons involved. Among such names are Archer, Baker, Barber, Bishop, Bowman, Brewer, Butcher, Carpenter, Carrier, Carter, Cooper, Farmer, Fisher, Harper, Hunter, Miller, Piper, Porter, Potter, Shoemaker, Tinker, Usher, Walker and Woodman.

Others have undergone slight modifications, as Cerf for Serf; Mayer for Mayor; Saylor for Sailor; Taylor for Tailor; Tyler for Tiler or Wagner for Wagoner. There are also names that represent a person's status more than occupation, as Bachelor, Benedict, Freeman, Friend, Gaylord, King, Prince or even Whistler.

To remember names in this category, simply link the person to the occupation or status that the name implies. You would imagine Mr. Carpenter working with hammer and saw; Mr. Farmer tilling a field; Mr. King wearing a crown; Mr. Walker striding along a road. If you happen to know these persons by sight, so much the better, but that comes later. For the present, consider those whom you know chiefly by name alone.

Effective though these links may seem, they are easily forgotten unless they serve as "hooks" to something equally tangible, so you must visualize that as well. Assuming that Mr. Carpenter lives near a stream called Mountain Creek, you would picture him building a bridge across it. If Mr. Farmer happened to be a book salesman, you would imagine books sprouting from the fields he tilled. Mr. King, as a jeweler, would be wearing a crown resplendent with all sorts of gems instead of simple gold. Mr. Walker, as a used car dealer, would be striding all around the lot.

2: Descriptive Names—A Further Step in Simple Memory Tabs

Similar to occupational names, those describing persons were also designed for individual identification and can serve the same purpose today. Here, again, the original connotations may be completely lost, but often they can be pictured and sometimes given a reverse twist.

Names of a distinctly descriptive type include Bold, Dark,

Darling, Gentle, Klinger, Light, Long, Priestly, Short, Small, Stout or Strong. So if you meet or hear of anyone with such a name, it can be pegged by visualizing him accordingly. Even though Mr. Light may be very heavy and Mr. Strong may be very weak, the hook will hold, and sometimes the more incongruous it turns out to be, the stronger the link will prove.

Names like Britten, English, French, Irish, Scott and Welch come in the descriptive category. Probably most of them had to do with a family's nationality, so you can apply the same rule to an individual, picturing him as a Briton, Irishman or Scot, as the name may imply. Names involving colors also can be effectively pegged: Black, Brown, Gray, Green, White and the like. Here, you might picture Mr. Black as wearing a somber black suit; Mr. Gray with gray hair; Mr. Green wearing a green necktie or whatever else might help.

3: Names of Things—A Wide Range of Advanced Memory Adjuncts

Dozens of names are taken from those of objects, both animate and inanimate. Rather than subdivide them into numerous classes, they can be covered as a single group, but with some appropriate modifications.

Animal names, for example, are subject to varied linkage. You can picture Mr. Fox as clever, like a fox; Mr. Lamb as gentle as his namesake; Mr. Lyons roaring like a lion and Mr. Wolf or Wolfe as hungry as wolves usually are. There are people with names of fish, as Bass, Pollock, Salmon, Trout and even Fish itself, all lending themselves to picturization, which may not always be flattering, but are more firmly retained in mind, the odder they become.

Both Bird and Byrd are common human names, as are others of the bird family, as Crane, Crowe, Dove, Finch, Grebe, Partridge, Pigeon, Swann and Wren. Know your birds and you will recall people whose names you simply must remember. Such edibles as Bacon, Basil, Garlick, Pepper and Rice form more or less familiar names; while the name Flowers is a reminder of Lilly and Rose. All these are first-rate material for memory hooks, as are many more.

Strictly inanimate objects yield names like Ball, Bell, Cash, Church, Diamond, Glass, Gold, Horn, House, Locke, Piazza,

Pitcher, Rock, Ruby, Steele, Temple, Webb. Picture these as they come, from Mr. Ball rolling a ball, to Mr. Webb being entangled in a spider's web. The more graphic the image, the better it will be retained.

4: Names of Places—A Proven Method of Remembering Personal Names

Have you ever heard of Jack London, the author? If you have —as most probably you have—his name will spring to your mind instantly. If you haven't, you have heard it now, and you will never forget it. Why? Because a name like London, a tremendous city, linked to a person's name, gives that person much of the importance that the city itself implies.

Similarly, the equally famous name of Irving Berlin links with the city of Berlin. But beyond that, there are few big cities with names that link with those of persons that you are anxious to remember. So you simply scale it down to lesser people and lesser places. The result is a real bonanza. For example:

You could think of a man named Fitch as coming from Fitchburg, Massachusetts; or a man named Myers from Myerstown, Pennsylvania. Harmon, New York; Marion, Kansas and Barstow, California, provide direct links to people's names, as does Scranton, Pennsylvania. It is easy to think of Mr. Gaines as coming from Gainesville, Florida; or Miss Sims taking a trip to Simsbury, Connecticut.

Such names may crop up often, as most of those places were named after some early resident or prominent citizen. If you are familiar with the towns in question, so much the better; but just noting one on a road map, or hearing about it in some minor way, may fix it in mind sufficiently for later use in tying in names of persons to whom you are introduced.

5: Famous Names—A Truly "Jump-to-Mind" Classification

If you are due to meet a man named Lincoln, chances are you will wonder if he is tall and rangy or wearing a beard. Such a link with Abraham Lincoln is automatic; and the same applies not only with historical figures, but stars of stage, screen and TV. If you are interested in sports, hobbies or any other specialities, your range of automatic linkage will be widened proportionately; so make the most of it.

6: Names of Products—Opening New Vistas in Memory Expansion

The amazing rule that the more things you memorize, the easier it becomes, is amply illustrated by the names of products, or trade names, with which the buying public is becoming more and more familiar. A few generations ago, customers went to a corner grocery and asked for a pound of coffee, a loaf of bread, a can of beans, a peck of peas and a bag of salt. Often, that was all that needed to be specified; if there happened to be a choice of individual items, the grocer generally only kept one in stock.

Today's array of supermarket products would utterly bewilder the buyer of yesteryear. There are a dozen brands of coffee, with a variety of grinds; dozens of bakeries with a multiplicity of products; canned beans are offered by ever increasing companies; even salt has a variety of trade names, while fresh peas and other vegetables now come in frozen form under another host of brand names.

Apply the same rule to the names of automobiles, gasoline, cigarettes, cigars, publishers, clothes, restaurants, motels and any number of varied industries emblazoned on billboards or in newspaper and magazine ads, and you will be amazed at the sum total. So, having acquired such a vast vocabulary, your next step is to put it to real use as a device toward remembering people's names that actually match the products, or can be stretched to the point where they are easily recognizable.

Here is a list of widely known brand names, which you can check for yourself while trying to visualize a product represented:

> Armour, Austin, Borden, Campbell, Coleman, Dodge, Ford, Gulden, Hartz, Heinz, Hershey, Hertz, Hilton, Kellogg, Knox, Libby, Lipton, Morton, Post, Remington, Reynolds, Sinclair, Swift, Tetley, Van Camp, Waldorf, Winston, Yale.

Dozens of others may come to your mind, particularly those of a local nature. Having visualized whatever the trade name represents, you can be ready to link it with any person of that name whom you happen to meet. For example: A Stetson is a make of hat, popular in the broad-brimmed, high-crowned style worn by Western ranchers, and called a "ten gallon hat." To remember a man named Stetson, you would simply picture him wearing a ten gallon hat.

7: Nicknames—A Compact Mental Index File in Themselves

From their very inception, nicknames have served as memory tabs, supplementing the occupational and descriptive names which represent the basic form of nomenclature. Such names as Wilson, for Will's, or the prefix Mac, to represent a similar relationship, may very well have marked a trend toward nicknames, because they suggested the use of other titles having to do with relationships, real or imagined.

The ancient Romans set a precedent in this field when they gave their great general, Publius Scipio, the name "Africanus" because of his victories in Africa. Later, when his brother Lucius Scipio, won victories in Asia, he adopted the title of "Asiaticus."

English history is replete with royal subtitles that bordered on nicknames, as Alfred the Great, Edward the Confessor, William the Conqueror, Richard the Lion Hearted, Good Queen Bess, Bonnie Prince Charlie and The Sailor Prince (later King George V). In American history, President Andrew Jackson was styled "Old Hickory," because of his rugged qualities; and his protégé, President James Polk, who furthered Jackson's aims, was appropriately nicknamed "Young Hickory."

Plays upon names have figured in modern politics as well. Calvin Coolidge ran for president backed by the slogan, "Keep Cool with Coolidge." With Herbert Hoover, it was "Who but Hoover?" Years later, President Dwight Eisenhower, popularly known as "Ike," gained many votes through the slogan based upon his nickname, "I like Ike"; while Lyndon B. Johnson did very well when his adherents chanted, "All the way with L.B.J."

You can apply nicknames of your own choosing to remember names of persons whom you meet. Think of a bearded man named Harry as "Hairy," or a girl named Georgine as "Gorgeous." You could picture a man named Eaton as always "Eating," or a chap named Drucker as a "Trucker." Note how these tie in with descriptive or occupational names. Trade names, too, can be stretched to advantage; for example, you could class a man named Wheaton as a person who is fond of "Wheaties," or a girl named Claire doing her hair with "Clairol."

Nicknames are very helpful in distinguishing between two

persons with the same last name, which works as well today as in the time of the Scipios. As an example, a man had two friends, both named Miller, whom he was always getting mixed. One, Charles Miller, was rotund of build and very amiable, which tied in with the old nursery rhyme, "Jolly is the Miller—" which in turn produced the nickname, "Jolly Cholly." The other, Hugh Miller, was tall and rangy, so it was easy to switch from "Hugh" to "huge" and think of him as a "Huge Miller."

8: First Names—How to Turn Them into Memory Tabs

From the example just given, it might seem that first names offer memory problems, which they occasionally do, when several persons have the same last name. In contrast, there are times when name similarities furnish a challenge that makes it easy to remember them. Nobody is apt to confuse Herbert Hoover, former president of the United States, with J. Edgar Hoover, chief of the F.B.I.; nor should two famous generals, Andrew Jackson and Thomas J. "Stonewall" Jackson be mistaken for one another. In each case, a simple checkup of the highlights of each individual career makes it easy to differentiate between them.

Apply that same rule to people of your own acquaintance and you will find that it works just as readily. Actually, by thinking in terms of various persons who have the same first name, you may make it easier to remember all of them. If you count the number of Bills, or Georges, or Maries whom you happen to know, you will find their last names springing to your mind as the essential points of difference.

Here, the linkage of first names with those of famous people or places can be handled as well as last names. You can picture a friend named George as being truthful like George Washington, or a girl named Greta as another Greta Garbo. You could think of a girl named Elizabeth as coming from Elizabeth, New Jersey, or a man named Lloyd as being connected with the famous Lloyds of London.

Jingles or catch phrases can often be used in memorizing first names, as "Mary, Mary, quite contrary" or "Silly Billy" or "Handy Andy" or "Georgie Porgie," provided of course that the terms apply. Sometimes, of course, they work in reverse, with Mary being anything but contrary, which makes the peg all the more effective. That is why today, in social circles, or on TV programs, it has become customary to introduce people by their first names, rather than their last. If you really hope to know somebody, you'll have to learn their first name eventually—so why not now?

Long ago, memory experts foresaw the coming wave and suggested that students of their systems should familiarize themselves with lists of first names, just to be ready. Today, however, we have gone beyond that stage. There is no need to bother with first names, unless they are those of people whom you already know, because first names have gone far beyond their former limits, particularly in the feminine field.

Call off your lists of men's names: Albert, Arthur, Benjamin, Charles and so on. With women's names, you have Abigail, Agatha, Agnes, Alice and there you may as well forget it. They just don't go that way today. First names like Bubbles, Candy, Dixie, Gima, Judy, Lisa, Mia, Sandy, Toby, and Zelda, are coming to the fore, with many others in-between. But that should not discourage you where remembering them is concerned.

Simply treat them as you would last names, as described under previous headings, and often, you can link the last name with them, simply reversing the process of remembering a last name and tying in a first name with it. Initials, too, are a help in remembering full names, one notable example being that of the Confederate cavalry general, James Ewell Brown Stuart, who was popularly styled J E B Stuart. Applied today, you could picture a man named Fred Martin as listening to FM radio; a girl named Gertrude Owens as being on the GO; a man named Edward T. Collins as ETCetera and so on.

9: Personal Linkage—Teaming the New with the Old

This is a very effective extension of the device of remembering two names by their similarity; but in this case, instead of balancing them up—as with Herbert Hoover and J. Edgar Hoover—you take a new name with which you are totally unfamiliar and link it with somebody whom you know very well, thus teaming the new with the old.

As an example: You are to meet a man whom everyone calls "Mac," but whose full name happens to be Mac Niece. You find yourself thinking of him as "Mac" and forgetting the rest, until you picture yourself introducing him to your niece Gwen, and saying, "Mac, I want you to meet my niece." Once you have fixed that scene in mind, you will never forget the name Mac Niece.

Similarly, you might meet a Mr. Willard and picture yourself introducing him to a friend of yours whose first name is Willard, saying, "Mr. Willard, meet Willard Smith." Other name links will suggest themselves, as your new friend, Mr. Silver, meeting your old friend Mr. Gold; or Mr. Squire meeting Mr. Knight; or Mr. Queen meeting Miss King.

Often, you can link a new friend with an old because they are in the same business, or have the same interest in sports, or have gone to the same places. Think of them meeting and talking over those mutual interests, thanks to you. Their names can be fitted into the conversation, thus linking them in your mind, regardless of how far removed they may be. Thus,two names like Mike Narleski (new) and Jim McDermott (old) will form a natural and permanent association through your interest in their mutual interest.

10:   Actual Connections—Letting Names Express Themselves

One of the best developed methods for remembering names is to link persons with things they do—or might do—and express it in the form of a statement, slogan or action picture, such as the following:

> PETTIT owns a dog and likes to *pet it*.
> HAMMOND is fond of *ham and eggs* (hammond eggs).
> MEYER is the company's *buyer*.
> STERRIT drinks coffee and likes to *stir it*.
> WARREN is opposed to *warring*.
> DU BOIS is very often *dubious*.

These follow the descriptive pattern given earlier, but instead of having a direct meaning (as Carpenter or Darling), the names are interpreted in some related term. Names based on a language other than English often lend themselves to such treatment. For example:

> KLEINBERG would be climbing a *hill*.
> (In German: *klein* = small; *Berg* = mountain.)
>
> LAMOREAUX would be swimming in a *lake*.
> (In French: *L'amour* = love; *eau* (plural eaux) = water.
>
> VILLAVERDE would be buying flowers in a *greenhouse*.
> (In Spanish: *villa* = large house; *verde* = green)

11:   Imaginary Connections—Forging Your Own Links

By stretching the meanings of names, or letting them suggest terms or interpretations, you can carry connections to almost any length. Stretching it too far may break the link, but often the more curious or incongruous it is, the better it stays in mind. Plays upon words are excellent, if they produce a definite image or an action scene. Here are some samples:

OSTERHAUT suggests the term *oyster house*, so think of someone named Osterhaut running an oyster house.

ANSBACH suggests the words *hands* and *back*, so picture Mr. Ansbach walking with his hands in back of him.

TOFFENETTI makes you think of an English *toff* bowing to a girl named *Nettie*.

GARAGIOLA suggests a *garage* man, putting *oil* in a car. Think of *Garage* + *Oil* = *Garagiola*.

WILLOUGHBY is pronounced *willow bee*. Think of *Willoughby* under a weeping *willow* tree dodging a buzzing *bee*.

These extensions from the actual to the imaginary are simply a transition to the next and final category in which real straining is required to meet the exigencies of names that just will not lend themselves to simpler treatment. There is no hard line of demarcation between them; in fact, many examples of mental picturization might fall into one or the other. But the harder they come, the more they belong under:

12:   Pictorial Sequence—The Rebus Method, a Veritable Memory Game

If you are familiar with the TV game called "Concentration," you are ready for what follows. If you aren't familiar with it, it is easily explained. A message is spelled out on a board, like:

A picture of a devil.	(Devil)
A smiling sailor.	(Mate)
A man holding his jaw.	(Ache)
An evergreen tree.	(Yew)

From *Devil Mate Ache Yew*, it is easy to spell out the message, "*Devil May Take You*." Often, if they need the word "to," they introduce the figure "2," or "for" with the figure "4." To remember hard names, you use the same devices, as:

BUCHANAN: Think of a *buck* (a male deer), eating a meal from a tin *can*, which is then eaten by a *nan* (or nanny) goat, which will eat anything: BUCK-CAN-NAN = BUCHANAN.

ELMENDORF: There was a famous poem that went, "Under the spreading chestnut tree—" but instead, you find an ELM tree, under which stand MEN, looking at a DOOR, marked with the initial F. Why should it say "F"? Because you want to remember ELM + MEN + DOOR + F = ELMENDORF.

GRUENWALD: They are *growing* and *groaning* while they build a *wall*. So it's GRUENWALD.

What else? Yes, it might be a name like:

HASSELTINE: Did you ever get into a *hassle?* Yes, that meant a quarrel, back when you were in your *teens*. Think of your friend *Hasseltine* getting into a *hassle* during his *teens* and you will never forget it. Maybe he won't, either.

KATZENBACH: Don't try to translate this or make it deep. Just take it as it is. There are *cats in back*. Think of Mr. *Katzenbach* calling to the *cats in a back* room. You'll never forget Mr. Katzenbach and he won't forget you; and neither of you will forget the cats, if there were any in back.

TERWILLIGER: A seemingly difficult name like this is simplified by reverting to the nickname process. Just think of TERWILLIGER as TWIG, and you have it for all time.

WINCKELBACH: We have picked this one because it is very unusual and at the same time, very adaptable. If you should meet anybody named Winckelbach, you should not just wink at him, you should winkle at him, which means an extra wink. In return, that person will surely *winkle back*. That's it: WINCKEL BACH.

That concludes the methods on names. Follow the rules as given and you should never forget any, provided you give them the P A I R treatment, as specified at the start.

*   *   *   *   *   *   *   *   *   *

CHAPTER 10

Let's Face It:
Memory Development at Its
Peak—Remembering Faces
and Linking Them with Names

The old saying, "Your face is your fortune," can be given a reverse twist where memory is concerned. In that field, the ability to remember other people's faces can prove valuable as well as fortunate to anyone possessing it. Why? Because if you can remember faces, you can remember people; and people like to be remembered. With such a power at your disposal, you have an open path toward popularity and profit, provided that you develop it, rather than let it lie latent, which too often happens.

The reason for this is that facial memory is a natural type, inherent in everyone. The result is that many persons boast about how easily they remember faces, yet in the same breath bemoan the fact that they can't recall names or anything else to go along with those faces. Their trouble is very easy to analyze. Such stress on faces indicates that they still rely primarily on natural memory and have done little to improve it or gear it to other aims.

In contrast, there are persons whose minds teem with facts and who can reel off names by the dozens, yet will stare blankly at someone whom they met only the night before, or will fail to recognize neighbors if they see them in a store or on a bus. This, too, is not difficult to understand. Such persons have so many things on their minds that they spend all their time trying to recall such data and fall down utterly where the most obvious form of natural memory is involved.

These examples represent opposite extremes, yet in neither case can it be said that the A I R formula is lacking, for if it were, neither of these types would remember the many things they do. It is just that the formula has been misdirected, or has become so limited that *attention* is neglected, because *interest* is lacking, which leaves no chance for *repetition* to supply its needed help.

Though this is often true in many instances where memory is involved, it looms to formidable proportions when dealing with natural memory as opposed to acquired memory, as emphasis on one often nullifies the other. You won't have to study extreme cases to uncover horrible examples. Through careful analysis, you may find, perhaps to your own horror, that you have fallen into the same fault of cancelling out your own efforts by separating vital elements instead of blending them.

That can be readily counteracted, by a series of three simple steps:

First, stop ignoring things that don't interest you.

Second, find out why they interest other people.

Third, from that, establish a mutual interest.

Obviously, the very first step brings other people into the picture, because you are trying to take interest in things that go beyond your own immediate interest. That plunges you into the second step, which automatically draws you into the third, because once you are interested in other people's ideas, you naturally begin to apply them to your own.

Setting Your Pace for the Future by a Selective Process of Facial Memory

Since the ability to remember faces represents perhaps the most natural form of memory, most people acquire it in infancy and some can even look back over many years and remember the slight differences in facial characteristics or expressions that they saw in different people, enabling them to distinguish one person from another. The same ability that you had in your own childhood is something that you can see in children today.

But with natural memory of that sort, its very strength can sometimes be its weakness. Here, more than ever, we find the A I R formula in action, yet operating in such subtle fashion that you may either take it totally for granted, or may not realize that it is functioning at all. Here is an excellent case in point:

A man past middle age came across an old photograph album containing a picture of his class at school when he was only twelve years old. He found other pictures: One of the boys at a summer camp which he had attended at the age of fifteen; another, of his high school class, when he was eighteen; finally, a college graduation picture, all of students with whom he had spent four years.

When he tried to name the people in each picture, he called off every member of the early class correctly, but he kept falling down more and more, as he proceeded through the later pictures.

Granting that this was a special case, it nevertheless applies to many people, and gives a good insight into the matter of natural memory. As a boy, this man had seen only the few companions in his school class; hence, they were vitally important in his life. He gave them *attention* from the moment that he met them; he took *interest* in the things they did, because his mind was in the formative state; and he went over and over the same routine with that same group, so in their limited sphere, *repetition* became a powerful factor.

With his camp life, he had given considerable attention to the boys he met, but took very little interest in them personally, because he didn't expect to see them again after that summer; hence, any memory links were also lacking in repetition.

Both in high school and in college, he gave very little attention to his classmates, until he found those with whom his interests coincided; then he concentrated on those almost to the exclusion of the others. From those pictures, he could pick out faces that belonged to smaller groups with which he was associated. He could name them, because he could recall frequent occasions when they had been engaged in mutual undertakings, hence repetition proved an aid. But with the great majority, even though he had seen many of them every day and heard their names called regularly in class, he couldn't remember them, because repetition had neither attention nor interest to work on, and his A I R formula had been reduced to a useless R.

In looking ahead, it is very easy to overlook people and things which are very close at hand. If you check back on your own experience, you will find lapses or lack of memory links that may surprise you. It is just as well that some of those should be obliterated, where they serve no useful purpose.

In short, there is no need to remember what you do not need to remember; and that can apply to people as well as things. But what you would like to do is either retain or recapture an ability that you once possessed. If you can go back to that point and apply the same procedure that you used then, you will have accomplished much toward improving your faculty of memory, from now on.

Typing Faces as an Adjunct to Your Personal Memory File

Here, again, we must reaffirm that your starting point is A I R. Also, you can take advantage of the pointer given in the last chapter, using the P A I R system. What you do with faces, is pair them, as you did with names. That is the preliminary step that will lead into others as you proceed.

First and foremost, is to link faces of people whom you meet with the faces of those whom you already know. You see someone who looks like your cousin Joe. So you think how nice it would be for him to meet Cousin Joe. You will find that this will develop your attention, interest and repetition (A I R) for this reason: every time that you see the person who reminds you of cousin Joe, you will automatically begin studying him to see how much further he may resemble—or differ from—cousin Joe, in lesser ways.

Not only that, but it can work the other way around. Whenever you see your cousin Joe, you compare his features with your mental image of the man who reminds you of him. Between times, if you happen to think of one, you will find yourself picturing the other as well, even imagining them meeting, whether or not they ever have. All this turns double attention into added interest, resulting in multiple repetition of a natural, effortless sort.

Expanding the "Double" System into a Specialized File

The "Double System," far from being limited to a few obvious cases of personal resemblance, is capable of remarkable expansion, the more you utilize it. Much has been written regarding the fact that practically everybody has an "identical twin"—so far as resemblance is concerned—and that you are sure to find that "twin" if you look far enough and long enough.

Years ago, newspapers and magazines used to run pictures to prove how many people had such "doubles." They amplified this with photos of celebrated people who could be made to look alike, by giving one a beard to match the other's or by having both strike the same pose. If you apply that rule of the "double" on the broadest possible scale, you will find points of similarity that will help amazingly; points that would ordinarily have passed totally unnoticed, until you begin looking for them.

Soon, you will find yourself putting the system in reverse; instead of concentrating only on faces that have an overall similarity, you will be looking for individual points that have something in common, no matter how trifling, then adding others as you note them and even imagining changes that would produce a close resemblance. In short, instead of working from the large to the small, you are working from the small to the large, even building up a synthetic resemblance.

As your next step in expansion, instead of simply linking new with old—that is, instead of only trying to link a stranger's features with those of someone you know well—you link those of two newcomers, associating them practically from the moment that you meet them. If they happen to be already well acquainted, points of similarity will crop up immediately and you can build from those as you go along, carefully noting their mutual interests. If they are not acquainted, you can inject some interests of your own, to see if it brings a similarity of response in their facial expressions.

Sometimes contrasts are every bit as good as similarities; it is always easy to remember a person who is long faced and morose as the opposite of someone whose features are roundish with a smile to match. The closer an overall resemblance between two people, the easier it is to remember them by some striking point of difference which marks them as distinct personalities, even in the case of twins.

Finally, as you continue with your study of faces, you can look for composite faces, which will afford the greatest scope of all. Suppose you meet a man named Mr. Quensett, who is dark-complexioned, like your brother-in-law. He has an upturned nose that reminds you of your nephew's boss; and his forehead is high and slightly baldish, like that of the janitor in the building where you work. Just picture all four getting together, with you introducing Mr. Quensett and watching for their reactions. You will find it harder to forget Mr. Quensett's face than to remember it.

Remembering Faces by the Celebrity Linkage Method

Once the pairing process is developed, it opens a whole new vista, with a proportionate development of facial memory. The speed of development depends upon constant attention, which stimulates interest to the point where repetition becomes automatic. Bank tellers, receptionists, secretaries of social organizations, must remember faces to hold down their jobs. Almost instinctively, they utilize the A I R formula, thereby improving their memory for faces as they proceed, often without ever analyzing the process. The fact that they are constantly seeing new faces and tabbing them for future reference, improves their facial memory all the more.

Yet even persons with such natural aptitude can profit by studying the actual techniques involved. Often, when questioned in regard to their method, such people will claim that they just "grew into it," which is true to some degree. What they usually overlook is the fact that it was some flash of their innate ability that gained them the job in the first place, or encouraged them to undertake it. But that makes it doubly difficult for the people who insist at the start that they just "can't remember faces" and therefore shy away from even giving it a try.

Having convinced themselves that they "couldn't remember," they cite their continued failure as proof of that fact, never realizing that they talked themselves out of the very opportunities that they needed. For memory, of all faculties, is one that depends on self-development. By dodging jobs that stimulate it, people lose out on the step-by-step training that is so essential.

So, again, it is a case of surmounting the first hurdle. By doing that, and applying the A I R formula throughout, anyone can gain the same confidence as a person who boasts of a "natural" memory for faces. What is more, through preliminary experimentation, you gain the marked advantage of learning how the process works, so you can apply its rules as you proceed. This mode of remembering faces has been styled the "Celebrity Linkage Method," because that aptly pegs it.

This method is not new. It has been going on ever since they began putting portraits of famous Americans and foreign rulers on postage stamps or currency. When you see such faces often enough, they register themselves indelibly in your memory. But until recent years, the scope was too limited. You saw the same faces over and over, often in miniature. Today, with modern newspapers, pictorial magazines, motion pictures and especially television programs, you are literally seeing hundreds of the number of famous faces that were commonly seen formerly.

You do not have to remember many of these faces; in fact, by trying to remember too many, you may be as badly off as you would be if you limited yourself to too few. The main thing is to concentrate on those that offer points of similarity or difference: newscasters, politicians, athletes, comedians; any who capture your attention, sustain your interest and appear often enough to provide good repetition. Try to keep linking them with faces of people whom you meet in everyday life. Again, you will have the A I R formula operating at full blast.

Advantage of Using Famous or Familiar Faces as Memory Models

One method of memorizing faces was to give a student pictures of persons chosen somewhat at random, with names accompanying them, the purpose being to link them and remember them, as an exercise toward memorizing real-life faces. While some such pictures might gain the observer's attention, few were distinctive enough to sustain interest, so that looking at the same pictures over and over became useless as a form of repetition.

That system was apparently based on the assumption that if the sample faces were too impressive, they would depart too far from the average, which would be a mistake, considering that most of the persons whom the student would actually meet would be representative of average types. Yet, to a marked degree, the situation is just the reverse. Any face can be impressive, if you have good reason to consider it so. Also, the faces that you see regularly in daily life have changing expressions, so that their smiles, frowns and other noteworthy points can register themselves in your mind, which is not the case with sample pictures.

If you could make home movies of people every time you met them, and run through them regularly, in order to refresh your recollections of them, you would have an ideal way of remembering their faces. Since that is impossible, the nearest equivalent is to use famous or familiar faces for memory models as already suggested. Its great advantage is that by seeing such faces often in photos or on TV, you get to recognize individual points and expressions; and you can automatically apply the same process to faces of people you see daily.

Applying the Rules of Physiognomy to Facial Memorization

As you become adept at "pairing" faces, or rather, linking your recollections of one face with those of another, you may be due for a surprise if you bring such persons together. Instead of the "near-twins" that you supposed them to be, you will find them so different that you may wonder how you ever came to think of them as doubles.

This has happened at meetings of organizations, where committee men are anxious to have a guest speaker meet one of their members who "looks like him," only to have the resemblance fade when they come face to face. Also, every now and then, a celebrity visits a night club and shakes hands with an entertainer who has just done a clever impersonation of him. But if a picture is taken of the pair, all the points of dissimilarity will come to the fore.

Far from detracting from the "pairing system," this is a great point in its favor. It shows that many people utilize that form of facial memory instinctively, using salient points as "tabs" which are so useful in every form of memory. As with other links that have been discussed, the more you exaggerate them, the better. If you can see points of similarity in two persons whom other people do not think are at all alike, you are that far ahead of the game.

It shows that you have been developing your ability for imagery, stretching your imagination and expanding your instinctive memory by gaining an awareness of factors that other persons overlook. These include watching for actions that help you remember and compare persons. Animals and children have that ability to an ingrown degree; and it is something that you should retain, rather than outgrow.

In addition, you may have unconsciously applied some rules relating to the study of physiognomy, a subject as time-honored as memory, but of a more speculative type. Physiognomy, in its pristine sense, refers to the study of facial types and formations; and in that form, it can be definitely utilized as a memory method. In its broader form, those outward aspects are supposed to reveal inner characteristics of the individual. Just how far they do is a very dubious question and one of no present concern, as typing faces is all that is needed toward improving your memory of them, according to the categories that follow.

Frontal Face Formations and Their Memorization: Square, Triangular, Oval

Viewed full-front, faces fall into one of three basic categories, which can be pictured mentally and automatically. The *Square Face* is equal in width at the temples and the jaws, with the cheeks following straight downward lines. In the fully square type, the top of the head is flattish and the jaws so heavy that they give the same squarish effect. Such rugged faces are seldom seen, however, so reasonable allowance can be made for a curvature at the top of the head and the chin. The squarish cheek lines remain essential.

The *Triangular Face* is very wide at the temples, tapering downward to a pointed chin, the longer the better. This type gains its name from its resemblance to an inverted triangle; and here again, as with the Square, a sharply marked Triangular Face is quite rare, but modified forms are often observed that for practical purposes can be tabbed as Triangular.

The *Oval Face* looks like what its name implies, a face which viewed frontally appears as an almost perfect oval, the top of the head and the chin following the same overall curve, so that the face curves outward between temples and jaws. In its fullest form, this is often termed a *Round Face*, because it has a circular appearance, but that is something of an exaggeration, though good to keep in mind for special cases.

Working from these three frontal types, *Square*, *Triangular* and *Oval*, you can gain an immediate impression of many faces at first sight, particularly those which you see on TV programs, as there it is often customary to look straight into the camera. If you want, you can cut out three cardboard frames: one square, another triangular, the third round, and apply them to faces that appear on your television screen, thus identifying or measuring them according to type.

Composite Types can also be pegged quite systematically— such as a *Square Face* with *Oval Chin*; a *Triangular Face* with *Square Chin* and so on. The nomenclature is important only as it helps you "key" the faces when you try to recall them. You might remember a TV personality by the fact that his face was definitely squarish, but with a rather high forehead and a tendency toward a rounded chin. Such exceptions will, in due course, become helpful, as they establish touches of individuality.

Three Types of Profiles That Can Be Automatically Remembered: Convex, Straight, Concave

Often, a good profile view of a face can etch it sharply in your memory, to stay. Here, again, by keeping three basic types in mind, you can have an instant and definitive rule that will apply directly in many instances, with modifications, as will be noted.

The *Convex Profile* follows a downward, outward curve, beginning with a sloping forehead and continuing out to the tip of a pointed nose, and continuing an inward curve past a protruding upper lip on past a receding chin. Just draw a semicircle from the top of the head to the throat and you have the type.

The *Straight Profile* is one that you can line up with a ruler, set vertically from top to bottom, allowing for a normal though often slight, projection of the nose. Forehead and chin are both strictly vertical, or so nearly so that they strongly convey that impression.

The *Concave Profile* consists of a bulging forehead, with the nose small and almost receding, and a chin that also bulges to match the forehead. This type somewhat resembles the familiar caricature of the "Man in the Moon" in the form of a crescent, with his profile following the inner curve. That, of course, is more exaggerated than it could ever be in real life, but as stated before, exaggeration helps with memory devices.

Composite Profiles are frequent and can be listed sectionally, as *Concave Forehead* with *Straight Nose* and *Convex Chin*, or *Straight Forehead* with *Convex Nose* and *Straight Chin* and so on. Just make sure that you have your definitions right at the start; a Concave Forehead, for example, would represent a bulging forehead, because it belongs to a Concave Profile. The same applies to the other terms.

Additional Features Helpful to Memorizing Faces

Observation of lesser or individual features is also valuable as an adjunct toward remembering faces. Among frontal features, a high forehead is often seen and is responsible for the word "highbrow" as a synonym for supposed intellectuality. A person with long jaws is sometimes described as "lantern-jawed" which serves as another memory jog. Eyes may be wide apart or deep-set; cheeks full or hollow; lips full or pursed and so on. Eyebrows are a study in themselves, from the "bushy-browed" type to those that are "pencil-thin."

Head shapes are viewed not only from the front, but from the sides and back. The term "egg-head" is a somewhat derogatory substitute for "highbrow"; and there are also large heads, small heads, long heads and short heads. This, in turn, leads to the study of ears, which are truly "earmarks" when it comes to memory tabs. The set of a person's ears—whether they are high or low on the head, close or protruding—may prove easy to remember. Pointed ears, or those with large lobes, also are apt to register in your mind, once you have learned to look for them.

There is no need, however, to take up physiognomy as a specialized branch of memory training simply because the two overlap. It is better to look for individual features that impress you personally than to endeavor to classify people in groups, which may prove confusing in the long run. Also, in memory work, your purpose is not to analyze people, but to remember them; therefore, you should look for salient features that can be quickly noted and remembered accordingly, rather than minor points requiring careful comparison.

Linking Names with Faces: The Art of Letting a Face Announce Its Owner

This brings us directly to the great aim of the Facial Memory System; namely, not just to remember faces, but to link them with names. Without that, you will find yourself at a loss; while in contrast, the ability to do the two together is wonderful indeed. Yet that, unfortunately, is where many persons fall down completely. They just say, "We can't do it." Once in such a mood, they can't; but once they adopt the slogan "I can!", they will find that it works.

Why? The answer is simple indeed. By teaming the two faculties discussed in the previous chapter and the present one, you will find that you have the perfect formula. If you have remembered a man named Fox by thinking of him as clever like a fox, now picture him with a sly expression, like a fox. If it fits the case, fine; if it doesn't, so much the better, as the very incongruity of the situation will forge links of its own. If Mr. Fox proves to be anything but clever and has no slyness whatever in his manner, you remember him for what he is not, instead of what he is, which works just as well. In short, if you play both ends against the middle, you will find that the system works both ways.

If you meet a man named Lord, think of him as someone important, like a lord; and expect him to be haughty. If he lives up to the part, perfect; if he falls short, that's perfect, too—from your standpoint. That's how nicknames frequently are coined: if a woman tries to boss the people working in an office, they are apt to refer to her as the "Queen Bee" or the "Duchess." In contrast, they refer to a shipping clerk as "Tiny" and when you come to meet him, you find that he is six feet three and weighs two hundred sixty pounds.

You just don't forget such people or their names. So it would be nice, indeed, if all people's names could be linked that easily with their faces. Or perhaps it would not be so good after all, because if all names dropped into line that easily, they would become so stylized that they would no longer command attention or sustain interest. It is often the unusual name as well as person that links more strongly in your mind the more you repeat it.

Linking Names and Faces by Step-by-Step Application of the A I R Formula

The primary requirement in all forms of memorization is that you must know something, or learn something, in order to remember it. This has been reiterated throughout the previous chapters, yet you may find that you still have a tendency to overlook it, perhaps because it may seem too obvious to matter. That is the case when it comes to forging fixed links between names and faces and it is the reason why many people fall down on that score.

In meeting a person, you should forge immediate links between the person's name and face. Make sure you have the name right and if need be, ask the person to repeat it. Repeat the name yourself, as part of the introduction, saying, "I am glad to meet you, Mr. Joyce," or "It's nice to meet you, Miss Maddox." At the same time, study the person's features for definite impressions. Thus, you are forming a postive *association* at first sight.

Keep that fixed in mind and avoid distractions while you forge additional links. Here, your process consists almost entirely of *attention* along established lines. If the person's name furnishes a natural tab, as "Baker" or "Carpenter," you naturally follow that through, as already described. An equally good tab is an overall impression, as "Mr. Small" being either small, or in contrast, large —as with the nickname "Tiny." Names like "Stout" and "Long" are naturally descriptive, and a husky man named "Burleigh" can be tabbed as burly.

Direct linkage of names and faces is often possible by adding imaginative touches. You remember a man named Eisner by concentrating on his eyes. You picture a person named Smiley as smiling broadly or else not smiling at all. You think of Mr. Mac-Pherson as "Mac—with furs on," picturing him as if wearing a beaver hat and a pair of ear muffs. Miss Deering would be wearing an "ear-ring." You might tab Mr. Loeb by his large ear-lobes or Mr. Moley by a mole on his forehead.

First names often serve as links: a bushy-haired man named Harry would give you "Hairy" as a tab; a tired-faced man named Walter would be "Falter." If a girl named Carol has a slightly Southern accent, you can think of her as "Carol from Carolina," whether she comes from there or not. Voice, manners, gestures, anything serving as an attention-getter, are all good tabs for later reference. These do not have to be flattering, provided you keep them to yourself.

The main thing is to peg the person effectively. First names are particularly important when a person has a fairly usual last name. Assume that you already have several friends named Jones and you meet a man named Washington Jones; you could picture all the Joneses of your acquaintance gathered around the Washington Monument, shaking hands with the new member of their clan.

Following Up the First Step of Attention with the Next Step: Interest

Good though attention-getters are, it is unwise to linger on them or overstrain them. Too many tabs of the same type may confuse the issue and time wasted in trying to add more may cause you to lose out on chances of another sort: those involving *interest* in the person whose name and face you are linking. Always you can come back to attention and begin another chain. So let's take it from the interest stage and see how nicely it might break your way.

You have been introduced to a man named Philip Markert, and you have fixed his face in mind, but have no way to link it to his name. So you casually ask, "Where do you come from, Phil?" He replies, "Why I live in Philadelphia." Immediately, you have a link: *Phil from Philly*. Further, if you are acquainted with Philadelphia, you know that *Market Street* is one of its principal thoroughfares. That ties in with *Market* and you picture yourself in Philadelphia, walking down Market Street with Philip Markert. That image is apt to stay with you indefinitely; in fact, years later, if you try to recall where you first met Phil Markert, you may remember the Market Street scene and not the place where you are actually meeting him now.

Naturally, names don't always link up as neatly as that; but you don't have to stop with your first question. Having learned where someone hails from, you can ask him how long he's lived there, or who he knows there, or any other relevant question. One good point of interest is to discuss the mutual friend who introduced you; how long each of you have known him or if you both know other friends of his. You may find that they met on a Caribbean cruise that your mutual friend often talks about and that enables you to picture them together in some tropical clime.

Often, the name of someone you meet suggests another person by that name. If you ask if they are related and they prove to be, that gives you the interest link you want. If they are not related, your new friend may go into some details of his family history. Sometimes a person's name suggests that of some prominent person, and if you ask about a possible relationship there, you are almost sure to strike a responsive chord. Mention of some business may forge unexpected links.

The more you rouse a person's own interest, the more points that person will provide for you to remember him by. Since most people are primarily interested in themselves, the farther you navigate that channel, the better. Meeting a person and exchanging no more than a few formal comments is as uninspiring as viewing a lumber yard. There is plenty of good material there, but you don't realize how good it is until it is sawed into proper lengths, nailed together, painted and given the required touches that turn it into a finished home. The same is true of memory building. Many other types of interest-rousing methods could be cited, but it is best to develop your own, just as you would plan your own home; for that in itself develops a personalized interest.

Repetition as a Final Independent Step in Linking Names and Faces

There is one rule regarding the linkage of names and faces that has been greatly overlooked or ignored. That is, the easier to remember one, the harder the other. This is not always true: at times, both are easy to remember; often both are hard. But the law of opposites applies in the vast majority of cases, though it is not always obvious.

For example: At a party, you meet a talkative, friendly man with bushy eyebrows, wide smile, long chin and warm handshake.

His name is Townsend, but somehow it doesn't register until everyone is about to leave. Then, while you are looking for a cab, Mr. Townsend claps you on the back and says, "Come in my car; I'll take you home." To that you respond, "But I don't want you to go out of your way" and he replies, "I can't go out of my way. I live in the last house down the line!"

That's it. *Town's end* is where Mr. Townsend lives. Now that you know that, his name is as easy to remember as his face. But until then, you were stumped, unless you pictured him as living on the outskirts. Think back to people whose faces you remember, but whose names you forget, and vice versa. You will soon recognize how this matter of imbalance presents a linkage problem.

If the man's name, instead of being Townsend, had been Domzalski, you would have had no satisfactory link. In that case, *repetition* would be your best adjunct, used almost entirely in its own right. This may seem at variance with most memory methods which provide short cuts rather than the hard way of learning something by rote. But names are something of an exception, for this reason: If you check back on names of old friends, you will find that quite a few "grew" on you, so to speak; at first, they tended to slip your mind, so that you had to ask older friends if they remembered the names of the persons in question.

That was a form of repetition in itself, but staggered at intervals, until eventually you had no trouble remembering those names; and some, when you come to think of them, may have been much longer and more difficult than that of your new friend, Mr. Domzalski. So in his case, you would apply the repetition as of now. If you find that a name has slipped you soon after you have heard it, ask someone who knows it, right then, instead of waiting until too late. With some people, it is a good plan to tell them that you have forgotten their names and would like them to repeat it, as your frankness is likely to please them.

In many cases, you can add power to repetition by picturing an urgent personal need on your part where remembering that name is concerned. In the case of the man who gave you the lift in his car, that need could be real enough, as you might be going to another party where you would be apt to meet him under similar circumstances.

So it is wise to prepare for such eventualities beforehand. When going to a party, find out who is going to be there, as well as which persons you should particularly meet. The more data you can learn, the better; for the more you know about people, the easier it is to turn any discussion into productive channels, where memory is concerned. If you forget a man's name before you meet him, the introduction itself will serve as a memory jog.

Keeping lists of persons whom you meet is always a good plan, as you can add the time and place, other persons involved, matters discussed and so on. The simplest way to do this is afterward, so that you can jot down names and descriptive details of faces and check how well you remembered them. A few days later, you can review the list mentally, then double-check it. Such practice enables you to decide which types of memory links have proven most effective, so you can use them as patterns for future occasions.

*   *   *   *   *   *   *   *   *   *

CHAPTER 11

Letting Memory Help You
Build and Spell Your
Word Power

The A I R formula, as a key to memory, attains its ultimate where word power is involved. Here, there are two distinct factors to be considered: *Vocal Vocabulary* and *Reading Vocabulary*. Yet each, if properly developed, follows a similar pattern, so far as memory retention is concerned. As usual, the trifold action—Attention—Interest—Repetition—asserts itself as definitively as ever, but in this case, even more so. There is a very simple reason; namely:

With language, either spoken or written, the A I R formula produces a multiple association of ideas, so interlocked or interwoven, that it becomes second nature. In short, this may be compared to Motor Memory, which is virtually automatic, with ideas springing to mind so rapidly that you almost begin to wonder where they came from, while at the same time you accept them because you know they are right. If you should pause or hesitate, you would be lost. So it is with language.

Distinguishing Between Vocabulary Types as Preliminary to Memory Expansion

The *Vocal Vocabulary*, which consists of the spoken word, is also termed the *Use Vocabulary*, as it is used for ordinary communication between two or more persons, regardless of their individual aims or educational levels. Somebody asks directions regarding how to get somewhere and hopes to receive a coherent reply. A person gives an order and expects it to be understood. You are using language to express a purpose or idea; hence, the term *Use Vocabulary* is very appropriate where the spoken word is concerned.

Naturally, it is not always that simple. Spoken words may lead to a clash of interests, involving spirited repartee. Two or more persons can exchange cutting or subtle remarks that go over the heads of innocent bystanders. Or it could bring a harmonious interchange of constructive ideas between persons with common interests of the same intellectual caliber. Such is the power of the *Vocal* or *Use Vocabulary*, as represented by the spoken word.

The *Reading Vocabulary*, known also as the *Recognition Vocabulary*, has much greater scope, yet needs a cautious approach.

It allows ideas to be expressed in full, with shades of meaning that can be interpreted still further by those who study and weigh them. Sometimes a written statement receives such repeated approval that it rises far beyond the hopes or intentions of the person who originally expressed it. That is why the term *Recognition Vocabulary* is applied to reading; but conversely, there are times when faults or fallacies become apparent in a written statement, no matter how skillfully it may be worded.

With the Vocal Vocabulary, all words must be on instant call. This is another reason why the term "Use Vocabulary" has been applied to this mode of expression, as any hesitation in speech reduces the effectiveness of whatever you are trying to say. But with the Reading Vocabulary, you can take all the time you need to choose a right word, or even change the phraseology of an entire statement in order to provide greater impact.

Synchronizing the Vocal and Reading Vocabularies Through A I R

Whole volumes have been written on how to develop a good vocabulary, but much of the advice so given can be boiled down to one vital factor: Memory. That applies either to the vocal vocabulary or the reading vocabulary—and for that matter, both. Yet here we encounter a situation which is slightly fantastic. Basic English, which was designed to reduce the vocal vocabulary to its most efficient terms of expression, is made up of only eight hundred fifty words, yet an abridged dictionary of "handy size" may contain more than eighty thousand words suited toward the expansion of a reading vocabulary.

Hence it would seem, at first glance, all but impossible to synchronize or adjust these two types of word studies so that each would help to develop the other. Yet that is exactly what the application of sound memory methods will enable you to do. The greatest speaker in the world will find himself at total loss if he suddenly lacks certain vital words required to do justice to some important subject under discussion. He is not likely to acquire those needed expressions through his vocal vocabulary; that is, by talking over the subject with persons who have already had their say. His only course is to expand his reading vocabulary in a selective search for fresh ideas or catch-phrases that will point up his vocal vocabulary.

Oscar Wilde was credited with making a quip so witty that a man who heard it remarked enviously, "I wish I had said that!" To that, Wilde instantly responded: "Don't worry, you will."

There, in essence, we have the formula for transmuting the broad coverage of the reading vocabulary into the compact format of the vocal vocabulary, with full emphasis on "use." Not that it means borrowing ideas outright from other people and converting them to your own purposes; far from it. Rather, we can accept Wilde's comment as an example of "a true word spoken in jest." What you really do is simply to stimulate new ideas that become definitely your own when reduced to a practical or epigrammatic state.

How Word Recognition Builds Word Power Through Word Use

Perfect timing in the vocabulary field is found in great orations and famous speeches, prepared beforehand through the reading vocabulary and then adapted to the vocal vocabulary. Here, recognition is given to words that have a definite or special use, so that statements carry an impact which impresses listeners more strongly than any that might be delivered without preliminary selection, or with no rehearsal for effect. But always, to be really great, these must be carefully reduced to terms so understandable and natural —or even so simple—that they do not sound overly prepared.

The greatest example of this was Lincoln's famous Gettysburg address, not just because of its simplicity, but also for its brevity. It followed a much longer oration by Edward Everett, the speaker chosen for the occasion, but he went into flowery rhetoric, well beyond the normal range of the spoken vocabulary, considering some of the simple folk among his listeners. In all, the oration ran about sixteen thousand words, and took two hours. Lincoln's address consisted of about two hundred fifty words that he spoke in two minutes. Yet one has been forgotten, while the other will live for all time.

Both used similar words or phrases, such as raising the question whether the Union should "endure" or "perish." Everett referred to "honored graves"; Lincoln to "honored dead." Everett referred to "those who nobly sacrificed their lives that their fellow-men might live in safety and honor"; whereas, Lincoln spoke of "those who gave their lives that the nation might live." But with Everett, those essential points were lost amid a verbal maze of classical allusions and prolonged references to the war and its issues; while with Lincoln, they were the keynotes of a vital message.

So the same choice was made from the recognition vocabulary to obtain words aptly suited to the use vocabulary; it was just a question of which to keep. Where Everett retained all that made good oratory, Lincoln limited himself to those that made sound sense. In short, the best way to apply recognition to use is to be short. Eliminate all frills, so that any additions to the vocal vocabulary will be natural and therefore emphatic.

Many great extemporaneous speakers have used an abbreviated variation of this system which is equally effective. Instead of culling their reading vocabulary for words that will blend with their vocal vocabulary and thereby amplify it, they look for special phrases or even coined expressions that can be injected into their usual flow of talk. Often, these are quoted as the highlight of a speech, causing people to regard the entire speech as having the same caliber.

Putting the Vocal Vocabulary to Special Use with the Reading Vocabulary

Here, the wheels turn the other way. Taking your Vocal Vocabulary as a basis, you put it to real use by expanding every word with which you are familiar into broader scope or understanding. That is, instead of drawing new words from your reading vocabulary and trying to fit them with your vocal vocabulary, you do it the other way around. This is particularly important to people who are avid readers—a category in which you unquestionably belong, or you would not be reading this book right now!—because the average avid reader has one trend, which often results in self-defeat; namely, over-reading.

Rather than become intrigued with words you don't know and try to gear them with words you do know, take words you do know and look for their equivalents, or any words that they may suggest, in whole or in part. Watch for shades of meaning that offer new extensions, so that you form an ever increasing series of links that will increase your vocabulary automatically. Don't worry about having to recall those links; they will forge themselves, because here you will be utilizing the A I R formula to the fullest degree, often winding up with an endless chain that makes it easy to remember the links wherever you happen to start.

For a good "starter," consider the word WORLD.

As synonyms for WORLD, we find EARTH and GLOBE, with the word SPHERE closely related. Taken in order, EARTH refers to our world, as a planet in the solar system, and signifies the ground as well. GLOBE means the world as a whole and the term "globular" applies to world affairs. SPHERE, though it refers to the world itself, is applied very often in the form "hemisphere," denoting a particular half of the world, as the northern, southern, eastern or western.

The term WORLDLY, however, does not signify world-wide, but concerns the affairs of earth, producing the related word, EARTHLY. This has two synonyms: one, MUNDANE, which comes from the Latin word MUNDUS, meaning "world"; and TERRESTRIAL, from another Latin word meaning "earth." The French equivalents of these are "monde" and "terre"; the Spanish, "mundo" and "tierra"; the Italian, "mondo" and "terra." These are linked to the Latin TERRA FIRMA, which has become an English term for "solid ground."

Reverting to the word WORLD, we find the slightly shortened WOLD, an Old English word for a large tract of land, which represented their world as they knew it then. So W-OLD becomes the "old world" and WOLD links with WILD, which the world was in those days. That is identical with the German word "wild," which by a slight switch becomes WELT, meaning WORLD. From that comes the Dutch South African "veld" or "veldt," which has become a better-known English word than "wold" and is akin to "field," which can be classed as the immediate WORLD around you. And getting down to EARTH, in German, it's "erde."

The Endless Chain of Memory Links and How You Can Apply It

Take any word like "world" and follow it through as just described. Does it become more complex? No. It becomes simpler. Why? Because there are more links involved. The more, the better, because if you find just one that leads to others, it will open a whole chain of new and productive thought.

In the example just cited, foreign words were introduced.

Those brought up immediate, direct derivatives. They showed how you can extend your knowledge into other fields or languages and even begin to learn from them, while learning your own. Just to prove it, take this statement:

> *Reposing* on my *couch* beside the *portal*, I *studied* the *verdant foliage* of the *vast forest* beyond the *placid mountain lake* that *mirrored* the *resplendent azure* of the *firmament* above.

Put in slightly simpler English, that would run:

> Resting on my cot by the door, I viewed the green leaves of the huge woods beyond the calm, hill-surrounded pond that reflected the sky-blue heavens above.

It sounds exactly the same, but with this difference: in the original statement, you weren't really talking English, you were talking French, because:

Reposing comes from the French *reposer:* To rest.

Couch is equivalent to *couche:* Couch, bed or cot.

Portal is derived from *porte:* Door, gate, entrance.

Studied closely resembles *étudier:* To study.

Verdant, rich in growth, comes from *vert:* Green.

Vast, as its name implies, is *vaste:* Great, spacious.

Forest is the French word *forêt:* A large woods or forest.

Placid in French, is *placide:* Calm and quiet.

Mountain finds its equivalent in *montagne:* Mountain.

Lake in English, is shortened to *lac* in French: Lake.

Mirrored is derived from the French *miroir:* To reflect.

Resplendent is the French *resplendissant:* To shine brightly.

Azure could only be the French *azur:* The color of the sky.

Firmament in English is the same as French: Heavens above.

So you see that all the while you were reading English, you were really thinking French, or vice versa. It is through links like these that word study becomes a story in itself, with each new adventure in the field of vocabulary opening still more vistas. Just watch for words or phrases of foreign origin in your daily reading and you will be surprised how they can improve your memory span.

Using Memory Keys to Increase Your Word-Span Ten to One Hundred Times

As indicated earlier, Basic English, with its eight hundred fifty vital words, is primarily intended as an aid for the vocal vocabulary. But the same rule of making one word do the work of anywhere from ten to one hundred can be applied to the reading vocabulary quite as readily. It is simply another instance of switching from use to recognition.

Statistically, nine-tenths of our English words are compounded or derived from lesser words. Evidently, the eighty thousand words in a sizable dictionary stem from approximately eight thousand roots. So by learning the roots, you should reap the fruit. Yet there, some judgment is required. Certain roots are more productive than others, with not just ten times as many derivatives, but up to one hundred times as many. The best of those roots to cultivate are prefixes and suffixes.

If ever a word defined itself, that word is prefix. It combines the Latin terms "pre," meaning before and "fixus," to make firm. From that comes many words, as preamble, precaution, precede, precipitate, preclude, on to preliminary, prelude, premeditate, on to prevail and preventive.

But the term "prefix" goes far beyond that. It includes any and all other introductory terms, like those given in the list that follows. Similarly, the term "suffix," from the Latin verb "suffigger," meaning to fasten on, applies to words formed by specialized endings; and they, too, are almost limitless in number, as the samples from the accompanying list will prove.

In a recent unabridged dictionary, you will find a listing of some six hundred words stemming from the prefix anti. Naturally, that does not necessarily mean that you have gained six hundred entirely new words from that lone prefix. In another sense, you have merely doubled a specific segment of your existing vocabulary. But if you work it the other way around, and apply more prefixes to a given word, it will multiply on that score.

For example: Like anti, the prefix super has a list of about six hundred words. But other prefixes go far beyond that; the same dictionary lists nearly five thousand words stemming from the prefix non and more than five thousand with the prefix un. Now a word like human happens to fall into all those classifications, so from human, you gain antihuman, superhuman, non-human, un-

human. As if that were not enough, you can add *subhuman* and *inhuman,* so that your original word has already increased to seven and can very well go beyond that.

Suffixes, in many cases, are far more productive than prefixes, and the more common suffixes would run up formidable lists if cataloged individually. That, fortunately, is unnecessary, because with a suffix, you use the basic word as a root; and in some cases, the addition of a suffix is so obvious or automatic that it doesn't have to be mentioned, particularly in an abridged dictionary.

From the word *small,* the addition of suffixes produces *smaller, smallest, smallish, smallness.* Only five words in all; but *large* produces an identical list, plus the word *largely,* making seven more. So do such words as *smart, short* and *long;* but by utilizing *long* as the basis for *length,* the chain is extended further. Hundreds of other adjectives can be treated in this manner.

From the noun *man,* suffixes produce *manful, manfully, manfulness, mankind, manless, manlessness, manlessly, manlike, manly, manness, mannishly, mannishness.* That makes thirteen words; and if *man* is extended to include *manage,* which leads into *manager* and *management,* along with their derivatives, the total will come close to thirty. Yet all such words are naturally formed and practically define themselves.

Further Exploration in the Twin Realms of Prefixes and Suffixes

Some people neglect the study of prefixes and suffixes, through the mistaken notion that a working knowledge of Latin and Greek is required to recognize them. It is true that most prefixes and suffixes come from those languages, but they are so anglicized that their origin does not greatly matter. In fact, they are used almost interchangeably: The prefix *ante,* for example, is from the Latin, while *anti* is from the Greek. The Latin prefix *ambi* is almost identical with the Greek *amphi.* Each means "both," so the word *ambidextrous* means a person who can use both hands equally well, while *amphibious* signifies a creature that can live both on land and in water.

Here, purists may point out that ambidextrous is formed from *ambo + dexter,* both Latin words, while *amphibious* is composed of *amphi + bios,* two terms of Greek origin. But our modern word, *automobile,* was coined from the Greek *auto,* for *self,* and the Latin

COMMON SUFFIXES *

able	inclining to, as capable
age	state or process, as tonnage or passage
an (ane, ain)	belonging to, as Grecian, mundane, terrain
ance, ence	an activity, as performance, existence
ary	occupation or place, as secretary, aviary
ary	pertaining to, as customary
al	pertaining, as musical
ant, ent	an operative force, as valiant, student
ate	agency, as pirate or delegate
ate	verbal form, as desecrate
dom	condition or control, as kingdom
en	small, as mitten
en	quality, as golden or broken
er	belonging to, as farmer, New Yorker
er	comparative, as larger
et, ette	small, as puppet or marionette
est	superlative, as finest
ess	feminine suffix, as hostess
ful	imbued with, as hopeful
ia	names of classes or places, as bacteria or Armenia
ian	practitioners or inhabitants, as musician, Parisian
ic	pertaining to, as gigantic or basic
id	a quality, as acid
ine	a compound, as chlorine
ion	a process or state, as in action, position, tension
ish	a similarity or relationship, as childish, greenish
ism	a result, as realism
ist	one who practices, as pessimist
ive	belonging to, as receptive
less	lacking, as fearless
lent	fulness, as violent
ly (like)	having the quality of, as softly, quickly
ment	a condition, as amusement
or	a state or action, as error, governor
ous	displaying a quality, as anxious, officious, vicious
some	a resemblance, as gladsome
tude	state or condition, as magnitude, gratitude
ward	direction, as outward
y	condition, as difficulty

* Many lesser suffixes or variations go into word formation. In looking for examples, any exceptions should also be noted.

COMMON PREFIXES *

a	at, in, on, as afloat	post	after or later, as postpone or posterior
ab, abs	from, as abdicate or abstain	pre	before, as prepaid
ad, ac, af, etc.	to, as advance, accede, affix	pro	forward, in favor of, as proceed or propound
ambi	both, around, as ambiguous	re	back, again, as return or revive
amphi	both, around, as amphitheater, amphibious	retro	backward, as retrograde
ante	before, as antedate	se	apart, as seclude, separate
anti	against, as antitoxic	semi	half, as semifinal
be	make, as belittle	sub	under, as submarine
bi	twice, as bicycle	super	above, over, as superintend
cata	down, as cataract	syn, syl, sym	with, together, as synonym, syllable, symphony
circum	around, as circumvent		
con	with, together, as confer		
contra	against, as contradict	trans	across, through, as transport or transparent
de	down, from, as descend or depart	ultra	beyond, as ultramarine
di, dia	twofold, as dilemma	un (in)	not, as undesirable (ineffective)
dis	apart, not, as disagree or disassociate		
en, em	in, as enter, emplace	under	below, as underfed
epi	upon, among, as epidermis or epidemic	vice	instead of, as viceroy
ex	out, from, as exit or exclude		
extra	beyond, as extraordinary		
fore	before, as foresee		
hemi	half, as hemisphere		
in	in, into, as inject		
in (un)	not, as inconsiderate		
inter	between, as intercept		
meta	beyond, as metaphysical		
mis	wrong, as mispronounce		
non	not, as nonsense		
ob	toward, or opposed to, as observe, or obstacle		
out	beyond, as outnumber		
over	above, as overburden		
per	through, as perforate		

* Many words also serve as prefixes, for instance *self* as in self-explanatory. Noting the occurrence of such words as prefixes is a great aid in word-building.

mobile, for *movable.* So the old order is definitely outmoded. Besides, some of the most-used prefixes are of English origin, as *en, mis* and *un.* The same applies to various suffixes, so the best plan is to regard them all as adjuncts to the English language and study them from that standpoint.

Indeed, English, with its acquired flexibility, can do things in this field that would have been totally impossible with Greek or Latin. One of the longest words in the English language is coined largely from prefixes and suffixes, namely:

Antidisestablishmentarianism.

It is quite simple to understand, considering how a person upholding the Establishment could make a doctrine of it, only to have someone else want to knock it down, which would naturally result in someone else objecting to that. It is also simple and legitimate to coin your own words by the prefix-suffix system, as with the man living in a hurricane zone who fixed cables to the corners of the roof that topped his bungalow and termed it a *non-blowable-off* roof.

Building These Adjuncts (Prefixes and Suffixes) into Easily Remembered Words

Actual English words have been enlisted as effective prefixes and are therefore plainly understandable, as:

FORE, in *forebode, forecast, foreclose, forego.*

OUT, in *outbreak, outcast, outrun, outwit.*

OVER, in *overcast, overlook, overtone, overwork.*

UNDER, in *underestimate, undermine, underscore.*

Especially noteworthy is the word *self,* which has some eight hundred entries as a prefix in the unabridged dictionary already mentioned. It is the equivalent of the Greek *auto* for *self* and occasionally, the two are used interchangeably; as an example, *autohypnosis* is the same thing as *self-hypnosis.* But *auto* has long been on the decline, except in specialized forms, while *self* is on the rise.

In the suffix department, ancient terms have become so prevalent that they have been coined into modern English words. The Greek *logos,* for "theory" or "science" has been combined with so many other forms, that the term *ology* has come to mean any branch of knowledge. Actually, it runs the gamut of more than one hundred scientific subjects, ranging from A to Z; such as *anthology, biology, cosmology,* through *geology, psychology* and on to *zoology.*

From the Greek *grapho,* for "write," comes the English word *graph,* meaning a chart; but it, too, has combined as a suffix with such subjects as *biography, geography, photography* and others. Here, as a striking sidelight, we find *graph* switched from a suffix to a prefix, to form the word *graphology,* which is applied to scientific handwriting analysis.

Also, the Greek word *Phobus,* denoting the classical god of fear, which was used very sparingly as a suffix in such words as *hydrophobia* and later *claustrophobia,* now runs from "A" for *acrophobia* to "Z" for *zoophobia,* with some seventy-five connotations in between. Since others are apt to crop up at any time, *phobia* as a synonym for *dread* of an irrational sort, has become a full-fledged English word.

Prefixes and suffixes are well suited to the A I R formula. Once proper attention is given to them, interest is stimulated and repetition becomes automatic. After using the same prefix a few dozen times, you won't have any trouble remembering it; the fact that you have combined it with perhaps a dozen different words, will keep the interest fresh and focus attention on those words as well.

Using Spelling as an Adjunct to Word Structure in Vocabulary Building

Where words themselves are involved, vocabulary building is a self-strengthening process. The reason is quite simple: Instead of piling new word upon new word, until the structure becomes top-heavy, you add them to those already solidly placed, thus providing additional foundations. The more you learn, the more you remember. That makes it all the more remarkable, yet all the more natural, since the multiplicity of the links thus forged makes memory all the easier.

However, any extensive development of the reading or recognition vocabulary simultaneously increases a new problem that demands a separate and highly complex series of memory processes of its own. That is spelling, a problem comparatively unimportant where the spoken word of the vocal vocabulary is concerned; but with the reading vocabulary, which requires response in the form of written words, spelling becomes essential to coherence.

This problem is actually much less pressing than some over-meticulous critics are apt to claim. Back in the heyday of radio, many writers were so closely geared to the spoken word that their scripts contained many misspelled words, but those made little difference if the actors who read them understood them. Sometimes such errors came closer to phonetic spelling, an artificial device to aid pronunciation, and were thereby all for the better.

This applies today with speeches or dictated statements intended to be read aloud. Often, the content of a sentence clarifies a doubtful word, but such errors must be corrected before finding their way into written or printed form. Otherwise, results may be serious, or even ludicrous, which may be worse. So in expanding your reading vocabulary through word recognition, try to keep pace by studying word structure, thus forming two interlocking chains.

Ways of Applying Memory Methods to Synonyms, Antonyms and Homonyms

Such a process of natural assimilation works nicely with synonyms, or words of identical meaning. For example: ORDER means COMMAND, forming a definition link. In appearance, COMMAND resembles DEMAND, forming a spelling link, but being stronger, COMMAND has two M's instead of only one. Similarly, dual links may be found with antonyms, or words that are opposite in meaning. ADVANCE finds its opposite in RE-TREAT, a definition link, while RETREAT, in structure, resembles RETRACT, an excellent spelling link. The fact that the two words are also similar in import forms an interlock between ADVANCE and RETRACT, adding to the natural memory factor.

However, there is another class of words called homonyms, which sound alike and may or may not be spelled differently. These have long been a problem, because the varied spellings, though often intended to distinguish between such words, as HEAR and HERE, only serve to confuse them. As a result, some grammarians have adopted the attitude that homonyms should be disregarded, in order to avoid such complications; but that is only begging the question, because sooner or later, a person is bound to meet up with such cases and be forced to meet the issue anyway.

So it is best to prepare beforehand. Since no natural memory links can be established with most homonyms, the proper way is to use artificial memory methods to form appropriate associations, in accordance with the systems already discussed. In the case of homonyms, it is very simple and remarkably effective. Your interest in such words is that you may have to use them, so the time to use them is now, by putting each member of the pair into a key-sentence, where each is self-defining, but with one point always in mind:

The two words must be placed in alphabetical order in the sentence, so that they will identify themselves as well.

In the example of HEAR and HERE, the words would be placed in that order, as H-E-A is ahead of H-E-R in alphabetical order. So your key-sentence could be:

We HEAR that our friends are coming HERE.

On this page, down below, you will find a list of such key-sentences, which literally put the troublesome homonyms in their proper place. Many more could be added, but it is better to form your own, for two reasons: First, because in thinking out a suitable

HOMONYM MEMORY SYSTEM

Through Alphabetical Arrangement

A *boar* is dangerous because it can *bore* victims with its tusks.
You can hear oars *creak* as you travel along the *creek*.
Of all *dear*, lovely animals, the *deer* is the loveliest.
To be perfectly *fair*, we insisted on paying our own *fare*.
A horse needs a fast *gait* to jump a high *gate*.
He became *hoarse* while shouting for his *horse* to win.
The *gnu* probably *knew* that it was in a *new* zoo.
The *mail* is usually delivered by a *male*.
They found the *knave* hiding in the *nave*.
The *main* feature of a horse is its *mane*.
Never give a *loan* on a *lone* signature.
He tripped over the *pail* and turned *pale*.
A *pair* of scissors can be used to *pare* a ripe *pear*.
Only *one* person ever *won* the grand prize.
He felt a *pain* when he broke the *pane*.
The *road* seemed longer, the farther he *rode*.
They *rode* across the plain and *rowed* across the lake.

If you sear a leaf, it will appear to be *sere.*
While you *shoe* a horse, you must *shoo* away flies.
We bought a *sail* for our boat at a special *sale.*
When a dog wags its *tail,* it tells a *tale.*
The tiny *vale* was hidden by a *veil* of mist.
We looked in *vain* for a weather *vane.*

phrase or sentence, you form a memory link that will be all the stronger; and second, you do not have to be bothered with key-phrases that you may not need. Just wait for the right time to form them.

Teaming Accepted Rules for Spelling with Simple Memory Devices

In contrast to the types of words just discussed, the English language actually follows well-defined rules in the formation and spelling of many compounded words. These are usually listed in the preliminary pages of various dictionaries under the heading of Orthography or Spelling and can therefore be checked along with any study of words themselves. Listed with the rules are their exceptions, perhaps more numerous than is desirable, yet not too formidable, if taken by degrees.

Again, it is largely a matter of noting odd spellings or word structures when you encounter them and pegging them mentally at that time. You will then find that systematic memory methods will be needed to remember the exceptions rather than the rules; and in some cases, only the exceptional exceptions. Here, any memory device or "dodge" that may prove helpful should be utilized accordingly, and the more you exercise your imagination or forge odd links between special words and their spelling, the better the results will be.

* * * * * * * * * *

CHAPTER 12

How to Read Faster and Remember Every Key Fact

Of all adjuncts to memory, reading is by far the most important. There are, of course, cases of illiterate persons possessed of remarkable memories, but they have been limited to mathematics or other specialized fields; while in contrast, most of the greatest mental prodigies have been noted for their ability in languages, historical data and literature, all outgrowths of extensive reading.

That, however, was long ago. Within the past few decades, the average person's amount of reading has increased anywhere from tenfold to a hundredfold. That seems a very wide range, but the more you study the factors involved, the more understandable it becomes. Since the chief of those factors is memory, the best course is to check back on the growth of reading through the years, showing how it has invariably kept pace with the tempo of life in general, until it has reached the point where it actually sets the pace.

To appreciate this development in full, it must be considered briefly from its inception onward, showing how speech, pictures and the printed word have been interwoven in a constantly expanding web to produce a memory span of a self-strengthening sort. Always, the aim is memory, with the remarkable feature that the more things you try to remember, the easier the rest become, provided you make full use of the memory links or "hooks" as mentioned earlier.

Using Pictures to Express Ideas: The Early Step Toward Reading

The upsurge of literacy in America can be traced directly to the all-out effort of one man: Benjamin Franklin. Primarily, Franklin was a printer and like every practical tradesman of his time, he was anxious to create a demand for his wares. In 1732—the year that George Washington was born!—Franklin produced *Poor Richard's Almanack*, which, like other such publications, contained monthly calendars, phases of the moon, times of the tides and other data familiar even to persons unable to read. But Franklin also included wit and wisdom in the form of proverbs which those

who could read might quote to those who couldn't, adding sub-
stantially to the circulation of his almanacs.

Even better, Franklin furthered the rebus, a mode of expressing
words by pictures of objects with similar names. Thus the word "I"
might be represented by a picture of an eye; the word "saw" by a
carpenter's saw; the word "cord" by a stack of wood, which was
measured by the cord in those days; "not" by a knotted rope and
so on. By interspersing these with printed words or syllables,
proverbs or phrases could be formed. Thus a person recognizing the
pictures and pronouncing them aloud could fill in the printed
words or syllables, first by guess-work, and later from memory.

Hence "Poor Richard," with all his other virtues, actually
taught people how to read, through the pages of his almanac. This
method, first advanced as a means of self-help for illiterate adults,
eventually became a means of instructing children in reading, for
nearly two centuries, when it finally dwindled into obscurity. That
transition, however, was gradual indeed; and even up until the early
days of the twentieth century, when the automobile began to bring
people closer together, reading was such a problem for many
simple country folk that they still relied on pictures to express
ideas.

Looking back to the advertisements of bygone years, we find
many in which the illustrations were most important, with printed
statements playing a very minor part; while along city streets where
small shops were prevalent, the scene was in striking contrast to
the present. Every store in those days was represented by some
pictorial sign or symbol. You could look above the dawdling horse-
cars or even the newly strung trolley wires and see all sorts of
objects that were for sale there. A huge wooden rifle, hanging
above the sidewalk, would stand for a gun shop; a large painted
watch, with its hands set permanently at twenty minutes past
eight, symbolized a jewelry store; while three golden balls be-
tokened a pawn shop, as they still do today.

A man in quest of a haircut or a shave would look along the
street itself for the familiar red and white striped sign of a barber
shop; but even while heading there, he might be waylaid by a life-
sized wooden Indian with a tomahawk raised in one hand and
a bundle of cigars extended in the other. Two colored glass jars
denoted a pharmacy; and if they flanked a bubbling glass globe, the
passer-by could quench his thirst at a new-fangled soda fountain,
unless he preferred to visit the corner opposite, where a pictured

stein of foaming lager bearing the legend 5¢ marked the equally popular beer saloon.

Supplanting the Hindering Habit of Vocalization with the Helpful Practice of Visualization

With such a start, it was not surprising that reading should have developed as *vocalization*. A physical object was regarded as existing in its own right; the word that represented it was simply built from letters of the alphabet. From that rose the tendency to "spell out" words, as C-A-T = cat, and so on. When words became polysyllabic, they had to be spelled out in detail, as:

Spell WILDERNESS.

"W-I-L, *will*. D-E-R, *der*. W-I-L-D-E-R, *wilder*. N-E-S-S, *ness*. *Will—wilder—wilderness*."

Great stuff, but very confusing. It should have been "Will" and "will-der," but the moment "wilder" cropped up, it became a word in itself and threw everything out of gear. But the hard way seemed to be the right way, because then there was no other way. So spelling became the art, rather than reading.

That brought up problems like the following:

- You pronounce BOUGH like *bow*, or PLOUGH as *plow*.
- You pronounce COUGH as *cawf*, or TROUGH as *trawf*.
- You pronounce DOUGH as *doe*, or THOROUGH as *thoro*.
- You pronounce ROUGH as *ruff*, or TOUGH as *tuff*.
- You pronounce THROUGH as *thru*.

Any effort to pronounce such words while reading them would simply slow the process, since all are common enough to be easily recognized. This shows quite plainly why *vocalization* should be superseded by *visualization* if speedier reading is desired. Instead of repeating words mentally, picture them, and improvement will be immediate, as the rule will apply to many words besides the samples just given. Nouns frequently picture themselves automatically, since they refer to things or actual objects. Adjectives provide additional impressions, rounding out such mental pictures. Verbs suggest action, producing impact and completion. Those, in turn, are amplified by adverbs, while conjunctions and prepositions naturally fall in line.

Take a simple sentence such as:

The black cat rapidly climbed the maple tree.

Color, appearance, action, purpose, are all included in such a direct statement; and far from having to "spell out" each word, the words themselves can be taken in a group, so that the entire sentence is literally read in a passing glance. That is the basis of modern "speed reading" which forges its own memory links.

Mapping Your Excursions in Reading as You Would a Trip over Modern Highways

Slow, painstaking reading dates back to the horse-and-buggy era, which raises an excellent point of comparison. Back then, people thought that if you tried to read fast, you couldn't even recognize the words you saw, let alone remember them. But those same people believed that if you drove an automobile at the madcap speed of fifteen miles an hour, the landscape would become so blurred that you would go dizzy and be unable to view the passing scene.

In those days, they had public readers, who appeared on platforms in town halls and read from famous works of literature, while an audience listened breathlessly. Note how *vocalization* held sway. The listeners *heard* the words but did not see them. Yet from that, they used *visualization* to form mental pictures of the things they heard. Similarly, when automobiles came into vogue, they had chauffeurs at the wheel, who kept a full mind on their jobs, just like the professional readers in the town halls. This enabled the palpitating passengers to enjoy the scenery that surged past at that incredible fifteen-mile-an-hour speed. Otherwise, they could not have enjoyed it, so they thought.

Today, we have outgrown both reading and driving limitations. The analogy between the two is so apt that it is worth pursuing further. By simply zoning your reading as you would your driving, you will find that both speed up in accordance with recognizable conditions, which offer a true form of comparison. The modern tempo is expressed in terms of modern action. With a horse and buggy, a man could describe a trip in terms of every rock he passed and every rill he crossed. Today, he gives them no more than passing notice. But he does see road signs all along the line and he heeds them, just as he heeds words and phrases when he reads.

Four Speed Zones of Modern Reading
with Memory Serving as Their Ultimate Aim

By classifying types of reading into convenient categories, you can gauge your speed beforehand, just as you would map out an automobile trip. Reading falls into four generally accepted zones, which can best be considered from the slowest on up, in keeping with the driving analogy. These run as follows:

Reading for Self-Improvement

This follows the old original reading pattern, even to "spelling out" unfamiliar words for future reference, or vocalizing those that may have to be quoted and therefore pronounced correctly. This is your fifteen-mile-an-hour driving zone; heavy traffic, stop lights, one-way streets, pedestrians, jay-walkers, everything to make it difficult. You can't speed up this type of reading any more than you can increase speed in driving of a similar nature; but you can become familiar with it and improve your technique by methods to be covered later.

Reading for Information

Here, you can speed the process within due limitations. Those depend partly on your knowledge of the subject at hand, and partly on how important it may be to you. For example, an item in a local newspaper or a national news weekly is something that you can absorb almost immediately, unless it brings up some vital or highly specialized point that is new to you. Informative writers frequently follow the formula of who, what, why, when, where, how, making sure that all their statements are focused on one or more of those vital points which makes it easier for the reader to follow their statements.

This can be compared with driving through a suburban area or along a secondary highway, with a thirty-five-mile-an-hour speed limit and various warning signs. The reader can go the limit if familiar with the route, but must be careful not to miss his turn or ignore the warnings. In this case, remembering what you read is like recalling landmarks or important places on a journey.

Reading for Cultural Development

Speed is a great adjunct in this type of reading, provided that you do not overtax it; otherwise, it will prove tiring, like driving along a main highway at the maximum speed of sixty miles an hour. The more familiar the subject, or the writer's style, the easier it is to step up the pace. Years ago, almost all reading was supposed to have some cultural value, otherwise it wasn't regarded as worthwhile. The result was that many people read the same books over and over, always pausing to let the same old message sink in. As a result, they limited their range of knowledge.

The modern trend is to read more books, expanding each cultural field as you go along. Through comparison of one writer's works, with the offerings of different authors on a given subject, you will find that you automatically recall many of the things you read previously, if only through the process of mental comparisons. Furthermore, modes, manners and opinions are changing rapidly today and anyone concerned with cultural development can not afford to become a back number. Here, the A I R formula works strongly, but be sure you give such reading due *attention* and sustain *interest* throughout a reading session, stopping as soon as it begins to slacken. In that way, you won't need the *repetition* once regarded as so vital and you can increase this type of reading both in scope and speed to a degree that would once have been regarded as impractical or even impossible.

Reading for Pleasure

Here, reading attains the speed of superhighway travel. It is like driving on a turnpike or a freeway at a speed of seventy miles an hour, or whatever the law allows. Fiction is the most popular type of pleasure reading and in keeping with its growth, modern writers long ago abandoned the ponderous, slow-moving style of the Victorian era and adopted a breezy, racy type of writing studded with sparkling dialogue that literally sped up reading by setting a pace of its own. Thus the reader finds himself drawn along at a continually increasing pace that becomes a stronger habit, the more he conforms to it. People didn't read that fast in the old days, because they couldn't; they didn't have the right sort of reading matter.

Turning the "One-Two-Three Word" Reading Processes into Multiplex Speed

Along with subject matter and style, techniques have been devised to speed up the reading process by widening the span of word recognition. This is easily and clearly explained by some comparative examples:

(1) *Single Word Process:* Reading words as underlined:
Like most interesting arts and endeavors, spying seems
to be as old as the legends of mankind.

That represents the old "word by word" method, slow, laborious and generally inadequate, as already described, only one step beyond "spelling out" words letter by letter.

(2) *Double Word Process:* Also termed "Duplex Speed":
Like most interesting arts and endeavors, spying seems
to be as old as the legends of mankind.

In this method, words are checked by pairs as underlined, with an occasional extra added. This is twice as fast as the "Single Word Process"; and often faster, as there are no severe short pauses.

(3) *Triple Word Process:* Also "Triplex" or "Multiplex Speed":
Like most interesting arts and endeavors, spying seems
to be as old as the legends of mankind.

Here, three or more words at a clip make the reading process three or more times as fast as the "Single Word." The "carry-over" indicated by the extended underline represents a "sweep" from one line to the next, so that instead of pausing, the eye keeps on, combining "spying seems . . . . to be" into "spying seems to be."

Letting "Key-Words" Serve as "Eye-Signals" for Still More Rapid Reading and Use as Memory Tabs

What has speed reading to do with memory? Everything!

You can quadruple or quintuple your reading speed and still register all that you see in a single glance, provided that you do not stretch your recognition span beyond its full capacity. The main point is, if you can remember one word at a glance, you can remember two, three or more—even a phrase or a sentence—quite as readily. Moreover, a phrase or sentence is more meaningful than a few loosely connected words and therefore forms a stronger memory tab. But there is a way of speeding reading and remembering even further; namely, by disregarding lesser or unimportant words and noting only those that tell the story, just like driving along a superhighway, where you are free of all distractions and can concentrate on the road alone.

This process is well illustrated by the following passage from *Roughing It*, by Mark Twain, whose style is particularly adapted to such a purpose. He is describing a highlight of his trip across the Great Plains in the Overland stage-coach, prior to the building of the transcontinental railway:

> We had had a consuming <u>desire,</u> from the beginning, to see a <u>pony-rider,</u> but somehow or other <u>all that passed us</u> and all that met us managed to streak by <u>in the night,</u> and so we heard only a <u>whiz</u> and a <u>hail,</u> and the swift phantom of the desert was <u>gone</u> before we could get our <u>heads</u> out of the <u>windows.</u> But now we were <u>expecting one</u> along every moment, and would see him in <u>broad daylight.</u> Presently the driver exclaims: "Here he comes!"

Taking only the underlined words as "keys," you gain the gist of the whole account with a rapidity rivalling the speed of the pony-rider himself. Not that the other words are superfluous; it merely depends on the reader's needs. If he wanted *information* about travel of that period, he might have read it at Duplex Speed; if studying Twain's literary style, Triplex or Multiplex; if he felt that he already knew enough about the Pony Express and its riders —all discussed earlier in the narrative—he could use the speedy "key-word" process as just given.

Specially Designed Techniques for Reading Faster and Remembering More

Various excellent systems have been devised to attain speed in reading and since their purpose is to combine comprehension with retention, they are actually memory methods as well. Hence, they are given here in brief:

The Five S System

You *select* the book or material that you want to read; then *sample* it by reading some for style and treatment; next you *skip* to whatever section seems most interesting; there you *skim* through the material to capture main ideas; finally, you *scan* the salient points more closely, thereby fixing them in your mind.

Note how the five S's follow the A I R pattern so essential in memory work. Selection is similar to *attention*, which merges with *interest* through sampling and skipping, with skimming and scanning paving the way to the *repetition* that is so valuable in pegging memory home. The same factors are found in:

The R T P System

Here, the letters stand for *Read The Problem*, which is vitally important with unfamiliar material of an instructive sort. Reading the problem thoroughly demands close *attention*, which in turn increases *interest*, so when you proceed with a full study of the subject, *repetition* swings into operation automatically, since you will be going over a familiar groundwork. This is developed further through:

The P E R U System

This starts with a *preview* of the material, as with the Five S System, up to the point where you can *enquire* into it, as with the R T P System. Then you *read* and rapidly, being so well up on the subject; and having thoroughly acquired it, you put it to *use*, which means remembering its essential points. The initial letters of those four steps spell P E R U, hence the system's name. Beyond that comes:

The P Q R S T System

This consists of the usual *preview*, followed by any *question* that may demand special reference. Next you *read* the material, pausing after each section to *state* what you have learned; and finally you *test* yourself by checking back on every point or having someone quiz you on the entire subject. This is not only a highly efficient formula for reading, it is practically a memory system in itself. The same applies to:

The S Q 3 R System

Known also as the "Survey Q 3 R," this starts with a survey of the material, either by general ideas, chapter headings, or any satisfactory runup. You then *question* all the points you have surveyed, putting yourself that much ahead. Then come the three R's, namely: *read, recite, revise,* in that order. If this extensive and sometimes exhaustive procedure works to perfection, as it can, the final stage of revision becomes unnecessary, so *revise* is supplanted by *review.*

These last two systems follow the A I R formula so closely that they are practically AIR-tight. Described as briefly as they have been, it may seem that there is an over-emphasis on repetition, but such is not the case. In each successive phase, the mind is directed upon some new point of attention, which in turn rouses new interest, so that the repetition that follows is actually a coordination of one phase with another, rather than the same old rote.

Adapting Reading Systems to Memorization of Poetry: How to Combine Theme with Rhyme

The systems just outlined are extremely valuable in memorizing poems and orations. With poetry, the old reliable method was to learn it practically line by line, depending on the rhymes to serve as memory tabs. But the longer the poem, the less the reliability, as one missing link could hold up all the rest or cause the person reciting the poem to backtrack or jump over an entire stanza. Hence the newer way was to try to commit the entire poem to memory, or at least memorize it in sizable sections. In the latter case, use of the Topical System (described in Chapter 4) is an important adjunct.

However, in memorizing "in whole" rather than "in part," you can still note links as you proceed. Rhyming words will assert themselves with each new reading; and you can give special attention to others. But along with links that form direct *rhyme,* you can forge others that pertain to *theme,* often displaying poetic quality of their own, like a verse within a verse. Often, this linkage may be stronger than the actual versification, giving *theme* preference over *rhyme.*

Take an excerpt from a poem by James Russell Lowell, in which the "theme links" are underlined and the "rhyme links" appear in capital letters:

> Now is the high-tide of the YEAR
> And whatever of life hath EBBED AWAY
> Comes flooding back with a RIPPLY CHEER
> Into every bare inlet and creek and BAY;
> Now the heart is so full that a drop OVERFILLS IT
> We are happy now because GOD WILLS IT.

At one reading, you could take the *whole stanza*, as it is. At another, you would pick the *theme*: High-tide of life—flooding back—inlet—heart full—happy. At still another, you would follow the *rhyme*: Year, away, cheer, bay, overfills it, God wills it. Another full reading could stress the *double linkage*, as evidenced by such words as "ebbed," "ripply," "overfills"—and possibly "creek" as a connection between "inlet" and "bay."

This, as you will see, conforms loosely to the general pattern of the "read and remember" systems that have just been discussed. You can apply those of any type from the "Five S" to the "S Q 3 R," according to which seems best suited to the case at hand. But in every case, the early stress on reading should wind up with final emphasis on remembering.

Pleasure Reading as a Step to Prestige: How to Read a Novel in a Few Hours

For many people, the most attractive feature of combining basic reading mechanics with memory methods is not only the pleasure but the prestige that they can gain by learning to read faster and remember more. Speed reading enables them to skip unimportant words or skim over irrelevant paragraphs with the efficiency of a skilled accountant running his eye down a column of figures. Actually you will find yourself reading *less words* and therefore remembering *more words* because you have eliminated those you didn't need, which speeds the process as well.

If you have never read a complete novel in a matter of a few hours, don't be surprised if you meet people who say they have. Instead, question them about the contents of the novel and your big surprise may come when they calmly reel off the essential details as if they had studied them. Why? Because fast reading develops that ability of recognizing and remembering essentials, just as fast driving along a turnpike increases ability in that line.

Apply the same A I R formula that you use in other ways to

pleasure reading as well, again keeping systems in mind, and you will acquire the same aptitude. Give *attention* to what you are about to read; make sure you are in a mood to *sustain* interest and if need be, apply *repetition* to the full by reading back over anything that you feel you may have missed by going too fast.

*   *   *   *   *   *   *   *   *   *

CHAPTER 13

Now Use Your Expert
Memory in High-Speed
Mathematics!

The most remarkable feature about memory is that many people become experts in the field without even realizing it. That can apply to you personally, a point that has been stressed continually throughout this book. If you are an avid reader, if you drive a car, if you play a good hand of bridge, if you go in for crafts or hobbies, you must be utilizing some specialized form of memory to a marked degree, otherwise you couldn't have developed the aptitude that you now possess.

The only problem, as you now should know, consists of stumbling blocks. We are back again to the absent-minded professor, whose mind is so full of the things he wants to remember and therefore can remember, that he feels himself incapable of remembering the very things that everyone else regards as commonplace. So the proper course is to pull yourself out of the deep old rut and say, "If I can remember *this*, I can remember *that*," and then proceed to do it. Give the new thing the same *attention* you gave to the old, show it the same *interest*, and good old *repetition* will do its duty, leaving you walking on A I R.

Oddly, the biggest stumbling block of all is mathematics. You will find many people who say, "I can remember anything except figures; I simply have no mind for math." What is more, they will go all out to prove it, by demonstrating their own inability, or citing cases of someone who is practically a human adding machine, indicating that it is somewhat beyond normal to have a mind for mathematics. Actually, such a person may just happen to be somebody who likes mathematics and therefore has utilized the A I R formula in a natural way. If the people who say they "can't figure" merely followed the same procedure, they might become math buffs in their own right.

A good parallel can be drawn between reading and mathematics. You, as a capable reader who has come this far in this book, are probably acquainted with some people who read very little and are always finding excuses for not reading more. They may say that it tires their eyes, or that they are too busy, or they can't find the books they want in the library. The real reason likely is that they are slow readers who still "spell out" words instead of recognizing them on sight. The same thing can happen in mathematics when people fail to go beyond the primary stage.

Applying the Memory Factor Toward Mathematical Efficiency

The important part that memory plays in high-speed mathematics is evidenced by the fact that the famous "lightning calculators" described in the first chapter depended on memory for their remarkable results. The added point that many were not skilled in mathematics alone is further proof that they depended on some special process. Indeed, some calculators of the "human calendar" type are actually mentally deficient and either unable or unwilling to explain how they reel off the exact days of the week on which certain dates will fall, over a wide range of years and centuries.

However, all mathematical procedures can be systematized, otherwise there would be no mechanical computers; so the first step is to see how far your own mind has become computerized. Don't laugh at the thought of yourself as a "human adding machine," for you may be well along the way to becoming one without knowing it, as a few simple tests will prove. As for the memory factor, in all work with figures, it is necessary to retain them in mind as long as needed and then erase them mentally when you go on with something else.

Doubling Your Speed in Simple Addition Through Acquired Memory

3	Note the column of figures at the left, all set to be added
6	up. In fact, adding them is just as simple as spelling C A T =
4	CAT. You can go down the column saying "3 and 6 are
5	9 and 4 are 13 and 5 are 18—" and so on. But why do it
9	that way? You know that C-A-T is CAT, and nobody has
2	to tell you that 3 and 6 are 9. You've certainly dealt with
1	enough figures to know they can't be anything else.

6	So, since you don't have to "spell" the letters, there is no
4	need to "count" the figures.

7	There are forty-five different ways of adding any two one-

```
5
2
3
4
8
1
3
5
—
```

figure numbers, from $1 + 1 = 2$, $1 + 2 = 3$, up to $9 + 9 = 18$. All are instantly recognizable, as they belong to a simple Addition Table, that you acquire automatically by repetition, through adding many columns of figures. So it is easy to "double" them as you run down the column, saying mentally: "9—18—29—36—47—54—61—70—78," totalling the pairs as you go along. That's using memory—already acquired!—to double your speed.

From Double to Triple Speed
Through Math Memory Methods

Practice the double speed system as described, using columns of figures of your own, and once you become familiar with it, you will find that it lives up to its title. Thinking in "pairs" is a very easy process, for it is just as natural to regard "3 + 6" as nine as it is to identify "36" as thirty-six. You can take the pairs slowly at first, for there are only half as many to be added, when compared to the old-style single figure addition.

Adding upward is often helpful toward attaining speed. In the example given, you would start with 8 (5 and 3) as your bottom pair; then go to 17 (from the next pair, 1 and 8); then 24 (from the next pair, 4 and 3) and so on to the top of the column. An intriguing exercise is to write out several columns on different sheets of paper; then time yourself by a clock with a second hand, to see how your speed is improving. Or you can do the same with a column of a dozen five-figure numbers, carrying over from one column to the next in the usual way.

You can then go into triple speed by treating numbers in groups of three. This is by no means difficult, as the highest total in such a group is only 27 $(9 + 9 + 9)$ which is one of the easiest to recognize. Taking the sample column already given, adding it from bottom up to top would run: "9—24—38—49—65—78." Here, again, practice is the ultimate factor.

Testing Your Numerical Span
in Terms of Instant Memory

Just as reading can be done at different speeds—simplex, duplex, triplex—so can figures be added. There are two differences, however. One difference is: in reading, you are working along the horizontal; in adding, on the vertical. The other is, that in reading, you are compounding words; while in adding, you are aiming for totals. So it seems odd to compare "reading span" with "numerical span," as though each had something of the same flow. Such, however, is the case. Just as the mind can form a word from a conglomerate of letters, so can it produce a total from a column of figures, all in a flash.

To prove this, have someone write a column of four or preferably five figures on a small pad and draw a line beneath. This is to be laid face down on the table, without your seeing the figures. For example:

$$5$$
$$8$$
$$6$$
$$2$$
$$\underline{7}$$

You then take the pad at the lower end, your fingers above and your thumb below, so your hand is palm down. In one continuous action, turn your palm upward, pad and all; then, with a reverse action, turn the pad down again, allowing only sufficient pause for a momentary glance. You will find that you can "read" the figures almost as you would a word. They run through your mind as you add them automatically, just as you might pronounce an odd name like "Jangrig" or a coined word like "Zatrex" if you happened to glimpse them while swinging a corner in a car.

Obviously, it is memory of the instant type that works in both cases, but applied to mathematics, it shows how fleeting impressions can be turned to advantage in rapid calculations. It also shows that groups of figures may be variable where speeded addition is concerned, which paves the way to further rapid processes.

Using "Catch Figures" as a Device in Paper-and-Pencil Addition

5	Here, starting with a simple column of figures, as	5
8	shown at the left, you add them downwards, in	8 −3
3	groups, as already described, but with this sole pur-	3
2	pose: To have each group form an individual total	2
3	between 10 and 20. This speeds the process, since	3
4	you do not have to add each total to the one before	4 −2

6   (as in the double and triple additions.) It also lets   6
2   you take advantage of the "memory flow" (as de-   2
9   scribed in the test with the pad).   9 −7

7   However, each time your group addition goes over   7
6   10, you drop the ten and write the unit as a small   6 −3
8   figure at the right of the column, marking the last   8

figure in the group. Thus with the column at the   23
left, the additions would run 13 $(5 + 8)$; 12 $(3 + 2$ 4

$+ 3 + 4)$; 17 $(6 + 2 + 9)$; 13 $(7 + 6)$; leaving an   63
8 unadded. This process is shown at the right.

You are now ready for the follow-up. Run down the column and add all the little figures (3, 2, 7, 3) and to that add the large left-over figure (8), which comes to $3 + 2 + 7 + 3 + 8 = 23$. Then run down the column again, counting the number of catch figures only, in this case four, and add that number (4) to your tens column. The tens and units are added (as shown at the right), giving you the answer to the entire addition, which is 63.

Carrying "Catch Figure Addition" to the Tens Column and Beyond

88   At the left is a column of two-figure num-   88
48 −6   bers to be added downward in "catch   2− 48 −6
38   figure" style. The units column is added in   38
61   the usual manner, exactly as shown. Then   61
98 −7   you proceed to add the tens column in the   8− 98 −7
24   same way, but set its total beneath and   24
13   one step to the left. This is illustrated by   13
62   the process on the right, in which the two   62
89 −8   totals have been added, giving the result.   7− 89 −8

23   With a column of three-figure numbers,   23

54   the procedure is continued into the hun-   54
    dreds column; with four-figure numbers,   49

    into the thousands and so on. In such   544
cases, the figures of each number should be written fairly well apart, to allow space for inserting the catch figures.

Speeding and Assuring Additions by Working from Left to Right

So far, we have departed widely from the old conventional form of addition that begins with the units, carries over to the tens, then to the hundreds and so on, working from right to left. Like spelling out a three-letter word, it. is still a good system if there are only a few numbers in the column; but the longer the column, the more irksome it becomes, because of the carry-over. If you forget what you carried, you have to backtrack and sometimes begin all over. Of course, you can write down the figures that you carry, in "catch figure" style, but even that can be avoided if you add from left to right.

Here is a simple example. You want to add the numbers 300, 60 and 5. So you set them down thus:

```
3 0 0
  6 0
    5
-------
3 6 5
```

No need to add them from right to left, saying "5 and carry 0; 6 and carry 0; 3." A glance from left to right tells you that it is 365 and you simply repeat, "Three hundred—sixty—five," getting the answer automatically.

How the simple "left to right" rule can be applied to a long and irregular column of numbers is shown under heading "A," below:

"A"			"B"			
			(1) (2) (3) (4)			
3 8 5				3	8	5
4 1 7 2			4	1	7	2
2 4 8				2	4	8
3 2 4 0			3	2	4	0
5 9 6				5	9	6
4 0 1				4	0	1
9 7 7 6				9	7	7	6

1 6 0 0 0	1st Col.	1 6 * 3 9 3rd Col.
2 4 0 0	2nd Col.	2 4 * 2 8 4th Col.
3 9 0		1 8 8 1 8
2 8		
1 8 8 1 8		

It's practically the same as $300 + 60 + 5$, except the ciphers are added in this case (Heading "A") to form 16,000, 2,400, 390 and 28. In adding those, you naturally work from right to left, as in the old conventional method, because sometimes you will have to carry 1, but never a higher figure, so the summing up is both rapid and rudimentary. To make it even faster, you can proceed as under Heading "B," leaving out the ciphers and putting down the total of the first column; then the second column beneath that; the third column in line with the first; and the fourth column in line with the second.

Summarized, the advantages of these specialized methods of addition are threefold: First, they are speedier and therefore more efficient. Second, a set of figures can be added by one method, then another, avoiding the same slip twice, and thereby providing a sure-fire check. Third, switching from one system to another provides relief from the monotony that frequently comes from adding long columns of figures in the same old way.

By giving each system a regular workout, memory becomes increasingly important, demanding *attention* to each new trial, thereby sustaining *interest*, and providing sufficient *repetition*, but not too much. Again, the A I R formula proves its worth.

Utilizing Memory Methods to Speed Up the Process of Subtraction

As with addition, a Subtraction Table can be formed, so that the difference between any two figures may be instantly recognized. Just as $5 + 3 = 8$ in the language of addition, so does $5 - 3 = 2$ where subtraction is involved, though the process is somewhat more complex. In adding two figures, it makes no difference which is placed above the other, as:

$$+\frac{5}{2} \text{ or } +\frac{2}{5} \text{ Or with larger numbers: } +\frac{62}{18} \text{ or } +\frac{18}{62}$$
$$\overline{7} \qquad \overline{7} \qquad\qquad\qquad\qquad \overline{80} \qquad \overline{80}$$

But with subtraction, it is customary to put the smaller below the larger, as with the following:

$$-\frac{7}{3} \text{ not } -\frac{3}{7} \text{ OR } -\frac{54}{45} \text{ not } -\frac{45}{54}$$

However, when it comes to speed subtraction, you should practice working upward as well as downward. Here, the memory factor enters. To you, when your mind is in a subtractive mood, 7 and 3 represent 4; and so do 3 and 7, whether you "read" them from left to right, right to left or downward or upward. But that raises another memory jog that must also be kept constantly in mind. In standardized subtraction, when the bottom figure in the unit column is larger than the top figure, you must "borrow" 10 from the tens column, thus:

$$-\frac{43}{26} \text{ is broken into } -\frac{30 + 13}{20 + 6} \text{ giving } -\frac{43}{26}$$
$$\overline{10 + 7} \qquad \overline{17}$$

Admittedly, this too is such simple arithmetic that it will prove commonplace to every reader; but here, the memory factor is again involved, and sometimes when something becomes second nature through rote or repetition, the real mechanics of the operation are overlooked. You must be familiar with those mechanics to apply the rules of speed subtraction.

Subtracting Two-Figure Numbers from Left to Right by Instant Sight

Take any two numbers of two figures each, place the larger above the smaller and subtract the left column first; then the right. If both upper figures are larger, this works automatically, as in "A":

$$
\begin{array}{cc}
\text{"A"} & \text{"B"} \\
8\ 6 & 7\ 3 \\
-\ 2\ 4 & -\ 4\ 8 \\
\hline
6\ 2 & 3 \\
& 2\ 5 \\
\end{array}
$$

However, if the upper figure on the right is smaller, as in "B," immediately deduct 1 more from the column on the left. That represents the 10 that was "borrowed" by the column on the right. But in this case, you simply "lend" it from the left column to the right, which is a shorter, speedier process.

Using Your Memory for Addition as an Adjunct to Quick Subtraction

Most people find it easier to add than to subtract; and if whatever subtraction is required involves only the deduction of the figure 1, it should be easy indeed. So first, let us consider how subtraction can be made easier by preliminary addition; then go on from there.

With any numbers in which only the final figure of the lower number is larger than the corresponding figure of the upper, you have simply to add enough to the lower number to raise it to the nearest multiple of 10, so it ends in a zero. Then add the same amount to the upper number and subtract the lower from the upper. As examples:

| $\begin{array}{r} 7\ 5 \\ 2\ 7 \\ \hline 4\ 8 \end{array}$ | Add "3" to both and subtract | $\begin{array}{r} 7\ 8 \\ 3\ 0 \\ \hline 4\ 8 \end{array}$ | $\begin{array}{r} 7\ 8\ 1 \\ 4\ 5\ 5 \\ \hline 3\ 2\ 6 \end{array}$ | Add "5" to both and subtract | $\begin{array}{r} 7\ 8\ 6 \\ 4\ 6\ 0 \\ \hline 3\ 2\ 6 \end{array}$ |

Note that in each case, the upper figure at the right was automatically raised to the point where it represented the final result of the subtraction, due to the lower figure becoming 0. In short, *addition* was used to produce *subtraction*. Now suppose, in the case of 75 − 27, you work from right to left, saying mentally: "7 and 3 are 10; 3 and 5 are 8," putting down 8. Then: "2 and 8 are 10; 8 and 7 are 5 (for 15), less 1, is 4." You would mark down the 4 at the left and have your answer, 48, through addition alone.

The reason for the "less 1" is to conform to the old "borrowing" principle. Now, taking the sample on the right, 781 − 455, you would proceed: "5 and 5 are 10; 1 and 5 are 6." Then: "5 and 5 are 10; 5 and 8 are 3 (for 13), less 1, is 2." Then: "4 and 6 are 10; 6 and 7 are 3 (for 13)." You would mark down 3 to complete your answer, 326. There was no "less 1" in this case, as there was no "carry-over" from the middle column.

Here is the same principle applied to a much longer pair of numbers, in which many of the figures in the lower number are larger than the corresponding figures in the upper:

$$\begin{array}{r} 8\ 5\ 7\ 3\ 2\ 8\ 4\ 0\ 1 \\ 5\ 9\ 2\ 7\ 6\ 3\ 7\ 6\ 8 \\ \hline 2\ 6\ 4\ 5\ 6\ 4\ 6\ 3\ 3 \end{array}$$

Here is how it would be "broken down" by the "add up" subtraction process in which there are actually no subtractions, other than the "less 1" carry-overs:

$(3-1)$	(6)	$(5-1)$	$(6-1)$	(6)	$(5-1)$	$(7-1)$	$(4-1)$	(3)
8	5	7	3	2	8	4	0	1
5	9	2	7	6	3	7	6	8
$(+5)$	$(+6)$	$(+8)$	$(+3)$	$(+4)$	$(+7)$	$(+3)$	$(+4)$	$(+2)$
2	6	4	5	6	4	6	3	3

All the figures in parentheses are simply carried mentally, adding the bottom row from right to left with each corresponding figure of the top row and then transcribing the total to the answer, below the line.

You Can Multiply Your Memory Power Through Multiple Memory Methods

The chances are about a million to one that you are already well acquainted with the greatest memory device of all time: The Multiplication Table. As commonly learned, running from $1 \times 1 = 1$ up to $12 \times 12 = 144$, the Multiplication Table is in one sense very limited, yet in another, practically unlimited. People who can glibly call off any total up to 12 times 12, may find that they have to "think it out" when asked, "How much is 13 times 14?"

Yet with our familiar decimal system, you don't actually have to go beyond $9 \times 9 = 81$. To multiply by 10, you merely attach a zero to any given number, so that $64 \times 10 = 640$, and so on. The fact that the common Multiplication Table goes as high as 12×12 is a carry-over from the duodecimal system, wherein 12 pence make a shilling, 12 inches a foot, and a dozen dozen (12×12), a gross (144). But all conventional multiplication methods can be reduced to single figures.

Hence there are ways to improve your ability in multiplication: one, to extend the range of the Multiplication Table; the other, to utilize shortcuts or devices in the multiplication process itself. Each of these requires individual consideration as a way to multiply your memory power.

Expanding the Multiplication Table
to Speed Specialized Calculations

Expansion of the Multiplication Table is a great help to accountants, salesmen, insurance agents, storekeepers and many other persons who must be prompt in coming up with the right figures or estimates when occasion so demands. The question is: How far should it be expanded? The answer, in most instances, depends on individual needs and inclinations.

The simplest course is to refer to such a table and go on beyond the multiple of 12, say to 15. That's almost automatic up to $13 \times 6 = 78$ and higher multiples such as $13 \times 11 = 143$ and $14 \times 11 = 154$, which follow an established pattern. The difficulty comes with higher numbers, such as $1 \times 13 = 13$, $2 \times 13 = 26$ and so on up to $13 \times 13 = 169$. However, by extending the lower multipliers first, you will be that much ahead when you reach the higher brackets.

For example, having extended your 7's to $15 \times 7 = 105$, and your 8's to $15 \times 8 = 120$, and your 9's to $15 \times 9 = 135$, you will be going over familiar ground as you commit your 15's to memory and come to $7 \times 15 = 105$, $8 \times 15 = 120$, $9 \times 15 = 135$. So if need and inclination provide sufficient urge, it is simple enough to expand to 20×20 or 25×25.

That will require time, however, for this is one case where you must revert to rote, in order to have the exact answers on immediate call, just as with the common Multiplication Table up to 12×12. There are, however, some specialized cases that require less effort. A printer, for example, thinks in terms of 16's as well as 32's and 64's, as printed sheets fold into pages composed of those numbers. So he can multiply by 8's, adding a doubling process; or, being so familiar with 16's, 32's and 64's, he can commit their tables to memory as far as needed, without worrying over the intervening stages.

How a New Look at Number Groups
Enables the Rapid Calculator
to Shine in Business

Since the great advantage of an expanded Multiplication Table is the aid it gives to business, it is quite obvious that any other modes of mental calculation can enable a man to shine in his chosen calling when figures loom as an essential item. There are many devices in this field, some entirely mental, others requiring pad and paper; but nearly all are easy to remember if you follow through with the A I R formula of noting them and then using them.

Here are some examples:

To multiply a number by:

2—Double it. $345 \times 2 = 345 + 345 = 690$

4—Double it again. $345 \times 4 = 690 + 690 = 1380$

5—Affix a zero and divide by 2. $92 \times 5 = 920 \div 2 = 460$

8—Double it three times. $26 \times 8 = 26 + 26 + 52 + 104 = 208$

9—Affix 0 and subtract original number. $65 \times 9 = 650 - 65 = 585$

10—Simply affix a zero. $83 \times 10 = 830$

11—Write the number beneath itself, but move it one column to the left; then add. $11 \times 18 = 18$

$$\begin{array}{r} 18 \\ \underline{18} \\ 198 \end{array}$$

15—Affix 0 and divide by 2. Again affix 0 to original number and add. $242 \times 15 = 2420 \div 2 = 1210$

$$\begin{array}{r} + 2420 \\ \hline 3630 \end{array}$$

19—Double the number, affix 0 and subtract original number. $28 \times 2 = 560 - 28 = 532$

20—Double the number and affix 0. $716 \times 2 = 716 + 716 = 14320$

25—Affix 00 and divide by 4. $66 \times 25 = 6600 \div 4 = 1650$
Or affix 00 and divide by 2 twice. $66 \times 25 = 6600 \div 2 = 3300 \div 2 = 1650$

The shortcuts listed can be combined in various ways for the multiplication of two numbers of two figures each, a need that often arises. Memory of the methods involved plays an important part in these excursions into mental mathematics.

Here are two typical examples:

To multiply 64 by 42:
Break it down to $64 \times 40 + 64 \times 2$.

Multiply 64×4 by doubling 64 twice; first to 128, then to 256.
Then attach a 0, making 2560, which is $64 \times 40 = 2560$.
Then multiply $64 \times 2 = 128$ or $64 + 64 = 128$.
Add $2560 + 128 = 2688$.

To multiply 36 by 51:
Break it down to $36 \times 50 + 36$ (or 36×1).
Attach 00 to 36, making 3600. Then:
Divide by 2, making 1800.
Multiply 36×1 and add: $1800 + 36 = 1836$.

Putting Multiplication Methods in Reverse to Speed the Division Process

Oddly, where division is concerned, the Multiplication Table is of prime importance. Yet actually, this is not as odd as it might seem. Multiplication and division are definitely interchangeable: When you think that $7 \times 6 = 42$, you automatically realize that $42 \div 7 = 6$. So familiarity with the Multiplication Table, sponsored by *attention*, sustained by *interest* and driven home through continued *repetition*, becomes a tremendous adjunct for division as well. That is a good reason for extending or expanding the range of the Multiplication Table, as already recommended.

There are, however, special rules regarding the divisibility of numbers; and if these are studied, with due consideration, and then gone over sufficiently, they can be so committed to memory by the A I R process that they will be constantly available for future reference. Those are:

A number can be exactly divided by:

2—if it ends in an even number (as 24, 38, 90).

3—if its figures add up to a number divisible by 3 (as 27 or 168).

4—if the last two figures are divisible by 4 (as 228).

5—if the last figure is 0 or 5 (as 100 or 37,295).

6—if divisible by both 2 and 3 (as 28,434).

8—if the last three figures are divisible by 8 (as 769,104 or 22,136).

9—if all the figures add up to a number divisible by 9 (as $325,638 = 3 + 2 + 5 + 6 + 3 + 8 = 27$).

10—if the number ends in 0 (as 20, 350, 1,630).

12—if divisible by both 3 and 4 (as 6,264).

Determining divisibility by 7 is an extremely complicated process and determining divisibility by 11 is somewhat difficult for general use, so those have been omitted from the list.

*   *   *   *   *   *   *   *   *   *

CHAPTER 14

Amaze Your Friends
with Memory Stunts
and Games

Perhaps the best part of building up a mighty memory is the fun that you can have in doing it. As soon as you study memory methods, you must utilize them in order to acquire new facility and expand your ability. In short, memory building is a cumulative process and should become a part of your daily life.

There is an old saying, "Nothing succeeds like success," and you will find that it applies particularly to memory, once you begin to display your new-found power. Some of the simplest of memory stunts can be built into apparently amazing feats if you demonstrate them boldly, as though they were really mental marvels. There's no need to worry if your friends think there's a trick to it. Let them try to guess the answer and when they find that they can't duplicate your work, they will admire it all the more.

Also, you can always follow up the simpler exhibitions with something more difficult or really complex, for as you progress in your memory study, you will gain new facility and confidence with it, resulting in proportionate improvement. From memory stunts you can go into memory games in which your friends participate, which will increase your popularity.

Here are types to choose from:

CALLING OFF FIGURES

This impressive memory stunt can be performed at a moment's notice with practically no preliminary practice. You write out a row of some twenty-odd figures; then, after concentrating on the long number, you turn your back and call off the figures in perfect order, while your friends check them by the list.

This trick used to be termed the "subway system" because that is where it originated. Many riders on Manhattan's West Side or Broadway Subway were familiar with the street numbers of the station: 14th, 23rd, 34th, 42nd, 50th, 59th, 66th, 72nd, 78th, 86th, up to the next express stop, 96th. Knowing those by rote, all you have to do is write down a long number taking them in order:

1 4 2 3 3 4 4 2 5 0 5 9 6 6 7 2 7 8 8 6 9 6

From then on, it is simply a matter of making something easy look difficult, by pretending to concentrate deeply as you call off the figures, pausing occasionally as though having trouble with the next figure, and then getting it correctly.

By way of variation, especially when repeating the stunt for some of the same friends, you can travel downtown on your mental subway trip, so your number would be written:

9 6 8 6 7 8 7 2 6 6 5 9 5 0 4 2 3 4 2 3 1 4

Street stations on other subways can be used as another variation; but if you aren't familiar with subways, you still can work the stunt. Just take a series of street addresses with which you are familiar, say your own, your brother's, your doctor's and a few more, as 707, 3516, 2332, 864, 334, 493, and imagine yourself making the rounds in that order as you write down:

7 0 7 3 5 1 6 2 3 3 2 8 6 4 3 3 4 4 9 3

Any time you want to change the number, picture yourself going to other places with familiar addresses. You can use telephone numbers instead, and here you can let your memory do double duty. Check a dozen or more phone numbers that are important enough to have on instant call; then go over them until you have memorized them practically by rote. When you want to do the stunt of "Calling Off Figures," just think of those "key" phone numbers and you will be set.

I'VE GOT YOUR NUMBER

Here is another stunt of calling off figures, but with a totally different twist and a distinctly personalized touch. You tell several friends that you have a remarkable faculty for remembering numbers rather than names and that you are willing to prove it. Suppose one of your friends is named James Passmore. You write the number 6309034 on a slip of paper and give it to him, saying, "Keep that number, Jim, and see how well I remember it."

Then you turn to another friend—say Millicent Busby—and write the number 35021909, telling her to keep it. You do this with half a dozen other people until they begin to wonder how you could even hope to remember all those numbers. But you do remember them. As each person says, "Give me my number," you concentrate and give it figure by figure while they check it off in amazed wonder.

What you do is use the Figure Alphabet, as described on page 128. You write each number slowly, as though concentrating on the figures to fix them firmly in mind. Actually, you are simply transcribing your friend's names into figures, as:

J A M E S   P A S S M O R E
6   3   0 9   0 3   4

M I L L I C E N T   B U S B Y
3   5   0   2 1 9   0 9

When each person asks you to call off his or her number, you simply spell that person's name mentally and transcribe the phonetic key letters back to the corresponding figures.

MASTER MEMORY

In this case, you validate your earliest tests by letting people call off figures of their own choice until you have about twenty-five in all. You write each figure on a card as you go along, so the number might read:

6 5 1 6 6 8 4 9 7 0 3 4 7 2 8 6 9 8 4 0 1 5 2 9 7

You then proceed to call them off, just as you did with the "subway system," but since these are anybody's numbers, people naturally believe that your earlier demonstration was just as legitimate. But this time, you use the Pictorial Alphabet System, described in Chapter 6, thus:

First you would think of *six apples*, like a pyramid. Next *five birds* sitting on the points of a star, being watched by *one* big *cat*. Next, *six dogs* forming a pyramid; *six elevators* running up in a real pyramid; a *family* living in an *eight*-sided house shaped like a cube and so on.

Take these slowly so as to form definite pictures for all the figures and you will find that it works perfectly. You can try it with ten to fifteen figures to start; then lengthen it to twenty-five as you become more proficient. In calling back the figures, simply visualize your apples, birds and so on, in terms of your numerical pictures.

As a climax, after calling off all the figures, say that you will repeat the number again, just to prove it wasn't luck. The second time is much easier, since you are merely reviewing your mental pictures. In fact, it is so much easier, that this time you can *add the figures* as you go along. So in the example just given, at the finish, you would say casually, as if in afterthought:

"By the way, if you would care to add up all the figures in

the number that you gave me, you will find that they come to 127."

When someone adds them and finds that you are right, they will be all the more amazed by your remarkable memory power.

FINDING CONCEALED NAMES

As a memory exercise, a search for names concealed in special sentences is very productive of results, provided the names all come under one head. Taking animals as the first example, this means that with each succeeding sentence, you will have to bring the names of more and more animals to mind. Here is a sample:

> Do not rush or serious results may follow.
> The concealed name of an animal is HORSE.
> (Do not rusH OR SErious results may follow.)

Now try to find a concealed animal in each of the following sentences:

  1: When I hear the bell I only go to sleep.

  2: Nothing but prestige remained for him.

  3: Despite the haze brave skippers sailed away.

  4: We gazed in awe as elevators sped up and down.

  5: Many creatures became lazy in hot weather.

  6: Send me three dozen boxes of towels.

  7: We saw the sampan there by the dock.

  8: He made error after error almost daily.

  9: Look at the nice new car I bought.

10: He took a picture of the house.

11: I want to go up on your roof.

12: He was lucky to draw a winning number.

(Answers to the above appear on page 229).

Now to proceed with the concealed names of a dozen different species of fish, one to each sentence:

  1: That would be the best route to take.

  2: I heard him whisper cheering words.

  3: He was badly shaken by the news.

  4: When I reached the top I kept on going.

  5: Of all nuts almonds are the tastiest.

  6: The new car purred very smoothly.

7: We must rush a delivery at once.

8: The comptroller and the bursar dined together.

9: He heard his brother ringing the bells.

10: They felt unable to proceed.

11: The theater manager found tickets for the new hit in great demand.

12: The spy decoded the message.

(Answers to the above appear on page 229).

Here is another group of sentences, each concealing the name of a modern country of the world. Try testing your memory on these as well:

1: With enough capital you can go into business.

2: We can go to the fair another time.

3: They put each in another place.

4: The journey was painless and speedy.

5: We sincerely hope rumors will cease.

6: He likes to scan a daily newspaper column.

7: The roof ran centrally toward the chimney.

8: He took the medals and pinned them on a coat.

9: He stroked his chin diagonally.

10: After lunch I leave for my vacation.

11: All of a sudden market prices fell.

12: They have taken yards of carpet for their house.

(Answers to the above appear on page 229).

I Doubt It

Although "bluff" plays a primary part in this card game, memory is usually the ultimate factor; hence, it is valuable as a "memory builder" along with providing good fun.

An ordinary pack of playing cards is used, and after being shuffled, it is divided about equally between three or four players. Each holds his cards as a hand, spreading it out so that the others cannot see its faces; that is, keeping the faces toward himself. He then arranges them in sets, according to their individual value: aces, twos, threes and on up to jack, queen and king, regardless of their suits.

The first player, starting to the left of the dealer, then lays

Answers to Names of Concealed Animals

1: LION (belL I ONly)
2: TIGER (presTIGE Remained)
3: ZEBRA (haZE BRAve)
4: WEASEL (aWE AS ELevators)
5: CAMEL (beCAME Lazy)
6: OX (bOXes)
7: PANTHER (samPAN THERe)
8: DEER (maDE ERror)
9: CARIBOU (CAR I BOUght)
10: OKAPI (toOK A PIcture)
11: PONY (uP ON Your)
12: GNU (winninG NUmber)

Answers to Names of Concealed Fish

1: TROUT (besT ROUTe)
2: PERCH (whisPER CHeering)
3: HAKE (sHAKEn)
4: PIKE (toP I KEpt)
5: SALMON (nutS ALMONds)
6: CARP (CAR Purred)
7: SHAD (ruSH A Delivery)
8: SARDINE (burSAR DINEd)
9: HERRING (brotHER RINGing)
10: TUNA (felT UNAble)
11: WHITING (neW HIT IN Great)
12: COD (deCODed)

Answers to Names of Concealed Countries

1: ITALY (capITAL You)
2: IRAN (faIR ANother)
3: CHINA (eaCH IN Another)
4: SPAIN (waS PAINless)
5: PERU (hoPE RUmors)
6: CANADA (sCAN A DAily)
7: FRANCE (rooF RAN CEntrally)
8: MONACO (theM ON A COat)
9: INDIA (chIN DIAgonally)
10: CHILE (lunCH I LEave)
11: DENMARK (sudDEN MARKet)
12: KENYA (taKEN YArds)

one, two, three or four cards face down, announcing "Aces," the assumption being that the cards are all aces. The second player does the same, announcing "Twos" on the same basis; the third follows with "Threes." In a three-player game, this would bring it back to the first player, who would lay down another card—or cards —saying, "Fours." It continues in this way, on up to kings.

However, a player is not compelled to lay down a card or cards of the particular value he announces. He can "bluff" his opponents by laying down any card he wants. Thus the first player could lay down a jack and a king and boldly assert, "Aces." The second player could lay down a five and say, "Twos." Often, this is necessary, because the player may not have a card of the particular value that he is forced to announce in accordance with his turn.

To offset such chicanery, the other players also have a privilege. If the second player doubts that the first player laid down nothing but aces, he can say, "I doubt it." In that case, the cards in question are turned face up. If they are aces, the second player must take them into his hand, along with any other cards that were previously discarded. But if they are not aces, the first player must take them back into his hand, with all other discards as well. If the second player doesn't use the doubting privilege, the third player can; or both can pass up the chance, if they think that the first player really laid down aces.

Once the play has gone as high as kings, the next player reverts to aces; the next follows with twos and upward. Sometimes the game is greatly prolonged because whenever a player is on the verge of going out, someone "doubts" him and catches him with a false discard, forcing him to pick up all the cards from the table.

A sample game could proceed thus:

First Player holds: 2 2 3 3 4 6 6 6 7 7 9 10 J J J Q K K
Second Player holds: A A 2 5 5 5 5 6 7 7 9 9 9 10 10 Q K
Third Player holds: A A 2 3 3 4 4 4 8 8 8 8 10 J Q Q K

First player lays down a jack and king, announcing "Aces," and gets away with it. Second player lays down a two and announces "Twos." Third player lays down an eight, announces "Threes" and gets away with it. First player lays down a four and announces "Fours." Second player lays down his four fives and announces, "Fives." Third player thinks that is just too nervy and says, "I doubt it." The cards are turned up, prove to be fives and the third player is forced to pick up all the discards. He continues from there by laying down an eight and meekly announcing, "Sixes." He now has so many new cards that no one challenges him.

So the game continues; but when it reaches eights, the second player, whose turn comes then, is sure to be caught by the third player. For whatever the second player lays down with the announcement, "Eights," his discard must be a bluff, for the third player had all four eights to start. There, memory enters the picture; and it would do so again if the second player should lay down two cards and announce "Jacks," when that turn came.

The first player, remembering that he had three jacks to start and that the one he falsely discarded was picked up by the third player, is sure that the second player could not really be laying down two jacks. So the first player says, "I doubt it," and the second player is forced to pick up the cards from the table. At times, however, a player may need to pick up discards, in order to obtain a card of some specific value that is missing from his hand, so he will have such a card when his turn comes to play it. That means more points to remember, making the game still more valuable as a memory builder.

As soon as one player has managed to dispose of his entire hand, he wins the game; and if a score is being kept, each of the other players is charged one point for every card remaining in his hand. Thus when play finally ends, the player with the lowest score is the winner. In that case, "game" can be set at a figure such as 50 points, ending when someone goes over that. With four to eight players in the game, a double pack is used, giving players an opportunity to discard up to eight cards at a time. With eight to twelve players, a third pack can be introduced, raising the discard level to a possible twelve, and adding that much more to the memory factor.

CONCENTRATION

Known also as "Memory," the game of "Concentration" lives up to both titles, for it needs increasingly intensive effort as it proceeds, though in the final stages it may become something of a runaway. Played with ordinary playing cards, it is probably the best game of that type, from the standpoint of memory development. Along with the 52-card pack, a full-sized card table is required for facility of operation.

The pack is shuffled and the cards are dealt face down in six rows of eight cards each, with the last four cards extending from each corner, to form the following layout:

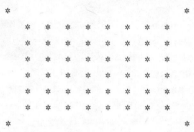

With two players participating, the first turns up any two cards in the big square. If they match in value and color—as two red kings, two black tens, he removes them from the layout and places them aside toward his score. He can then turn up another pair on the same basis. It does not matter if the cards are close together or far apart; that is up to the player to decide for himself. But if a turned-up pair fail to match as described, the player's turn ends and the two cards must be turned face down in their original positions.

It is then the second player's turn, and he proceeds on exactly the same terms until he fails to match a pair, when play reverts to the first player. This goes on, turn by turn, until the pairs have all been matched, when the player with the most cards wins.

Obviously, the advantage is with the player who is better able to remember any cards that have been turned up. Players turn up random cards at the start, hoping for lucky matches. So at the end of say three turns, the following six cards might show up: Q H, 10 S, 9 D, 7 C, 7 H, 3 C. If on the next turn, a player should turn up the 10 C, he would naturally turn up the 10 S, to match it. The same would apply if he turned up the Q D, 9 H, 7 S, 7 D or 3 S, since he knows the positions of the cards that match them (Q H, 9 D, 7 C, 7 H, 3 C).

That is, he *should* know the positions of those cards, for he has seen them, but as the game goes on, it becomes increasingly difficult for a player to recall where a needed card is; and if he turns up a wrong one by mistake, the opportunity of turning up the right one reverts to his adversary. With three or more players, each takes his turn in clockwise rotation around the table. If desired, a score can be kept according to the number of cards taken by each player, with game set at 50 or 100 points. This means shuffling the pack and dealing a new layout after each round.

Concentration forms the basis for the elaborate and highly popular television game of the same title, in which participants win prizes by matching squares on a board, while members of the TV audience test their memories as well. A version of the TV game has also been marketed in the form of a complete outfit suitable for home play.

AUTHORS

This game is usually played with a special pack of cards, bearing the names of authors and their works. Use of such cards is particularly good, as they increase the memory factor. However, since the game can be played with ordinary playing cards, it will be described in that form first, giving readers an opportunity to test it before taking it up on a more elaborate scale.

An entire pack of cards is dealt face down to anywhere from three to eight players, each receiving approximately the same number of cards. For example: With five players, the 52-card pack might be divided so that each player received totals as follows: Andy, 11; Bob, 11; Charley, 10; Ellen, 10; Fran, 10. Each player looks at his or her hand and arranges its cards in groups according to values, as aces, kings, queens and all the rest, though there is no order of sequence in this game.

Then, the first player, Andy, can order some other player to give him a specific card, provided he already has one of that value in his hand. To simplify this, suppose Andy holds:

A H, K C, K D, 10 C, 9 D, 9 H, 9 C, 5 H, 4 H, 3 H, 3 C

Andy could say, "Ellen, give me the King of Hearts," and if Ellen had it, she would have to hand it over. Andy could then say, "Charley, give me the Three of Spades," and that demand, too, would have to be fulfilled. But if Charley didn't have the Three of Spades, Andy's turn would end and it would become Bob's turn to demand cards from other players, provided of course that he held one of whatever value he named. So the play continues around the table and each time a player completes a set of four cards of the same value, he lays it face up in front of him. Sometimes a player is lucky enough to be dealt a complete set, which he lays down automatically when his turn comes; but in any event, the game keeps on until all sets have been completed and the player with the most sets wins. Often, this is a tie, but the game can be continued over a predetermined number of rounds, or until one player has reached a specified total of say, 25 sets.

Where memory enters the game, and powerfully, is whenever the turn moves to the next player. For example, Andy, in asking Charley for the "Three of Spades," is forced to reveal that he already has a Three. Now if Fran happened to be holding the 3 S, she would know that Andy held at least one Three. So in her turn, Fran might say, "Andy, give me the Three of Hearts," and getting it, Fran could continue, "Andy, give me the Three of Clubs," and getting that, Fran might happily add, "Andy, give me the Three of Diamonds," which would complete the set for Fran.

But Andy doesn't have the 3 D, so Fran, far from being a winner where Threes are concerned, is a sure loser. Assuming that Bob holds the 3 D, when his turn comes, he simply calls upon Fran to deliver the Threes in whatever order he chooses, completing the set for himself; and he can still call for some other card from another player. Hence as the round progresses, it zigzags more from one player to another; the game now switches from sheer guess-work to absolute memory.

In the standard game of *Authors*, each group of four cards bears the portrait of an author, as *Louisa Alcott*, with the name of one of the author's works above; so the four cards of the set would be *An Old-Fashioned Girl, Eight Cousins, Little Men, Little Women*. The names of the other three cards in the set are listed below the portrait, so that players can refer to them when calling for cards. This not only makes the game more interesting but also it gives it a special value where memory is concerned, for after several sessions of *Authors*, the average player can recall the various books of the different authors almost automatically. It is just another case of the A I R formula working to perfection, as the *attention* given to the game and the *interest* it stimulates, enable *repetition* to supply the final touch.

The original game of *Authors* is more than a century old, and the fact that it has retained its popularity through all those years is proof of its worth as a memory builder. Various offshoots of the game have been derived during that period, one of the best being the use of cards that enable the players to remember words in a foreign language, such as French. For example: one set of four cards would depict a cat, a dog, a horse and a cow, topped by the words CHAT, CHIEN, CHEVAL and VACHE, respectively, with the other members of the group listed below each picture.

Thus a player holding the cat card would recognize that the word "chat" was French for "cat": and he could ask for any of the three cards listed beneath, *Chien, Cheval, Vache,* without knowing what they actually were, until such cards were handed to him, when the top name would link with the picture, as VACHE with cow. After playing a while with these language cards, players find that they have acquired a French vocabulary which, though limited, will be firmly fixed in mind.

* * * * * * * * * *

INDEX

A

Ability, individual, 81

"Above," 134

Absent-mindedness, 88–89 (see also Topical Method)

Accents, 172

Action, 58–60, 74, 75, 81, 134, 167

Actors, 98

Addition:
  advantages of special methods, 214
  aiming for totals, 211
  "catch figures," 211–212
  checking, 214
  double speed system, 209–210
  groups of three numbers, 210
  left to right, 213–214
  makes subtraction easier, 216–217
  "numerical span," 211
  relief from monotony, 214
  speed and efficiency, 214
  speeding and assuring, 213–214
  thinking in "pairs," 210
  triple speed system, 210
  upward, 210
  working on vertical, 211

Addresses, street, 121

Aids:
  alphabet, 102–111 (see also Alphabet)
  animated picture, 40
  Chain System, 56–68 (see also Links)

Aids (contd.)
  Cicero's, 71–82
  "cross-file," 43
  interlocking of lists, 35–38
  "Link-Place System," 83–86 (see also "Link-Place System")
  linking places with images, 71–82
  pairing items, 35–38
  personalized pairing process, 39–40
  senses, 43–54 (see also Senses)
  Topical Method, 71–82 (see also Topical Method)
  visualization process, 40–43

AIR:
  application, 25
  connecting links, 29, 65–66
  expanding formula, 115–123 (see also under specific headings)
    audio-visual memory, 121–123
    catch phrases, 119–121
    ten picture method, 116–119
  faces linked with names, 160–165
  file the right way, 24
  Homophonic Method, 121–123
  mathematics, 208
  Morphy, Paul, 28
  Phonetic Numeral Code, 126
  reading, 199, 202, 203
  Thompson, John, 27
  Topical Method, 89, 98
  word power, 178–180, 182, 189

Alphabet:
  group of objects, 109–111

239

Alphabet (*contd.*)
    alphabetical key-words, 110
        example, 110
        extra time taken, 111
        keeping list in mind, 110
        link and interlock, 110
        retaining over prolonged period, 111
        unrelated items, 110
        weak associations, 110
    numerical memory system, 107–109
        "A-Z" into "1" to "0," 107
        new wipes out old, 109
        test immediately, 109
        thirteen figure number, 107
        using different picture alphabet, 109
        visualization, 108
        weak links, 109
    pictorial, 105–106
        aphabetical, pictorial chain, 106
        links succeeding letters, 105
        permanent chain, 106
        test immediately after reading, 105
        twenty-six linked objects, 106
        visualizing, 105–106
    telephone numbers, 102–105
        code-words, 103
        examples, 103–105
        "jog words," 103
        letters in parentheses, 103
        seven letters or figures, 102
        standard dial, 103
        tabbing, 103
Antonyms, 190
Aphorisms, 21
Appointment schedule, 139
Association, 29, 58, 75
Audio-visual memory:
    extending key-list, 123
    homophonic method, 121–123
    intriguing feature, 122
    list, 122
    picturing items, 123
    remembering items, 123
    sounds translated into figures, 122
    twenties or beyond, 123

Authors, game, 233–235
Automobile, driver's seat, 96–98

B

"Below," 134
Bentham, Jeremy, 26
Bidder, George Park, 25–26
Biographical writers, 21
Bottell, William John, 28
Business, 173
Business data, 139–141
Buxton, Jedediah, 25

C

Calculator, rapid, 219–220
Calculators, lightning, 25–26
Calendar count:
    fingers and knuckles, 91–92
    "long" or "short" months, 92
    months of year, 91
Calling Off Figures, stunt, 224–225
Camillo, Giulio, 81
Car, 96–98
Cardiac, Jean Louis, 26
"Catch figures," 211–212
Catch phrases:
    dates, 119
    names, 155
    samples, 120–121
    simple picture, 121
    statistics, 119
    street addresses, 121
Celebrity Linkage Method:
    constant attention, 164
    natural aptitude, 165
    not new, 165
    not too many faces, 165
    recent years, 165
    self-development of memory, 165
    similarity or difference, 165
    speed of development, 164
    step-by-step training, 165
Chain, 20
Chain system, 56–68 (*see also* Links)
Character tags, 98
Children, 161
Chronological items, 60

Cicero, 71, 72, 73, 76, 79, 81, 82
Colburn, Zerah, 25
Colors, names, 150
Composites, faces and profiles, 164, 168, 169
Comprehension, reading, 194–205 (*see also* Reading)
Concave Profile, 169
Concentration, game, 231–233
Confidence, 29
Connections, names:
  actual, 156
  imaginary, 157
Connotations, names, 149
Continuity of pairs, 57
Contrasts, 164
Convex Profile, 168–169
"Cross-file," senses, 43
Cross-indexing, 22
Cross-reference name file, 148–158
Cultural development, reading, 198–199

D

Da Signa, Boncompagno, 82
Dates, 119, 128
Days of week, 90–91
De Oratore, 71, 72, 82
Decimal system, 217
Descriptive names, 149–150
Divisibility of numbers, 220–221
Division:
  divisibility of numbers, rules, 220–221
  interchangeable with multiplication, 220
  Multiplication Table important, 220
Double speed system, addition, 209–210

E

Ears, 169
Elderly people, 161–162
Eyebrows, 169
Eyes, 169

F

Face formations, frontal, 167–168
Faces linked with names:
  AIR formula, 171–175
    accents, 172
    attention, 171
    business, 173
    direct linkage, 171
    family history, 173
    first names, 172
    forgotten names, 174
    gestures, 172
    imbalance, 174
    interest, 172–173
    law of opposites, 173–174
    lists of persons, 175
    manners, 172
    meeting a person, 171
    mutual friends, 173
    ordinary last name, 172
    peg person effectively, 172
    positive *association*, 171
    questions, 172, 173
    repetition, 173–174
    urgent personal need, 174
    voice, 172
  "Celebrity Linkage Method," 164–165 (*see also* Celebrity Linkage Method)
  "Double System," expansion, 163–164
    changes producing resemblance, 163
    composite faces, 164
    contrasts, 164
    features of two newcomers, 164
    "identical twin," 163
    individual points, 163
    work from small to large, 164
  establish mutual interests, 161
  extreme memory types, 160
  face announces owner, 170–171
  facial memory, 160
  faculties, teaming two, 170
  famous or familiar faces, 166
  interests of others, 161
  memory models, 166
  misdirection of AIR formula, 160

Faces (*contd.*)
nicknames, 170
PAIR system, 162
physiognomy, 166–170 (*see also* Physiognomy)
popularity and profit, 160
remembering proves valuable, 160
selective process, 161–162
  attention, 162
  infants and children, 161
  interest, 162
  need to remember, 162
  older people, 161–162
  people close at hand, 162
  repetition, 162
  stop ignoring things, 161
typing faces, 162–163
vital elements blended, 160–161
vital elements separated, 161
watch for actions, 167
Family history, 173
Famous names, 151
Feminine touch, 95–96
Figure Alphabet, 127 (*see also* Phonetic Numeral Code)
File, memory:
acrostic, 30–31
AIR formula, 24, 25, 27, 28, 29, 65, 66
aphorisms, 21
association, 29
biographical writers, 21
calculators, 25–26
chain of recollections, 20
forming and using, 22
historians, 21
historic cases, 25–28
  Bentham, Jeremy, 26–27
  Bidder, George Parker, 25–26
  Bottell, William John, 28
  Buxton, Jedediah, 25
  Cardiac, Jean Louis, 26
  Colburn, Zerah, 25
  Heinecken, Christian Friedrich, 26
  Macaulay, Thomas Babington, 27
  Morphy, Paul, 27–28
  Thompson, John, 27

File, memory (*contd.*)
key-word from initial letters, 30
links, 29
list of items, 30
proverbs, 21
putting articles into verse, 21
quotations, 21
recognizing potential, 22–24
rules of profession or trade, 21–22
self-confidence, 29
tabs (*see* Tabs)
Filing system, names, 147
"Finger count," 90–92 (*see also* Topical Method)
First names, 154–155, 172
Five S System, reading, 201–202
Fixed objects, 89–90
Floor plans, 76
Forehead, 169
Forgetfulness, 88–99 (*see also* Topical Method)
Franklin, Benjamin, 21, 194
Frontal face formations, 167–168

G

Games and stunts:
Authors, 233–235
Calling Off Figures, 224–225
Concentration, 231–233
Finding Concealed Names, 227
I Doubt It, 228–231
I've Got Your Number, 225–226
Master Memory, 226–227
Gestures, 172
Group of objects, 109–111

H

Handbag, 95
Handkerchief, "stopper," 94
Head shapes, 169
Heads and subheads, 22
Hearing:
blind people, 48
learn to hear more, 48–49
sight supplants, 48
supplement to sight, 49–51
touch aids, 51

Heinecken, Christian Friedrich, 26,
Hippocrates, 21
Historians, 21
Historical data, 61–63
Homonyms, 190
Homophonic Method, 121–123 (see also Audio-visual memory)
"Hooks," 149
"Human calendars," 209
Humor, 63–64

I

I Doubt It, card game, 229–231
Imagination, exercise, 56–68
Incongruity, 57–58, 74, 75, 95
Individual ability, 81
Infants, 161
Information, reading, 198
Initials, 155
Interests, personal, 146
Interlocking of lists, 35–38
I've Got Your Number, 225–226

J

Jaws, 169
Jingles, 154
Jogs, 88–99 (see also Topical Method)

K

Key-links, AIR formula, 66–68
"Key-words" as "eye-signals," 200–201
Knots, 89
Knuckles, 91–92

L

"Large," 134
Large items, picture, 96
License numbers, 117
"Lightning calculators," 209
Likes, personal, 95
"Link-Place System":
    imagination, 86
    past Number 50, 86

"Link-Place System" (contd.)
    picturization, 84–85
    placing images, 84
    type of room visualized, 83
    up to 50 items, 83–86
Linkage, personal, 155–156
Links:
    action and practicality, 58–60
    chronological items, 60
    connecting by AIR formula, 29
    continuity of pairs, 57
    essential facts, 60–63
    extending to everyday life, 56–58
    forge into chain, 57
    historical data, 61–63
    humor, 63–64
    imagination, 56–68
    incongruous, 57–58
    key-links, 66–68
    motor memory, 56–57
    natural pairs, 57
    nonsense, 63–64
    overall theme, 63
    paired objects in succession, 57
    personal needs, 64–66
    proper order, 61
    purposeful application, 65
    reason for remembering, 59
    strengthen with minor associations, 58
    use of AIR formula, 66–68
Lips, 169
Lists of persons, 175
Lowell, James Russell, 203

M

Macaulay, Thomas Babington, 27
Main association, 75
Manners, 172
Master Memory, 226–227
Mathematics, high-speed:
    addition, 208–214, 216–217 (see also Addition)
    AIR, 208
    computerized mind, 209
    division, 220–221 (see also Division)
    "human calendars," 209

Mathematics, high-speed (contd.)
  "lightning calculators," 209
  multiplication, 217–220 (see also
      Multiplication)
  "numerical span," 211
  procedures systematized, 209
  subtraction, 214–216 (see also
      Subtraction)
  tables, 214, 217, 218, 219, 220
    Multiplication, 217, 218, 219,
        220
    Subtraction, 214
Memory Jogs, 88–99 (see also Topi-
    cal Method)
Memory span, 34–35
Men's suits, 93
Mental images, 43
Millions, 135–138 (see also Phonetic
    Numerical Code)
Months, 91–92
Morphy, Paul, 27–28
"Motor memory":
  link method, 56–57
  touch, 52
Multiplex speed, reading, 199–200
Multiplication:
  decimal system, 217
  expanding table, 218
  interchangeable with division, 220
  new look at number groups, 219–
      220
  rapid calculator, 219–220
  speeding specialized calculations,
      218
  table, 217

N

Names:
  actual connections, 156
  AIR, 144
  attention, 147
  broaden personal interests, 146
  concealed, 227–228
  cross-reference index, 147
  descriptive, 149–150
    colors, 150
    nationality, 150
    distinctly descriptive type, 149

Names (contd.)
  individual identification, 149
  original connotations, 149
  famous, 151
  first, 154–155
    catch phrases, 155
    initials, 155
    jingles, 154
    similarities, 154
  imaginary connections, 157
  interest, 147
  linking faces, 160–175 (see also
      Faces linked with names)
  mental filing system, 147
  nicknames, 153–154
  occupational, 148–149
    "hooks," 149
    names become secondary, 149
    slight modifications, 149
    small communities, 148
  PAIR, 147, 158, 162
  personal linkage, 155–156
  personal relations to fore, 146
  pictorial sequence, 157–158
  places, 151
  Rebus Method, 157–158
  remembering people, 145–146
    association, 145
    constant turnover, 145, 146
    contacts not face to face, 145
    contacts through agents, 145
    facial memory, 145
    immediate needs, 145
    lesser links as tabs, 145
    preparation, 145, 147
    references to departments, 145
    telephone contacts, 145
  repetition, 147
  suggested classifications, 148–158
  things, 150–151
Napier, 70–72, 75, 82
Nationality, names, 150
Natural pairs, 57
Needs, personal, 64–66, 174
Neighborhood system, 79–80
Nicknames, 153–154, 170
Nonsense, 63–64
Novel, reading, 204–205
Number groups, 219–220

Numbers, telephone, 102–105, 129, 138
Numerical memory system, 107–109
"Numerical span," 211

O

Objective Sensations, 43
Objects, group, 109–111
Occupational names, 148–149
Older people, 161–162
Opposites, law, 173–174
Order, proper, 61, 117
Oval Face, 168

P

PAIR, 147, 158, 162
Pairing items:
    chronological, 60
    continuity of pairs, 57
    imagination and ingenuity, 38–40
    incongruous links, 57
    instant aid to memory, 35–38
    natural pairs, 57
    succession, 57
"Pairs," addition, 210
Personal linkage, 155–156
Personal needs, 64–66, 174
Personalized memory system, 99
Personalized pairing process, 39–40
PERU System, reading, 202
Phone number, 117
Phonetic Numeral Code:
    AIR, 126
    basic sounds are consonants, 128
    business data, 139–141
        appointment schedule, 139
        examples, 139–141
        price list, 141
    "cipher," 127
    dates, 128–129
    double letters, 129
    Figure Alphabet, 127
    lettered code, 127
    links, 128
    longer numbers, 129
    millions using paired lists, 135–138
        association, 135

Phonetic Numeral Code (*contd.*)
    companion list, 135
    differentiating words, 135
    original list, 135
    paired lists, 136–137
    supplementary paired list, 137
    10,000, numbers up to, 137
    utilizing two lists, 135
    "naught," 127
    numerical code, 127
    practicing, 129
    seven-figure number, 138–139
        population figures, 139
        telephone numbers, 138
    telephone numbers, 129, 138
    ten word key-list, 130–134
        "above" and "below," 133, 134
        action pictures, 134
        basic function, 133
        imagery, practice, 134
        key-list of 100 words, 132–133
        "large" and "small," 133, 134
        memorizing list, 132
        mental pictures, 131
        nine items, 131
        numbers of two figures, 133
        pegging words permanently, 130
        practical uses, 133
        running chain formed, 131
        single consonant words, 130
        starter letter "H," 130
        supplementary list, 133
        10,000, numbers up to, 134
        three or four figures, 133
        up to 99, 132
        vowels as fillers, 128
        "zero," 127
Physiognomy:
    Composite Types, 168
    Composite Profiles, 169
    Concave Profile, 169
    Convex Profile, 168–169
    ears, 169
    eyebrows, 169
    eyes, 169
    facial memorization, 166–170
    forehead, 169
    frontal face types, 167–168
    head shapes, 169

Physiognomy (*contd.*)
  impression at first sight, 168
  jaws, 169
  lips, 169
  Oval Face, 168
  profiles, 168–169
  Square Face, 167
  Straight Profile, 169
  Triangular Face, 168
Pictures, reading, 194–196
Pictorial alphabet, 105–106
Pictorial sequence, names, 157–158
Places, names, 151
Places with *images*, 71–82 (see also
  Topical Method)
Pleasure, reading, 199, 204
Pockets, 93–95
Poetry, memorization, 203–204
Poor Richard's Almanac, 194
Population figures, 139
PQRST System, reading, 202
Practicality, 58–60
Prefixes:
  apply more to given word, 184
  definition, 184
  English origin, 188
  English words used as, 188
  list, 187
  most from Latin or Greek, 185
  most-used, 188
  suited to AIR formula, 189
Preparation, 145, 147
Price list, 141
Prodigies, 26–28
Products, names, 152–153
Profiles, 168–169
Projecting mind ahead, 98
Projection of mental image, 43
Proverbs, 21
Public buildings or places, 77–79

Q

Quintilian, 79, 80
Quotations, 21

R

Reading:
  AIR, 199, 202, 203

Reading (*contd.*)
  compounding words, 211
  comprehension and retention, 201–
    203
  cultural development, 198–199
  Five S System, 201–202
  information, 198
  "key-words" as "eye-signals," 200–
    201
  mapping or zoning, 197
  multiplex speed, 199–200
  novel, 204–205
  PERU System, 202
  pictures express ideas, 194–196
  pleasure, 199, 204
  poetry, memorization, 203–204
  PQRST System, 202
  "reading span," 211
  RTP System, 202
  self-improvement, 198
  speeds, 198–200
  SQ3R System, 202–203
  visualization, 196–197
  vocalization, 196
  working along horizontal, 210–211
"Reading span," 211
Reading vocabulary, 178–182 (see
  also Reading)
Reason for remembering, 59
Rebus Method, 157–158
Recognition vocabulary, 178–182
  (see also Reading)
Recollections, 20
Rehearsals, 98
Relatedness of objects, 89
Resemblance, 163–164
Retention:
  image, 43
  reading, 194–205 (see also Reading)
Romano, Jacques, 67–68
RTP System, reading, 202

S

Schedule, appointment, 139
Self-confidence, 29
Self-improvement, reading, 198
Senses:
  "cross-file," 43

Senses (*contd.*)
　details of mental image, 43
　hearing, 48–51 (*see also* Hearing)
　Objective Sensations, 43
　over-dependence on one, 43
　projection of image, 43
　retention of mental images, 43
　"sensations," 43
　sight, 44–48 (*see also* Sight)
　smell, 52–53
　Subjective Sensations, 43
　taste, 53–54 (*see also* Taste)
　touch, 50–52 (*see also* Touch)
Seven-figure numbers, 138–139
Shirt pockets, 94
Sight:
　action supplies details, 46
　application to memory, 47–48
　check "everyday" use, 47
　hearing supplants, 48
　hearing supplements, 49–51
　learn to see more, 44
　over-trust, 44
　pictorial test, 47–48
　see as others see, 46
　test, 44–45
"Small," 134
Smell, 52–53
Span, memory, 34, 35
Speeds, reading:
　cultural development, 198–199
　information, 198
　multiplex, 199–200
　pleasure, 199, 204
　self-improvement, 198
Spelling, 189–190, 192
SQ3R System, reading, 202–203
Square Face, 167
Statistics, 119
"Stopper," handkerchief, 94
Straight Profile, 169
Street addresses, 121
String, 88–89
Stunts and games, 224–235 (*see also*
　　Games and stunts)
Subheads and heads, 22
Subjective Sensations, 43
Subtraction:
　facilitated by addition, 216

Subtraction (*contd.*)
　left to right, 215
　table, 214
　two-figure numbers, 215
　upward and downward, 215
Success, importance of memory, 20
Succession, paired objects, 57
Suffixes:
　addition, 185
　ancient terms, 188–189
　definition, 185
　English origin, 188
　list, 186
　most from Latin or Greek, 185
　most-used, 188
　suited to AIR formula, 189
Suits, men's, 93
Supplementary associations, 75
Symbol, double, 117–118
Synonyms, 190

T

Tables:
　Multiplication, 217, 218, 219,
　　220
　Subtraction, 214
Tabs:
　adding new ones, 22
　AIR, 29
　cross-indexing, 22
　heads and subheads, 22
　inadequate, 23
　"keys," 22
　look for, 22
　names, 147
　telephone numbers and addresses,
　　102–105
　tested ones as patterns, 30–32
　value, 20–22
　　aphorisms, 21
　　biographical writers, 21
　　chain of recollections, 20
　　historians, 21
　　instant delivery of information,
　　　20
　　proverbs, 21
　　putting articles into verse, 21
　　quotations, 21

Tabs (*contd.*)
  rules of profession or trade, 21–22
  you have multitude, 20
Tags, character, 98
Targets, aiming for, 98–99
  almost-forgotten experiences, 53
  smell and taste interrelated, 53
Telephone numbers, 102–105, 129, 138
Ten picture method:
  action, 117
  developing imaginative faculty, 116
  double symbol, 117–118
  figures 1–0, 116–117
  final picturization, 118
  fixing images in mind, 117
  license numbers, 117
  order, 117
  phone number, 117
  picture figures as objects, 116–117
  retaining figures visually, 116–119
  running sequence, 117
  several important items, 116
  short numbers, 116
  ten articles, and more, 118–119
    more composite numbers, 118–119
    more than ten, 118
    series of articles, 118
    specimen series, 118
    ten to fifteen enough, 119
  worthwhile in own right, 116
Ten word key list, 130–134 (*see also* Phonetic Numeral Code)
Theme, overall, 63
Things, names, 150–151
Thompson, John, 27, 79
Topical Method:
  action, 75
  actors, 98
  actual rooms unnecessary, 76
  add objects, 75
  AIR treatment, 89, 98
  application, 80
  automobile driver's seat, 96–98
  booster for memory, 81
  closeness to system, 95
  dependence on lesser links, 75

Topical Method (*contd.*)
  device itself, 80
  erasure, 75
  extended to broader scenes, 77–79
  familiar scene, 74, 75
  "finger count," 90–92
    calendar count, 91–92 (*see also* Calendar count)
    days of week, 90–91
    weeks, months, years, 91
  floor plans, 76
  handbag, 95
  images imprinted upon *places*, 78
  incongruity important, 75, 95
  individual ability, 81
  individuality of places, 79
  knot, 89
  knuckles, 91–92
  link is association, 75
  linking things, 89
  main associations, 75
  memory jogs, 88–99
  memory to stimulate memory, 88
  mental trip around room, 75
  more than one room, 76
  neighborhood system, 79–80
  new sequence obliterates old, 79
  personal likes, 95
  personalized memory system, 99
  picture items on large scale, 96
  "place plus image," 74
  pockets, 93–95
    feminine touch, 95–96
    form mental pictures, 93–94
    handkerchief as "stopper," 94
    men's suits, 93
    shirt pockets added, 94
    ten or dozen items, 93
  progressive scene, 77
  projecting mind ahead, 98
  public buildings or places, 77
  regular sequence of places, 77, 80
  rehearsals, 98
  related objects, 89
  simplification, 80–82
  stimulus to individual initiative, 77
  string around finger, 88–89
  supplementary associations, 75
  targets, aiming for, 98–99

Topical Method (*contd.*)
ten fixed objects, 89–90
ten places, 75, 76
tote bag, 95
"utility bag," 95
varied neighborhood, 79
writer's character tags, 98
Tote bag, 95
Touch:
aids hearing and sight, 51
dial phone, 51
driving a car, 52
"groping in the dark," 51
"motor memory," 52
specialized functions, 51
typewriter, 52
Triangular Face, 168
Triple speed system, addition, 210
Twins, identical, 163

U

Use vocabulary, 178–182 (*see also* Reading)
"Utility bag," 95

V

Verse, 21
Visualization:
process, 40–43
reading, 196–197
Vocabulary, 178–191 (*see also* Word power)
Vocal vocabulary, 178–182 (*see also* Reading)
Vocalization in reading, 196
Voice, 172

W

Weeks, 91
Word power:
AIR, 178–180, 182, 189
adjust types of word studies, 179–180
attains its ultimate, 178

Word Power (*contd.*)
multiple associations, 178
prefixes and suffixes, 189
utilized to fullest degree, 182
antonyms, 190
apply memory links, 182–183
avid readers, 181
coin own words, 188
homonyms, 190
increase word-span, 184–185
over-reading, 181
prefixes, 184–189 (*see also* Prefixes)
Reading Vocabulary, 178–182
known as Recognition Vocabulary, 178–182
take time to choose word, 179
recognition applied to use, 180–181
eliminate frills, 181
impact, 180
rehearsal, 180
timing, 180
understandable, natural terms, 180
shades of meaning, 181
spelling, 189–190, 192
suffixes, 184–189 (*see also* Suffixes)
synchronizing two vocabularies, 178
synonyms, 190
use to recognition, 184
vocabulary types, 178–182
Vocal Vocabulary, 178–182
consists of spoken word, 178
purpose or idea, 178
termed Use Vocabulary, 178–180
use with Reading Vocabulary, 181–182
words on instant call, 179
Wright, Harold, 59
Writer, character tags, 98

Y

Years, 91